Sarah M. Zaides

Tevye's Ottoman Daughter:
Ashkenazi and
Sephardi Jews at the End of Empire

LİBRA KİTAP: 545

HISTORY: 465

© Libra Kitapçılık ve Yayıncılık

Layout: Özgü Simay Kızılelma
Cover Design: Mehmet Cevdet Kösemen
Front cover: Galata Bridge, Constantinople. View from Karaköy.

1st edition: 2022

ISBN 978-625-8472-45-5

Printing and Binding
Birlik Fotokopi Baskı Ozalit ve Büro Malzemeleri
Sanayi ve Ticaret Ltd. Şti.
Nispetiye Mah. Birlik Sokak No: 2
Nevin Arıcan Plaza
34340 Levent / İstanbul
Tel: (212) 269 30 00
Certificate No: 52846

Libra Kitapçılık ve Yayıncılık Ticaret A.Ş.
Ebe Kızı Sok. Günaydın Apt. No: 9/2
Osmanbey / İstanbul
Certificate No: 48556
Tel: 90- 212-232 99 04/05
Fax: 90- 212-231 11 29
E-posta: info@librakitap.com.tr
www.librakitap.com.tr

Sarah M. Zaides

Tevye's Ottoman Daughter:
Ashkenazi and
Sephardi Jews at the End of Empire

Sarah M. ZAIDES,

received her PhD from the Department of History at the University of Washington and her BA from the University of California San Diego. She was a Fellow at the Woodrow Wilson Foundation in 2015-2016. Additionally, her work has been supported by the Memorial Foundation for Jewish Culture, the Genesis Institute at Brandeis University, and the Vidal Sassoon Center at the Hebrew University of Jerusalem. She has also held the Joff Hanauer Fellowship for the Study of Western Civilization and the Titus Ellison Fellowship from the University of Washington. She has lived and studied in Oxford, Amman, and in Jerusalem. Dr. Zaides is currently the Associate Director of the Stroum Center for Jewish Studies at the Henry M. Jackson School of International Studies at the University of Washington in Seattle, Washington.

TABLE OF CONTENTS

TABLES AND FIGURES

For my mother, and my grandmothers

ABBREVIATIONS

AIU	:	Alliance Israélite Universelle
CAHJP	:	Central Archives for the History of the Jewish People
CUP	:	Committee of Union and Progress
CZA	:	Central Zionist Archives
JCA or ICA	:	Jewish Colonization Association
JDC	:	Jewish Joint Distribution Committee
WZO	:	World Zionist Organisation

ACKNOWLEDGEMENTS

So many people, ideas, and institutions assisted in the publication of this manuscript. Thank you to the University of Washington Department of History, and especially to the Stroum Center for Jewish Studies at the University of Washington for supporting this research at the dissertation stage and for granting me leave of administrative responsibilities to prepare the manuscript. My original dissertation was supported by the Woodrow Wilson Foundation's Charlotte Newcombe Fellowship, the Fritz-Boeing Fellowship from the University of Washington, the Schwartz and Hanauer Fellowships at the University of Washington, the Vidal Sassoon Center for the Study of Anti-Semitism, Brandeis University's Genesis Institute, and the Memorial Foundation for Jewish Culture. Thanks is also owed to the Henry M. Jackson School of International Studies' Ellison Center for awarding me the Titus Ellison Fellowship, which allowed me to pursue language study unencumbered by the commitments of teaching in the most formative years of graduate study. A scholarship from the Department of State's Critical Language Scholarship Program to study Arabic in Amman in 2011 was both personally and intellectually transformational. Thank you to my many mentors, including Devin Naar, Noam Pianko, Glennys Young, Elena Campbell, Mika Ahuvia, Selim Sırrı Kuru, Gershon Shafir, Michael Provence, and Luis Alvarez. I thought of my first history teachers at University High School, John Kessler and Bill Ives, frequently while writing my dissertation.

Rıfat Bali's contributions to the field of Ottoman Jewish history – both as a scholar and also as a publisher and editor- must be recognized. Thank you to the archivists and professionals that allow new histories to be written. At the Central Archives for the History of the Jewish People and the Central Zionist Archives, Yochai Ben-Ghedalia gave me unprecedented access to unarchived materials. Denise Rein expertly prepared the ICA-Turkey guide for my use—much of this material served as the foundation for this project. Eli Ben-Yosef made extra trips to the storage units in Talpiot to gather my materials (and even brought me a critical mass of rugelach to get through long afternoons squinting at microfilm machines). Josef Gelston was always welcoming with a word of encouragement and made sure I was neither too hot nor too cold, and always reminded me to break for lunch. Olga Shraberman made sure to introduce me to every scholar at work in the archives that might know something about my project. In Istanbul, I would like to thank Robert Schild, a true intellectual, who thoughtfully toured me around Istanbul and introduced me to real life descendants of Tevye's Ottoman Daughter. He also taught me how to use the Turkish metro. Thank you also to Rabbi Mendy Chitrik, who pointed out books in the Ashkenazi Synagogue with Chassidic liturgy and artifacts from Russia, and let me dig through bags of old papers in the Beit Midrash. Christina Sztajnkrycer, Canan Bolel and Elly Moseson assisted thoughtfully in translations of primary source materials that spanned languages and continents. Thank you to Julian Smith-Newman who first encouraged me to think about history's connection to prose and for reading so many books with me. You changed everything. Of course, thank you to my family most of all, who have supported me in all of my endeavors, and especially to my husband Adam Rosen, who makes all of my dreams possible.

INTRODUCTION

"One is always at home in one's past."

Vladimir Nabokov

In Shalom Aleichem's *Tevye the Dairyman*, later adapted as the classic musical and 1964 film *Fiddler On The Roof*, Tevye's daughters represent three of the typical fates of Russia's Jews on the eve of the Bolshevik Revolution. Jews living in the Pale of Settlement could, like Tsatyl, marry a tailor and presumably remain in the *shtetl*. They could follow Beilke and her husband to North America, or, like Hodl and her husband Perchik, they could move to St. Petersburg and join the Bolshevik Revolution (1917) and its promises of legal and social emancipation. Yuri Slezkine, a scholar of Russian and Jewish history, has noted that Shalom Aleichem's characters depicted the paths of twentieth-century Russian Jewish migration. In his 2004 monograph *The Jewish Century,* Slezkine controversially argues that Jews were the most visible embodiment of modernity during a twentieth century characterized by increased urbanism, mobility, and literacy, so that consequently "modernization is about everyone becoming Jewish."[1]

But what both Aleichem and Slezkine overlook in their typography of Russian Jewry are those who made their way to Odessa and found passage aboard a steamship crossing the Black Sea to the Russian Empire's centuries-

---

1   Yuri Slezkine, *The Jewish Century* (Princeton, NJ: Princeton University Press, 1984), 1, 206. For Slezkine, Russian Jews' enthusiastic participation in the Bolshevik Revolution (the path of Tevye's daughter Hodl) was just another route to emancipation, as "conversion to Communism was not a conversion at all. Abandoning Judaism for Christianity was an act of apostasy," but abandoning Judaism for "the human race was a family affair." Notice, also, that he uses modernity and modernization interchangeably.

old neighbor and foe, the Ottoman Empire, which also happened to control a land that some argued was the Jewish homeland: Palestine.[2]

If Shalom Aleichem had created another daughter for Tevye, she would have arrived in Constantinople sometime in between 1882 and 1919 and would have been met by a mostly Sephardic Jewish community, proudly commemorating four centuries since their own arrival in the Ottoman Empire.[3] Russian Jews would have either stayed and settled in the imperial métropole or could have moved on to agricultural settlements financed by the Jewish Colonization Association near the Aegean port of Smyrna (Izmir).[4] There, Russian Jews lived and worked on collective farming projects like Or Yehuda ("Light of Judah") about one hundred kilometers from the city as they awaited the Ottoman citizenship necessary before moving on to Palestine. Some found their way back to Constantinople, and others traveled on to the major cities of Western Europe and North America. Tevye's story is a complicated one in its own right: In Aleichem's *Tevye Goes to the Land of Israel*, Tevye himself leaves the village of Anatekva for Palestine, where his wealthy son-in-law Padhatzur suggests that he continue on to the United States. When Tevye refuses, Padhatzur asks Tevye, "If not America, why not Palestine? All old Jews go to Palestine!"

This project tells the story of Tevye's other daughter, the Ottoman daughter whom I have taken the liberty of imagining and writing back into the saga of the twilight years of Imperial Russian Jewry that Shalom Aleichem so astutely captured. Yet the title of this project is something of a bait-and-switch; by "daughter," I mean Russian Jewish men, women, and children—just as Aleichem did in his stories at the turn of the twentieth century. And really, Tevye had *many* Ottoman daughters (and sons) who led varied lives once they

---

2   There exist a number of excellent comparative works on the histories of the Ottoman and Russian Empires. For an analysis of the Russian and Ottoman borderlands, see Lucien J. Frary and Mara Kozelsky, *Russian-Ottoman Borderlands: The Eastern Question Reconsidered* (Madison: University of Wisconsin Press, 2014). For a military history of the Ottoman and Russian Empires in the nineteenth century, see Edward Michael Fitzgibbon, *Alexander I and the Near East: The Ottoman Empire in Russia's Foreign Relations, 1801–1807* (Columbus: Ohio State University Press, 1974). For a confessional history of the two empires, see Victor Taki, "Limits of Protection: Russia and the Orthodox Coreligionists in the Ottoman Empire," *Carl Beck Papers in Russian and East European Studies* 2401 (2015). For a comparative study of Jewish media, see Sarah Abrevaya Stein, *Making Jews Modern: The Yiddish and Ladino Press in the Russian and Ottoman Empires* (Bloomington: Indiana University Press, 2004), a landmark work discussed below.

3   Julia Phillips Cohen, *Becoming Ottomans: Sephardi Jews and Imperial Citizenship in the Modern Era* (Oxford: Oxford University Press, 2014).

4   For an overview of the activities of the Jewish Colonization Association, see Theodor Norman, *An Outstretched Arm: A History of the Jewish Colonization Association* (Routledge: London, 1985).

arrived in the Ottoman Empire, and he had other daughters who chose even *other* routes of exit to South America, Africa, and Australia. But his *Ottoman* daughter had many decisions to make once she arrived in Constantinople. Some became agriculturalists, while others settled in Constantinople; some moved on to Palestine, while others migrated to the Jewish Colonization Association's colonies in Argentina and Brazil; some even became brothel keepers and prostitutes, like the two former prostitutes who purchased what was known as the "Pimp's Synagogue" in the Galata quarter of Constantinople and turned it into a refuge for former prostitutes.[5] Others returned to St. Petersburg after the end of the Russian Civil War (1917-1922).[6]

The Sephardi and Ashkenazi Jews who Tevye's Ottoman daughter would have encountered turn out to be complex characters as well. This project follows Russian Jews' arrival in Constantinople as they navigated what initially may appear to be two distinct Jewish worlds, Sephardi and Ashkenazi, which have traditionally been treated as two separate Jewish histories, but these two communities were themselves subdivided even further. German Jews, Russian Jews, Polish Jews, Italian Jews, and Sephardic Jews each constituted a Jewish community whose boundaries were too porous to understand in dichotomous terms like Sephardi or Ashkenazi.[7] It is in this diverse Jewish milieu that the subjects of this monograph undertake a fascinating historical project: they begin to fashion the contours, the very boundaries, of these subcategories of Ottoman Jews. This self-fashioning occurs among Jewish subjects of the Austro-Hungarian Empire, Jewish subjects of the Ottoman Empire, and Russian Jewish subjects of the Russian Empire – all living in the cities and borderlands of Constantinople.

The term *ashkenaz* occurs in the Hebrew Bible three times, and refers loosely to the German Rhineland, although Ashkenazi came to mean "eastern European" Jews more broadly.[8] Sephardi Jews, from the Hebrew word for Spain, *sefarad*, are generally understood as Jews who trace their roots to the Iberian

---

5   Aslan Yahni, ed., *90 Yıl Kuruluşundan Bugüne İhtiyarlara Yardım Derneği* (Istanbul: İhtiyarlara Yardım Derneği, 2006), 29.

6   See, for example, Alfred Kant's friend Danyusha in Albert Kant, *Mémoires d'un Fermier Juif en Turquie*, ed. by Rıfat N. Bali (Istanbul: Libra Kitap, 2013).

7   I interchangeably use Sephardi and Sephardic or Ashkenazi and Ashkenazic as adjectives, and use Sephardim or Ashkenazim as the Hebrew plural of Sephardi/Ashkenazi.

8   See Genesis 10:3, in I Chronicles 1:6 and in Jeremiah 51:27.

Peninsula prior to the Spanish Expulsion of 1492, but also sometimes refers to non-Ashkenazi or non-European Jews, in general. German Jews, Polish Jews, and Russian Jews refer to themselves and others at times as Ashkenazi, and other times call themselves simply "German Jews" or "Russians."[9] Confusion is inevitable, as the Jews of the Ottoman Empire were themselves attempting to sort out what each of these terms mean. Indeed "Ashkenazi" and "Sephardi" and even "German" and "Russian" meant different things, to different people, at different points in time.[10] At times, it was socially (and therefore politically) more beneficial to define oneself as a German Jew, especially as Russian migrants became more visibly present in the Ottoman Empire, while at times when migration was less significant, Ashkenazi seemed to be the preferred category. Thus, Constantinople's Jews at the turn of the century are working out the very contours of these Jewish identities, and it is the contested and constructed nature of these terms that is one of the foci of this study.

I refrain from referring to these categories as "imperial groups," "national groups," or "ethno-religious groups" because the constitutive meaning of these categories was being developed during this time period and was contingent upon who was using them. Bedross Der Matossian has argued in his monograph on early nationalism in the Young Turk Revolution that "in the nineteenth century, the majority of the Ottoman Empire's constituent groups did not see themselves as a part of a nation but as rather a part of an ethno-religious community" that was informed by "overlapping identities, highlighted by religious, linguistic, and cultural loyalties on the one hand, and regional and local loyalties on the other."[11] I hesitate to use either of these terms (nation or ethno-religious group), however, because the sources spanning nearly thirty years, from the vantage points of Sephardic Ottoman

---

9   In this monograph, I make every attempt to historicize these terms and note the language used by the sources and historical actors. Thus while noting the problems with these categories, in my attempt to accurately represent the sources, I will nonetheless use Sephardi and Ashkenazi throughout the monograph.

10   Although not the central focus of this study, this monograph also begins to unravel the diversity of Sephardic, Italian, Karaite and Romaniote Jews who were considered to be under the auspices of the *Haham Başı*, the Chief Rabbi, who was always Sephardic and acted as the interlocutor between the Jewish community and the Ottoman administration. See Esther Benbassa, *A Sephardic Chief Rabbi in Politics, 1892–1923*, trans. Miriam Kochan (Tuscaloosa: University of Alabama Press, 1995) and Aron Rodrigue, *French Jews, Turkish Jews: The Alliance Israélite Universelle and the Politics of Jewish Schooling in Turkey, 1860-1925* (Indiana: Indiana University Press, 1990).

11   Bedross Der Matossian, *Shattered Dreams of Revolution: From Liberty to Violence in the Late Ottoman Empire* (Stanford: Stanford University Press, 2014), 5–6.

Jews, Ashkenazi Ottoman Jews, as well as Russian Jews, indicate that they often did not consider themselves as part of the same "ethno-religious group" at all. There are certainly occurrences of self-designation and othering, usually in the context of increased migration of Russian Jews especially after 1891, but it is my intent to understand exactly what these historical actors *meant* by using what *appear* to be "imperial" or "national" categories. Their use of such terms coincides with the various political, economic, and personal agendas of German, Russian, and Sephardi Jewish groups in Constantinople that changed over the course of the late Ottoman period, and their allegiances to one another changed along with those agendas.

According to an article by Alphons Sussnitski in a 1912 issue of the Berlin Jewish newspaper *Allgemeine Zeitung des Judentums,* Ashkenazi Jews and particularly the German Jews of Constantinople had a presence in the Ottoman Empire reaching back nearly half a millennium. Sussnitski claimed that their arrival in 1483 with a specific "connection to Frankfurt" even predated the arrival of Sephardic Jews following the formal invitation of Sultan Bayezid II (1481–1512) to Jews expelled from Spain and Portugal.[12] The term "German Jew" carried a particular cultural cachet. Even though many of the Jews were from the Austro-Hungarian Empire, these Ashkenazi Jews may have called themselves "German Jews" to invoke the Vienna-Berlin axis that comprised the intellectual center of the *Haskalah,* the Jewish Enlightenment. German Jews are often described in the historical literature as more educated and cultivated than their eastern European or Middle Eastern coreligionists.[13] German Jews living in Constantinople engaged in various trades and commercial activities. Some entered the garment business, others owned central department stores in downtown Constantinople, and, according to a recurring motif about the high regard for German Jews in Ottoman society, a German Jew even

---

12 Alphons J. Sussnitski, "Die Wirtschaftliche Lage der Juden in Konstantinopel," *Allgemeine Zeitung des Judentums,* 5 January 1912. Retrieved online 27 January 2017. http://sammlungen.ub.uni-frankfurt.de/cm/periodical/titleinfo/3229015.

13 For example, see Steven E. Aschheim, *Brothers and Strangers: The East European Jew in German and German Jewish Consciousness, 1800–1923* (Madison: University of Wisconsin Press, 1982); Steven M. Lowenstein, *Frankfurt on the Hudson: The German Jewish Community of Washington Heights, 1933–1983, its Structure and Culture* (Detroit: Wayne State University Press, 1989); Hasia R. Diner, *A Time for Gathering: The Second Migration, 1820-1880* (Baltimore: The Johns Hopkins University Press, 1995); Naomi Wiener Cohen, *Encounter With Emancipation: The German Jews in the United States, 1830–1914* (Philadelphia: Jewish Publication Society, 1984); Daniel Soyer, *Jewish Immigrant Associations and American Identity in New York, 1880–1939* (Detroit: Wayne State University Press, 2001); and Jeffrey S. Gurock, *When Harlem Was Jewish, 1870–1930* (New York: Columbia University Press, 1979).

served as the personal tailor to the sultan.[14] Even a synagogue, which opened to accommodate new Russian migrants in Constantinople, was named the *habeit knesset tofre begadim*, or the Tailor's Synagogue, in honor of this highly regarded position.

This process of self-fashioning invokes the politics, language, and ideas of the theater of nineteenth century modernity. I bring up this elusive concept because my sources do, using proxy discussions about nations, nationalism, citizenship, and identity. The anthropologist Paul Rabinow has pointed out that "debates about modernity are endless: since it refers to so many diverse things, it seems futile, or simply part of the modernizing process-to worry about abstract definitions."[15] "It would seem more heuristic," he argues, "to explore how the term is understood and used by its self-proclaimed practitioners."[16] The Jews of the *fin de siècle* Ottoman Empire demonstrate that there is no such "thing" as modernity, only claims to it.

Indeed, Jews in the Ottoman Empire went to great lengths to identify themselves as German Jews in order to demonstrate a political and cultural allegiance to Austria-Hungary (1867) or the newly unified Germany (1871) in order to claim a status for themselves as more modern and European than other Jews they encountered in the Ottoman Empire. Politically, many Ashkenazi Jews retained Austro-Hungarian citizenship and loyalty, even dedicating the Ashkenazi Synagogue on Yüksek Kaldırım to the Emperor of Austria, Francis Joseph I, when it reopened on September 8, 1894.[17] The system of Capitulations, in which the Ottoman Empire excused non-Muslim subjects of foreign (Christian) nations from Ottoman jurisdiction, allowed Jews living in the Ottoman Empire to maintain foreign citizenship and remain subject to the laws of foreign consulates.[18]

---

14 Yavuz Köse "Vertical Bazaars of Modernity: Western Department Stores and their Staff in Istanbul, 1889–1921. *International Review of Social History* 54, S17 (2009): 91-114.

15 Paul Rabinow, *The French Modern* (Chicago: The University of Chicago Press, 1989), 9.

16 Ibid.

17 The old wooden synagogue that had burnt down was called the Österreichischer Synagogue—the Austrian Synagogue. It was renamed the "Ashkenazi Synagogue" after it was rebuilt and rededicated. See Robert Schild et. al., *A Hundred Year Old Synagogue* (Istanbul: Galata Ashkenazi Cultural Association, 2000).

18 See Maurits H. Van Den Boogert, *The Capitulations and the Ottoman Legal System: Qadis, Consuls and Beratlis in the 18th Century*. Studies in Islamic Law and Society (Leiden: Brill, 2005).

For the opening of the synagogue, the Ashkenazi community invited foreign dignitaries including the Austro-Hungarian ambassador, and a distinguished member of the community, Dr. Adolph Rosenthal, who gave his opening speech in both Turkish and German.[19] The dedication coincided with the opening of another synagogue built expressly for accommodating new Russian immigrants in 1895, the "Schneider Tempel," just down the street from the Ashkenazi Synagogue. As Russian Jews began arriving in Constantinople in larger numbers, Ashkenazi Jews already living in the city made increasing efforts to define themselves as German Jews, distinct from the impoverished and sometimes revolutionary and politically subversive Russian migrants who had arrived in the Jewish neighborhoods of Constantinople. These efforts further increased as the Jewish community of Constantinople came under scrutiny from Jewish communities abroad, especially as Russian Jews became involved in prostitution and, to use the parlance of the time, the white slave trade (see Chapter 2 for an extensive discussion of Russian Jews' participation in prostitution in Constantinople).

This project is an examination of Jewish communities in Constantinople and in the Anatolian borderlands and how they attempted to define the boundaries of Jewish identities. It is the first integrative history of Sephardi and Ashkenazi Jews that examines their points of contact in the Ottoman Empire. Historian Sarah Abrevaya Stein made the first attempt to consider the two worlds together. Her landmark book *Making Jews Modern* is a comparative history of the Ladino and Yiddish Press in the Ottoman and Russian empires, respectively, but she does not consider the possibility of cultural, social, and political permeability between two of the major Jewish communities of the two major Eastern European empires, who spoke two mutually unintelligible Jewish vernaculars, Yiddish and Ladino. My effort is also to examine the socially constructed nature of these identities. This project explores inter- and intra-Jewish religious relationships, as well as these groups' relationship with the Ottoman administration and with Jewish organizations like the Jewish Colonization Association and the Alliance Israélite Universelle. It is a study of citizenship and empire and how Jewish groups negotiated power with the Ottoman center under the *millet* system. It helps us understand questions of Jewish identity in a gray zone between religious and national identities, the

---

19   Ibid., 65

complexities and nuances within religious groups, and how every other has its own *other* (see Chapter 2 for a discussion of Usamma Makdisi's "Ottoman Orientalism" as well as Milica Bakić-Hayden's "Nesting Orientalisms," and how both Sephardi and German Ashkenazi Jews designated Russian Jews as their *other*).[20] It is therefore a story about religious politics, about the ways in which Jews constructed community and meaning in a time of political and social uncertainty.

This project offers a discursive analysis of the Ladino press in which I trace shifting Sephardic representations of Russian Jews from persecuted Jewish pogrom victim to enemy revolutionaries designated as "foreign Jews" as Zionism took hold in the Ottoman Empire. I argue that these evolving representations are indicative of shifting political tides in this unique Jewish world within the Ottoman Empire: the Empire was home to a spectrum of Jewish politics, including Jewish nationalists advocating for a separate Jewish state in Palestine, other Jewish nationalists who argued for a Jewish national autonomy within the Ottoman framework, and others connected with the French-Jewish Alliance Israélite Universelle, who were pro-Empire, and while they supported Jewish projects in Palestine like Mikveh Israel (see chapter four) actively opposed sovereign statehood. Some of the subjects of this study moved fluidly along these political spectrums, often working for multiple organizations with seemingly conflicting political ideologies. Indeed, upon closer examination, the categories that emerge are closely correlated to a particular political and communal context constructed at the intersection of ethnicity, citizenship, and gender.[21]

Focusing not on the experience of Jews from the Russian Empire who took routes of exit typified by Tevye's descendants, but rather on the more than ten thousand Russian Jews who found their way to the major cities and agricultural colonies of the Ottoman Empire (and not only Ottoman Palestine),

---

20   Milica Bakić-Hayden, "Nesting Orientalisms: The Case of Former Yugoslavia," *Slavic Review* 54, no. 4 (1995): 917–31, Ussama Makdisi, "Ottoman Orientalism," *The American Historical Review*, 107 (3), 768-796.

21   Advances in critical theory have demonstrated that these discursively constructed categories are often mutually constitutive. While much of the discussion of these terms has emerged from the field of American Studies, research over the past decade has applied critical theory to non-Western fields, especially concerning the processes of early state-building. See for example Frederic Cooper, *Citizenship Between Empire and Nation: Remaking France and French Africa, 1945–1960* (Princeton: Princeton University Press, 2014). See also Faye Yuan Kleeman, *Gender, Ethnicity, and the Spectacles of the Empire* (Honolulu: University of Hawaii Press, 2014).

demonstrates the potential of looking beyond the vertical interaction between Jews and the state to consider the horizontal relationships among diverse Jewish groups in Constantinople.[22] In doing so, we can see how these religious and ethnic minorities developed their own institutions and responses to the political and social climate in the fin de siècle, and we can gain insight into the complex identities and intracommunal tensions in the twilight years of the Ottoman Empire. Using the beginnings of mass Jewish emigration from the Russian Empire in the 1880s and the mutual year of Turkish and Soviet Statehood (1923) as historical bookends, I follow a story that includes Russian migrants in Constantinople and in the Ottoman borderlands, as well as everyday Ottoman, Italian, German, and Russian Jews who variously created competing and overlapping senses of community, principally as "Sephardim" and "Ashkenazim." These subjects were civic and community leaders, intellectuals, writers, and newspaper editors.[23] I examine their communal organizations, their philanthropies, their schools, their synagogues, and even their brothels, as they interacted with and interpreted the politics of the late Ottoman Empire. My intention is not to reify historical epochs but rather to argue that these final years, between empire and nation-state, are fundamental to our understanding of Jewish geographies in the twentieth century more broadly. The myriad routes of exit available to Tevye's daughters were not just paths of migration, but also paths of ideas and politics.

Paths of Migration and Difficulties of Religious Designations

Understanding the demographics and points of origin of Russian Jewish migrants is quite difficult, because they traveled with various kinds of documents, if any at all. Ottoman authorities also did not ask for migrants'

---

22 Yosef Yerushalmi sees a "vertical alliance" in which the Jews of Europe entrusted their fate to their sovereigns. See Yosef Hayim Yerushalmi, "Exile and Expulsion in Jewish History," in *Crisis and Creativity in the Sephardic World, 1391-1648*, ed. B. Gampbel (New York: Columbia University Press, 1997), 3–23; Yosef Hayim Yerushalmi, "Servants of the Kings and Not Servants of Servants: Some Aspects of the Political History of the Jews," in *The Faith of Fallen Jews: Yosef Hayim Yerushalmi and the Writing of Jewish History*, ed. D. Myers and A. Kaye (Waltham: Brandeis University Press, 2013), 245–76. According to Benedict Anderson, the "nation is always conceived of as a deep, horizontal comradeship." Benedict Anderson, *Imagined Communities: Reflections on the Origin and the Spread of Nationalism* (New York: Verso, 2006), 7.

23 Although these years overlap with the First and Second Aliyah, I am avoiding using these periodizations because none of my sources use these terms. The term *aliyah* has been retroactively applied by contemporary historians. Its literally Hebrew meaning is "to ascend" and comes from Genesis 50:13 when Jacob's bones are "brought up" to the Land of Israel.

religion at their point of entry. Kemal Karpat has used the Ottoman archives to estimate that the number of Russian migrants who came to Constantinople is at least 11,500 documented men and women between 1880-1913, but likely more came either illegally or claiming they were "en route" to other cities in the Ottoman Empire and beyond.[24] We know from the records of the Jewish Colonization Association that immigrants came from places like Bessarabia, Kiev, Odessa, and Novoselytsia, and possibly others in the Russian Empire.[25] Congressional records in the United States in support of Jewish migration tell us that they also came from places like Podolia and outside of Moscow.[26] And Jews were not the only subjects migrating to the Ottoman Empire from the Russian Empire. At the end of the 19th century, approximately one million Muslim refugees entered Ottoman lands from Crimea and the Northern Caucuses, and, after the end of the First World War, they were joined by Tatars, Circassians, and Turks from the Russian Empire.[27] The newly formed Turkish State was particularly interested in accepting emigrants who were religiously Muslim and Turkish speaking.[28] Political turmoil – namely the Bolshevik Revolution, World War I, and the Russian Civil War, and consequent mass emigration, led to the moniker "Russia abroad" in the Ottoman Empire and many other places in Europe. Constantinople (and later Istanbul) became one of the pivotal centers for "white or anti-Bolshevik" emigres, namely Paris, Berlin, Prague, Sofia, Belgrade, and Harbin.[29] Interestingly, Russian Jews – who had for generations been restricted to settle largely only in the Pale of Settlement (with exception for the Crimea and Odessa) for the first time, encountered non-Jewish Russians in these major European cities.

The Jewish Colonization Association, founded by the Austrian Jewish Baron Maurice de Hirsch, was the first organization in the Russian Empire to help migrants and advise them free of charge, having received official

---

24   Kemal H. Karpat, *Ottoman Population, 1830-1914: Demographic and Social Characteristics* (Madison: University of Wisconsin Press, 1985).

25   ICA/Turkey CAHJP ICA/Tur 237-2. See also Letter to Monsieurs Taranto, 19 Janvier 1911, from Férnandez, CAHJP ICA/Tur 237-2.
      Ibid.

26   *Congressional Record* (Senate), February 15, 1892, vol. 33, pt. 2 (52nd Congress,. 1st session), 1132 (speech of Senator W.E. Chandler); *New York Sun,* February 12, 1892, *opt. cite* in Markel, *Quarantine,* 1997

27   Yelena Lykova, "Russian Emigration to Turkey in the 1920s: A Case Study," Hacettepe Üniversitesi *İktisadi ve İdari Bilimler Fakültesi Dergisi,* Cilt 25, Sayı 1, (2007): 323-341

28   Ibid.

29   Ibid., 332

authorization from Russian authorities in 1891 after the work of a Arnold White, a British Member of Parliament and fairly well-known anti-Semite, discussed in chapter four, and David Feinberg, who became the executive chairman of the JCA Russia.[30] The chairman of the central committee of the JCA was Baron Horace Ginsburg (1833-1909), a famous Russian philanthropist and patron of the St. Petersburg Grand Choral Synagogue. The JCA began circulating informational pamphlets in Yiddish, Russian, and Hebrew, covering a range of immigration topics such as how to exchange money, required documentation, passage, etc.[31] Ginsburg and another employee, Janovsky, set policies for the information bureaus to warn the would-be immigrants not to rely on the "recommendations of relatives to travel specifically to the places where they work, not to be drawn to the large and beautiful cities over the ocean to which emigration naturally flows."[32] By 1906, there were 160 information bureaus in the Pale of Settlement, and by 1913, there were 507.[33] These regional information bureaus communicated back to the JCA office and sometimes to the JCA Turkey office, and served as a communication point between Jewish communities, often forwarding information of Jewish law to the Office of the Chief Rabbi.[34] The Bureaus aided immigrants (to places beyond the Ottoman Empire) in all matters concerning emigration including medical assistance, financial assistance for purchasing tickets and passports, and securing bodily protection for women immigrants.[35]

In 1890–91, approximately 45,393 Jews lived in Istanbul Province, and 44,361 in Istanbul City. By 1893–94, that number had increased to 46,440, and 45,369, respectively, and by 1911–12, the population had grown to 53,606 in the Province and 51,721 in Istanbul City. Istanbul Province accounted

30   Gur Alroey, *An Unpromising Land: Jewish Migration to Palestine in the Early Twentieth Century* (Stanford: Stanford University Press, 2014), 66. See Norman, *An Outstretched Arm*, 20.

31   Ibid, 66-68. See also CAHJP ICA/Lon 67-1. I have been unable to determine Janovsky's first name.

32   Ibid, 68.

33   Ibid, 67.

34   Ibid. See also CAHJP ICA/Tur 237-2, and CAHJP HM2/9070-1

35   Ibid. 70.

for approximately 15% of the Empire's Jewish population.[36] This population growth took place in the context of major catastrophic events and over a decade of war, including the Balkan Wars (1912–13), the First World War (1914–18), the Armenian Genocide (1915), and the subsequent forced removal of millions of people under "population exchanges" in order to fit national populations into new boundaries according to the Treaty of Lausanne (1923).[37]

The Galata neighborhood was the religious and ethnic *entrepôt* of Constantinople, and its urban image was quite different from that of the Istanbul peninsula. It was a densely populated settlement surrounded by fifteenth-century walls, 2.80 kilometers long and 2.00 meters thick and built over five periods, demarcated it as an independent Genoese suburb and divided it into five zones. In 1863, an Ottoman imperial order mandated the walls to be torn down after the European model to gain access to new streets and widen existing ones. New neighborhoods, Tophane and Fındıklı, were built along the Bosporus, and Kasımpaşa along the Golden Horn (Haliç), and they quickly became the most densely populated. The inhabitants of Galata included a cosmopolitan blend of Armenians, Greeks, Europeans and Jews. The Jews lived primarily along the eastern part of the waterfront, just outside the city walls. The three new outposts were exclusively Muslim.

Tevye's Ottoman daughter would have walked along Yüksek Kaldırım, "synagogue street," which connected Galata to Pera (north of the Galata Tower, see figure 1.0, literally meaning *beyond* in Turkish) via the Grand Rue de Pera and continues to do so to this day. Jewish life in Galata was concentrated in these and neighboring streets, housing at least three Ashkenazi synagogues, and a number of brothels. From the Ashkenazi Synagogue, she would have looked up and seen the Galata Tower to the northwest. The romanesque Galata Tower, or *Tower of Christ*, was built in 1348 while Galata was still a

---

36   Justin McCarthy, "Jewish Population in the Late Ottoman Period," in *The Jews of the Ottoman Empire*, ed. Avigdor Levy (Princeton: Darwin Press, 1994), 377–78. Scholars such as McCarthy and Karpat have used Ottoman sources to determine populations of multiple ethnic groups. Jews were "somewhat better recorded than Muslims and Armenians, and approximately as well recorded as Greeks. This was due to the essentially urban character of the Jewish population." Women and children were systematically underrepresented in the Ottoman census, and their numbers were likely higher than indicated in census figures.

37   See Devin E. Naar *Jewish Salonica: Between the Ottoman Empire and Modern Greece* (Stanford: Stanford University Press, 2016), 5; see also Reşat Kasaba, *A Moveable Empire: Ottoman Nomads, Migrants, and Migrants* (Seattle: University of Washington Press, 2009).

Figure 1.0:

Old map of Constantinople (Istanbul) Center - Pera of Constantinople in Turkey
by Wagner & Debes, Leipzig (1905)

Genoese colony.[38] Albert Kant, a Russian Jew who left the Russian Empire with his family to start a farm in Western Anatolia, writes of his impressions of Galata during the First World War while on a guided tour by Joseph Niego (1863–1945), who worked for the Jewish Colonization Association and the Alliance:

> The official language was Turkish, but the Greek, Armenian, Judeo-Spanish, French, English and German languages were widespread in the district. The Russian restaurants swarmed every way you looked, ranging from the simple to the elegant, and the diverse population came to taste the delicious Russian dishes: borsch, kasha, blinis, shashlik, and other specialties. There were even Jewish restaurants that served stuffed fish, chicken bouillon with pasta, paté and other dishes specific to Russian Jews.[39]

During her stay in Galata, she would have encountered various ethnic and religious groups conducting business, including European expatriates, Armenians, Greeks, and, after the Balkan Wars (1912–13), many Sephardic Jews who had sought refuge in Constantinople. Religious groups with a presence in Galata included the Armenian Evangelical Church (established in 1846 in Constantinople), the Bulgarian Catholic Church (where services were conducted in Old Slavic according to the rites of the Eastern Church), Bulgarian Orthodox, and French Roman Catholic Church.[40] Jews in Ottoman Istanbul worked in tobacco factories or had small shops serving their surrounding communities.[41] By the twentieth century, they owned many of the important department stores in downtown Istanbul.[42]

The Jewish *millet*, from the Arabic word *milah,* or nation, was one of six official *millets* in the Ottoman Empire after the *Tanzimat* Reforms in the mid-nineteenth century. Roman Catholics, Syriac Christians, Greek Orthodox, Armenians, and Muslims were governed by the principle that each religious community had religious and some legal jurisdiction over its

---

38   Alexander Kazhan, ed., *Oxford Dictionary of Byzantium* (New York: Oxford University Press, 1991), 815.

39   Albert Kant, *Mèmoires d'un Fermier Juif en Turquie*, ed. by Rıfat N. Bali (Istanbul: Libra Kitap, 2013), 124.

40   Clarence Richard Johnson, *Constantinople Today; Or, The Pathfinder Survey of Constantinople: A Study in Oriental Social Life* (New York: Macmillan, 1922), 149–55.

41   Ibid.; see also Marie-Christine Bornes-Varol, "The Balat Quarter and its Image: A Study of a Jewish Neighborhood in Istanbul," trans. by Eric Fassin and Avigdor Levy in *The Jews of the Ottoman Empire*, ed. Avigdor Levy (Princeton: Darwin, 1994), 633–46.

42   Yavuz Köse, "Vertical Bazaars of Modernity: Western Department Stores and Their Staff in Istanbul (1889–1921)," *International Review of Social History* 54, no. S17 (2009): 91–114.

subjects.[43] The *Haham Başı* or Chief Rabbi served as an interlocutor between the Ottoman state and the Jewish population. As was the case with other *millets* in the Ottoman Empire, the administration did not distinguish among ethnic groups, and despite the existence of at least five types of Jews in the Empire (Ashkenazi, including Russian and German Jews, Sephardic, Italian, and Karaite), a Chief Rabbi had jurisdiction over all civil and religious matters involving the Empire's Jews.[44]

In 1890, emboldened by the growing Russian Jewish population in Constantinople, already established German Jews joined forces, however tentatively, with the newly-arriving Russian Jews under the rubric of "Ashkenazi Jews" in order to challenge the primacy of the Chief Rabbi, who had been Sephardic and prioritized the interests of the demographically dominant Sephardic Jews in the empire. For the first time, the *Haham Başı* (then Moshe Halévy (1827–1910)) issued a statement citing the responsibilities between the office of the *Haham Başı* and the Ashkenazi Jewish community and created a new position, called the *Baş Haham* ("Principle Rabbi").[45] Now with more formal and recognized status, the Ashkenazi community searched for a rabbi who could both lead the new congregation and assume the position of headmaster at the German Jewish secondary school, the Goldschmidt School. That rabbi was David Feivel Markus (1870–1944), a young rabbi born in Russia but educated in Austria-Hungary who could appeal to the predominantly Russian constituency but could also speak to the Austro-Hungarian orientation of the German Jews.

---

43   See Stanford J. Shaw et. al., *History of the Ottoman Empire and Modern Turkey* (Cambridge: Cambridge University Press, 1976).

44   Avigdor Levy "The Appointment of a Chief Rabbi in 1835," in *The Jews of the Ottoman Empire*, ed. Avigdor Levy (Princeton: Darwin, 1994), 425–39.

45   "Una Convension entre el *Haham Başı* y los Senores Rubenthal, Friedman, y Mayefayr," *El Tiempo*, 30 June 1890; see also D Gershon Lewental, "Levi (Ha-Levi), Moshe," in: *Encyclopedia of Jews in the Islamic World*, ed. Norman A. Stillman. Consulted online 21 September 2016.

Rabbi David Markus,
photograph courtesy of Robert Schild

Rabbi Markus arrived in 1900 in the Galata quarter of Constantinople, became head of the Goldschmidt School, and began working and accepting leadership positions within several Jewish organizations, including the newly built Tailor's Synagogue. Markus and community leaders became concerned with what they saw as high rates of conversion among Jews and the presence of Protestant missionaries from Western Europe and set up programming to resist conversion.[46]

Tensions between Ashkenazim and Sephardim reached its peak in the wake of the Young Turk Revolution (1908), which stimulated the proliferation and visibility of various Jewish nationalisms through the abolition of censorship in the press, when Rabbi Markus appeared to be at the helm of Zionist movements

---

46   See Rachel Saba Wolfe, "From Protestant Missionaries to Jewish Educators: Children's Textbooks in Judeo Spanish," *Neue Romania* 40 (2011): 135–51. For conversion in the interwar period, see Naar, *Jewish Salonica*, 67.

in the city.[47] At the height of political instability, Ashkenazi Jews and especially Russian Jews became denoted as "foreign Jews" in the Ladino language press, with political ideas (of Jewish national statehood) that were fundamentally opposed to the editors' interpretation of the Young Turk Revolution and the political future of the Ottoman Empire. For the first time, the Jewish community *elected* a new *Haham Başı*, Haim Nahum, six months after the Young Turk Revolution. As a protégé of the Alliance Israélite Universelle, which was anti-nationalist and pro-integrationist, Nahum shaped the official policy of the Ottoman Jewish community as anti-Zionist, and most of all, pro-Empire.[48] Markus' Zionism therefore placed him at odds with Nahum and the Ottoman Jewish (Sephardic) establishment. Many Sephardim, however, including those educated by the Alliance, did not see Jewish migration to Palestine as a threat to the Ottoman Empire as long as Jewish colonization was not accompanied by calls for Jewish political independence. Instead, Palestine was conceptualized rather as a kind of Jewish "outpost" in the Ottoman Empire that maintained the empire's territorial integrity.[49]

Additionally, none of the Russian sources specifically raise the prospect of a sovereign Jewish state in Palestine, which is consistent with the agendas of other Jewish nationalist thinkers and migrants who anticipated the creation of a Jewish home within the framework of Ottoman Palestine. In 1911, with the help of Joseph Niego (the same person who served as a tour guide to Kant during his time in Constantinople), a prominent Ottoman Sephardic Jewish leader, the Ashkenazi community helped found the local Lodge of the B'nai B'rith ("people of the covenant") organization, which, in addition to providing aid for the needy, was an attempt to bring together Sephardim and Ashkenazim in the Ottoman Empire. Despite the heightened tensions between the communities in Constantinople, the B'nai B'rith Lodge hoped to foster community between the two groups, to "combine the scruples and self-esteem and the fiery Castilian pride [of the Sephardim] with the spirit of enterprise, endurance to persecution, as Ashkenazim bring with them the

---

47   See for example, issues of *L'Aurore* from 1908, and 23 July 1909

48   Esther Benbassa, *A Sephardic Chief Rabbi in Politics, 1892–1923*, trans. Miriam Kochan (Tuscaloosa: University of Alabama Press, 1995) and Aron Rodrigue, *French Jews, Turkish Jews: The Alliance Israélite Universelle and the Politics of Jewish Schooling in Turkey, 1860-1925* (Indiana: Indiana University Press, 1990).

49   See Abigail Johnson, *From Empire to Empire: Between Ottoman and British Rule* (Syracuse: Syracuse University Press, 2011); Michelle U. Campos, *Ottoman Brothers: Muslims, Christians, and Jews in Early Twentieth-Century Palestine* (Stanford: Stanford University Press, 2011).

cultivated circles of the places in Europe in which they have lived," as Joseph Niego stated in a speech in 1913.[50] This telling excerpt is telling of the kind of orientalist essentializations at work in these claims to Sephardi and Ashkenazi identities.

Confronting Archival Silences: Jewish History, Historiography, and the Limits of an Archive

This book is named for Tevye's Ottoman *daughters* not only as an allusion to the work of Shalom Aleichem, but also to underscore the silence of the incomplete historical record. My naming this study as such reflects my desire to remind my reader that despite the fact that many of the protagonists of my narrative are men, this is a result of the unfortunate reality that Russian Jewish women, both as marginalized migrants and as women, were not obviously visible in the archive.[51] Each archive is limited and the challenges I faced are common to researchers working across many fields. While the Ladino press and archives in Jerusalem and in Turkey rarely mention Russian Jewish women, there was one startling exception: several Jewish communities in Constantinople and abroad became increasingly alarmed with growing numbers of Russian Jewish prostitutes in the Ottoman capital.

The Black Sea port was a gateway to North America, South America, and the Middle East for migrants of all kinds, including Russian Jewish prostitutes. The prostitution trade became a topic for debate and a target for suppression among at least three Jewish communities: Western European Jews, German Jews in Constantinople, and Sephardi Jews in Constantinople. Groups of prominent Jewish philanthropists from Western Europe, interested in maintaining their own positions in Europe by combating anti-Semitic tropes that Jews "dealt with finance and in flesh," formed the Jewish Association for the Protection of Girls and Women in 1883. The Austrian-Jewish feminist Bertha Pappenheim (whom students of Freud will recognize as "Anna O."), succinctly described this problem at the Jewish Conference on the White Slave Traffic in London in 1910: "If we admit the existence of this traffic our enemies

---

50   *Bulletin de la Grande Loge de District XI et de la Loge de Constantinople, No. 678* (1913), 112.

51   Emma Perez, "Queering the Borderlands: The Challenges of Excavating the Invisible and Unheard," *Frontiers: A Journal of Women Studies* 24 (2003): 122–31.

decry us; if we deny it they say we are trying to conceal it."[52] As Paula Hyman noted in her study of Jewish immigrants in the United States at the turn of the century, the urgency to eradicate Jewish entanglement in prostitution coincided with Jewish embourgeoisement; in other words, "their concern was heightened by their awareness that their own status and image were linked in the public imagination with the ... newcomers."[53] Therefore, "Jewish social workers, reformers, and philanthropists were particularly sensitive to the mores and image of women, for the entire group's honor could be called into question by the disreputable conduct of its women."[54] The list of concerned parties in the Ottoman context included Lady Constance Rothschild Battersea, Pappenheim, and members of the German Jewish community in Constantinople. One of the reasons that Constantinople's Ashkenazi Jews began to refer to themselves as German Jews was in fact to distance themselves from Russian Jews. Pappenheim and other Western European Jews had criticized the Ashkenazi Jews of Constantinople for allowing prostitution to spread unchecked throughout the city. She described this laissez-faire attitude as a result of a "moral defect [of allowing prostitution to prevail in the city] that ... derives from living together with the Turks, or—what appears to me as more probable—a hereditary mindset among the oriental Jews."[55]

Imagining Tevye's Ottoman daughter helps us to understand this apparent paradox: why were Russian Jews, specifically Russian Jewish women, at the center of a transnational discourse surrounding prostitution, yet simultaneously occluded from traditional tellings of Jewish history? As Irving Howe noticed: "communities struggling for survival seldom rush to announce their failures."[56]

An additional layer that also must be considered is the complex work of conducting historical scholarship in the Ottoman Empire. Scholars such as Aron Rodrigue, Sarah Abrevaya Stein, Julia Phillips Cohen, and Devin E. Naar have begun to correct the scholarly asymmetry that has favored "European"

---

52 Bertha Pappenheim, "The Burning Shame of a Terrible Scandal: Jewish Conference in London on the White Slave Traffic," *The Jewish Chronicle*, 23 April 1910.

53 Paula Hyman, *Gender and Assimilation in Modern Jewish History: The Roles and Representation of Women* (Seattle: University of Washington Press, 1995), 106.

54 Ibid.

55 Pappenheim, "Burning Shame of a Terrible Scandal", 40-42

56 Irving Howe, *World of Our Fathers* (Harcourt: New York, 1976), 96.

Jewish Studies, wherein a kind of "double erasure" has occurred (an erasure of Sephardic history, and within that, an erasure of the history of Russian Jewish migration to the Sephardic Ottoman world). Indeed, the story of Russian Jewish migrants in the Ottoman Empire has been therefore occluded by the two principal Jewish historiographies: the Sephardic history of the Ottoman Empire and the teleological foundational narrative of the State of Israel. As the eminent scholar of Jewish History Yosef Yerushalmi (1932–2009) commented on the particularly important relationship between Jewish history and Jewish memory, and how the establishment of the State of Israel obfuscated Jews' "perception of how they got there and where they are," which is "most often more mythical than real."[57] This teleology that Yerushalmi hints at precludes certain histories from traditional Jewish historiography.[58]

Over the past decade, there has been a surge of publications on alternative Jewish nationalist projects, from the Soviet Far East in Birobidzhan to agricultural projects in New Jersey.[59] Sovereign Jewish statehood was one vision among several for Jewish life in the age of European-style nationalism, yet because this vision prevailed, histories of Zionism dominated the historiography. Indeed, this dominance was born out of the Israeli state building project and the deeply rooted relationship between history and historiography.[60] Imagining Tevye's Ottoman daughter is therefore an act of historical recovery.

The geographic imaginations of Russian Jews who migrated to the Ottoman Empire because it was in the vicinity of the Land of Israel may challenge our own understanding of the geographical boundaries of the Land of Israel. Some sources suggest that many Russian Jews considered any part of the Ottoman

---

57   Yosef Yerushalmi, *Zakhor: Jewish History and Jewish Memory* (Seattle: University of Washington Press, 1982), 99.

58   See Devin E. Naar, "Fashioning the 'Mother of Israel': The Ottoman Jewish Historical Narrative and the Image of Jewish Salonica,"*Jewish History* 28, no. 3 (2014): 337–72.

59   See, for example, Jonathan Dekel-Chen, *Farming the Red Land: Jewish Agricultural Colonization and Local Soviet Power, 1924–1941* (New Haven: Yale University Press, 2005); Henry Felix Srebrnik, *Jerusalem on the Amur: Birobidzhan and the Canadian Jewish Communist Movement, 1924–1951* (Montreal: McGill-Queen's University Press, 2008); Adam Rovner, *In the Shadow of Zion: Promised Lands Before Israel* (New York: New York University Press, 2014).

60   The trials of the Israeli "New Historians" or "Post-Zionists" is a case in point. For commentary on the New Historians' work, see Edward Said, "New History, Old Ideas," *Al-Ahram*, 27 May 1998; Benny Morris, *The Birth of the Palestinian Refugee Problem 1947–1949* (Cambridge: Cambridge University Press 1989); Ilan Pappé, *A History of Modern Palestine: One Land Two Peoples* (Cambrige: Cambridge University Press, 2006).

Empire, not only the Land of Israel, to be desirable for settlement precisely because Palestine was part of the Ottoman Empire.[61] Migrating to the Ottoman borderlands or Constantinople was a better option than avoiding the region entirely. An agricultural colony on the Aegean Sea was an attractive option for families like that of Albert Kant's, who came to the Ottoman Empire because it was "in the domain of the holy land" to begin a farming business with his parents and siblings in 1913. Kant became infatuated by Zionist politics during the First World War, but abandoned the idea after experiencing the rigors of agricultural life and settled into life in Constantinople. From newly arrived immigrants to rabbis, we will also meet figures like the aforementioned Joseph Niego (1863–1945) and Isaac Férnandez (1889–1929), Sephardic Jews with close connections to the major Jewish organizations of Constantinople who proved integral to the shaping of policy and practice on the ground in the Ottoman Empire.

While the Ottoman Empire was the destination for some Russians, for others it was a stepping-stone to North America or to Western Europe, and sometimes Tevye's Ottoman daughter returned to the Russian Empire. Migration is not unidirectional; migrants' experiences in various locales affected their politics and identities and impacted their decisions to move from one place to the next. While Tevye's Ottoman daughter may have set out for the Ottoman Empire for a variety of reasons, the late Ottoman milieu she encountered would have provided a swirling confrontation of multiple political ideas and ideologies, especially Zionism, Territorialism, Ottomanism, and the ideas of the Young Turk Revolution. Additionally, she would have been confronted with various kinds of economic opportunities that may have encouraged her to make one decision over another, regardless of political or ideological affiliation. Her potential responses included options to return to the Russian Empire.[62]

Although two of the most discussed versions of Jewish nationalism—Zionism and Territorialism—proposed competing solutions to the problem of "Jewish homelessness" (to borrow from historian Adam Rovner), this project suggests that the people and organizations who implemented and supported

---

61   See, for example, Albert Kant, *Mèmoires d'un Fermier Juif*, 23, and See Letters from Migrants to JCA, CAHJP ICA/Turk 067-1

62   For example, Albert Kant's Uncle Oyser returned to Bessarabia after the end of the First World War. Kant, *Mèmoires d'un Fermier Juif*, 102.

the various movements frequently overlapped. Zionism, rudimentarily defined as Jewish national statehood in the "Land of Israel" or *Eretz Yisrael*, has traditionally been understood as at odds with Territorialism, an ideological movement(s) that advocated for Jewish autonomy and self-reliance, but not in *Eretz Yisrael*. Sephardic Jews did not see Zionism and Territorialism as two distinct options, but rather understood the Ottoman Empire as already having served as a refuge for Europe's homeless Jews (*kibbutz galuyot*), a point to be further explored in Chapter 2.[63] After the 1908 Young Turk Revolution lifted censorship of the press, Zionism began to be discussed more openly and Sephardi and Ashkenazi Jews debated its multiple forms.[64] In his study of Jewish Territorialist projects from Angola to New Jersey, Rovner points out that Territorialists and Zionists "both said *there was a land;* they just couldn't agree on where it was located or how it was to be constituted."[65] What Rovner alludes to, and as this study also finds, is that the actual migrants and those who carried out the logistical work of Jewish nationalism often overlapped from one nationalist or territorialist project to another. Although intellectuals, politicians, and journalists may have disagreed as to where the boundaries of the Land of Israel were, the projects turned out to have much in common with one another.

Historians of Jewish nationalism may be surprised to find a host of familiar names and organizations in this monograph. Israel Zangwill, Edmond de Rothschild, Vladimir Jabotinsky, and even Theodor Herzl himself appear here, and all participated in familiar organizations such as the Alliance, the Jewish Colonization Association, and the B'nai B'rith Movement. In addition to these leaders synonymous with Jewish nationalism, I have pursued the perspective of both ordinary Jews in Constantinople and in the Ottoman borderlands. To superimpose contemporary terms on this time period, "program managers" such as Joseph Niego and Issaac Férnandez were employed by organizations like the Alliance Israélite Universelle and the Jewish Colonization Association to assist Russian Jews and migrants in the Ottoman Empire, but unwittingly helped set in motion pro-nationalist ideas despite their marching orders.

---

63   See also Cohen, *Becoming Ottoman*, and Naar, *Jewish Salonica*.

64   See Michelle U. Campos, *Ottoman Brothers*, and Julia Phillips Cohen, *Becoming Ottomans*.

65   Rovner, *In the Shadow of Zion*, 2–5. Rovner uses an allusion to the German Jewish poet Shaul Tchernichovsky's 1923 poem "They Say: There is a Land," written in 1923: "How / have we gone astray? / When will we be unmolested? / That land of sun, / That land never found."

My project is situated in the midst of some of the greatest political and social upheavals in modern history: war, revolution, and population exchanges among the ruins of the two last great empires in Eastern Europe. These are the classic examples of *shatterzones*, a concept elucidated in two recent monographs. Michael A. Reynold's *Shattering Empires* (2011) examines the dual collapse of the Russian and Ottoman Empires from the vantage point of the borderlands. Reynolds notes that existing historiography on both empires, aided in part by the post-1991 dissolution of the Soviet Union along national borders, casts the blame for imperial (and Soviet) collapse on a kind of dormant nationalism. He argues that scholars have grown to be "comfortable with the idea of nationalism" at the cost of undervaluing other dynamics.[66] I similarly reconsider the "prison of nations" narrative found in both Russian and Ottoman history, and my project demonstrates, as Rogers Brubaker has argued, that nationalism was not a primordial sentiment that lay dormant, but rather was "induced ... by political fields of particular kinds."[67] By examining the late Ottoman milieu, we see that the Jewish nationalism that resulted in Israeli statehood was not a pre-existing goal of Ashkenazi and Sephardi Jews, but instead became both "cause and effect" by the turn of the century, aided in part by the practices of the reforming Ottoman Empire and the Young Turk Revolution.[68]

The second essential work on shatterzones is a volume by Omer Bartov and Eric Weitz, *Shatterzones of Empires: Coexistence and Violence in the German, Habsburg, Russian and Ottoman Borderlands*. They observe that by examining these shatterzones, we can "gain a much greater understanding of how the many populations of this borderland managed to coexist and how they eventually descended into and became objects of the worst violence imaginable."[69] As the Ottoman Empire and the Russian Empires transitioned

---

66   Michael A. Reynolds, *Shattering Empires: The Clash and Collapse of the Ottoman and Russian Empires 1908–1918* (Cambridge: Cambridge University Press, 2011), 5–6.

67   Rogers Brubaker, *Nationalism Reframed: Nationhood and the National Question in the New Europe* (Cambridge: Cambridge University Press, 1996), 15.

68   Brubaker, *Nationalism Reframed*, 4. For more on this process in the Soviet Union, see Ronald Suny, *The Revenge of the Past: Nationalism, Revolution, and the Collapse of the Soviet Union* (Stanford: Stanford University Press, 1993); Francine Hirsch, *Empire of Nations: Ethnographic Knowledge and the Making of the Soviet Union* (Ithaca: Cornell University Press, 2014); and Terry Dean Martin, *The Affirmative Action Empire: Nations and Nationalism in the Soviet Union, 1923–1939* (Ithaca: Cornell University Press, 2001).

69   Omer Bartov and Eric D. Weitz, *Shatterzone of Empires: Coexistence and Violence in the German, Habsburg, Russian, and Ottoman Borderlands* (Bloomington: Indiana University Press, 2013), 2. See also Reynolds, *Shattering Empires*.

from multiethnic empires into nation-states, how did Jews conceptualize their identities, citizenships, and roles in this new landscape?[70] What was their relationship to the many forms of nationalism (including Zionism) that circulated throughout the Jewish world? How can we conceptualize these relationships if we view nationalism as "expansive, indeed revolutionary, in its claim that the conformity of territorial and ethnic borders was the natural state of being," which directly challenged "the multiethnic and multiconfessional empires with their far more extensive borders?"[71]

While Bartov and Weitz emphasize that borderlands, because they are "far from the seat of power," become shatterzones, the critical relationship that the borderlands have with the center requires further investigation. This project shows that the identities of Jewish agriculturalists like Kant were not "made or unmade" solely in the borderlands. Identity was rather the result of a constitutive process determined by the relationships between many places, including the Ottoman métropole.

In other words, this book is about porosity, not only of borders, but of ideas, people, and institutions. The boundaries between the Ottoman Empire and the Russian Empire were porous, as were the boundaries between Palestine and (the rest of) the Ottoman Empire. So too were the boundaries among Jewish communal organizations, even ones that claimed one political allegiance over the other. Despite tensions and attempts to delineate national (and political) difference, Jewish life in the twilight years of the Ottoman Empire was far more diverse and far more porous than Jews of the Ottoman and Russian Empires held them to be, or Jewish, Russian and Ottoman history has claimed it to be.[72] This book is about recovering what it meant to be one of Tevye's daughters.

---

70   For the Soviet Union as an empire versus a nation-state, see Martin, *The Affirmative Action Empire*, and Hirsch, *Empire of Nations*.

71   Bartov and Weitz, *Shatterzone of Empires*, 5.

72   See, for example, See Devi Mays, *Forging Ties, Forging Passports: Migration and the Modern Sephardi Diaspora* (Stanford: Stanford University Press, 2020) and Devin E. Naar, "Fashioning the 'Mother of Israel': The Ottoman Jewish Historical Narrative and the Image of Jewish Salonica," *Jewish History* 28, no. 3 (2014): 337–72.

Sources, Methods, Memory, and Memoir

Recovering migrants' motivations to leave one's home for another place is one of the most difficult tasks that a historian can undertake. In official paperwork, immigrants might obscure their true reasons for leaving in order to more easily move past officials at the port or cut through bureaucratic red tape. Thus the letters from Jewish migrants to information bureaus in North America and Western Europe, collected and published by Guy Alroey, are all the more remarkable. They document the "dramatic moment when a family came to the decision that there was no longer any hope for them in Eastern Europe and they would have to move to a new land—despite all the difficulties—and build a new, safer life." Alroey astutely notices that while acculturation, assimilation, and migrants' life in their new locales has received much scholarly attention, a lack of source material has made it difficult to identify "why some Jews acted on these urgent motives and others did not," as Irving Howe has formulated this important question.[73]

This book relies on multiple types of sources primarily collected in Jerusalem, Istanbul, and also in Seattle. Regarding Jerusalem, I rely on a few principal archival collections, including incoming letters from the Ashkenazi community to the *Haham Başı*, the collections of the Jewish Colonization Association in Turkey and in London, as well as select publications from the Alliance Israélite Universelle. I also gained access to some objects of material culture in Istanbul as well as some unarchived material there, including Torah curtains made by Russian migrants, religious books published in Odessa and brought to the Synagogue by Russian migrants, and (partial) registries from the Ashkenazi Synagogue. The languages of these sources are as diverse as the Jews were at the turn of the century, which include Judeo-Spanish or Ladino, Russian, Yiddish, German, Hebrew, English, and French, the Mediterranean basin's *lingua franca*.[74]

Memoir, as its name suggests, relies on *memory*, which entails a processes of self-fashioning, of reimagining the past. Historian Yosef Yerushalmi famously remarked that "memory is always problematic, usually deceptive,

---

73   Guy Alroey, *Bread to Eat and Clothes to Wear: Letters from Jewish Migrants in the Early Twentieth Century* (Detroit: Wayne State University Press, 2011), 2–3.

74   "Judeo-Spanish" is the term most frequently used in my sources. The language is usually referred to as Ladino in the United States, and is sometimes also called Judezmo.

and sometimes treacherous."[75] The Russian novelist Vladimir Nabokov complained, "Mnemosyne, one must admit, has shown herself to be a very careless girl."[76] Despite Nabokov's observations, I have decided to incorporate Kant's memoir because it gives us rare insight into the perspective of typical Russian Jews who immigrated to the Ottoman Empire. In an archive brimming with official correspondence, Kant's memoir is particularly important precisely *because* it is such a problematic source. Through it, we have a glimpse of the process of self-fashioning – how a memoirist justified his decision to remain in the Ottoman Empire or, after 1923, in Turkey – and how he positioned himself as a Russian émigré discussing high Russian culture despite living on a farm in Western Anatolia. And we follow Kant as he struggles with his Zionist ideals despite not being able to follow through with them.

This book is split into four principle chapters. Through its structure, I have mirrored the path that Tevye's Ottoman daughter may have taken from her home in the Russian Empire to Odessa to Constantinople, to the Ottoman borderlands, and perhaps back to Constantinople.

The first chapter, "*Los Rusos* in the Jewish Entrepôt," traces representations of Russian Jews in the Sephardic (Ladino) press during pivotal years, including the "Fourth Centennial of Spanish Expulsion," a new civic holiday commemorating Sephardic Jews' arrival in the Ottoman Empire that also coincided with the two hundredth anniversary of Jewish emancipation in France through the French Revolution. During this period, Russian Jews came to serve as a foil for the Sephardic "emancipated" Jewish experience in the Ottoman Empire. Sephardic Jews' preoccupation with the "Centenary of the French Revolution" indicated that they saw themselves as inheritors of the "Paris" model of Jewish emancipation. This chapter develops the idea that Jews in the Ottoman Empire understood themselves in relationship with other, specifically Russian, Jews, and that these "horizontal" relationships were as important to their understandings of themselves as subjects of the Ottoman Empire as were their "vertical" relationship with the sultan and the Ottoman State.

---

75   Yosef Yerushalmi, *Zakhor*, 10.

76   Vladimir Nabokov, *Speak, Memory: An Autobiography Revisited* (New York: Knopf, 1999), 6–7. Nabokov recalls that after the publication of his autobiography, friends and relatives would constantly remind him of how he erred: "Certain matters were dismissed by my advisers as legends or rumors or, if genuine, were proven to be related to events and periods other than those to which frail memory had attached them."

The second chapter, "Tevye's Ottoman Daughters" revisits the title of the book in order to focus on what I see as a central piece of Ottoman Jewish history. The chapter is an analysis of the various discourses surrounding the "white slave trade" among Western European Jewish philanthropists, Ashkenazi Jews in Constantinople, and Sephardi Jews in Constantinople, and the various political and social contexts for their anxieties in the wake of significant demographic changes in Europe, North America, and in the Ottoman Empire. The chapter examines discourses concerning prostitution, the highly gendered moral categories by which it was analyzed, and the influence of ideas such as the *eishet chayil* ("woman of valor") for the transmitters of tradition. These discourses serve as examples of "nesting Orientalisms," which, as Usamma Makdisi has pointed out, are a consequence of internalized Orientalism.[77] Various categories, including "German Jew," begin to emerge from these discourses.

Chapter 3, "Under One Great Fraternal Flag: Ashkenazi Jews in Constantinople," examines the ways in which Ashkenazi Jews and Jews from Russia helped to erode Sephardic hegemony in the capital's institutions, including houses of prayer, communal gathering and camaraderie, as well as in the print media. This chapter examines the growing power of political Zionism in this time period and how conflicting ideas about the future of Ottoman Jewry contributed to schisms in the Jewish community that were largely blamed on (perceived) national divisions. In the pages of the post-1908 press, free of censorship for the first time, Sephardim, Ashkenazim, and many in the middle debated what political vision would inherit the legacy of the Young Turk Revolution, an event by which "under one great fraternal flag, thirty years of hatred was abolished," as journalist Lucien Sciuto reported in a new periodical published in the Ottoman Empire, *L'Aurore*.[78]

Finally, we conclude with the fourth chapter in the borderlands of Anatolia, "A Nursery Ground for Palestine? Russian Jews in the Ottoman Borderlands," which follows Russian Jewish movement from Constantinople to the Ottoman borderlands, specifically in the Aegean region just outside of Smyrna (Izmir). Here we follow the story of Russian migrants, such as Kant (1901–1972),

---

77   Milica Bakić-Hayden, "Nesting Orientalisms: The Case of Former Yugoslavia," *Slavic Review* 54, no. 4 (1995): 917–31. See also Edward Said, *Orientalism* (New York: Vintage Books, 1979), and Edward Said, *Culture and Imperialism* (Vintage Books: New York, 1994).

78   *L'Aurore*, 23 July 1909

Alfred Goldenberg (1907–1999) and how these migrants interpreted and reinterpreted their Jewish nationalist ideas in conjunction with political ideas and realities both in the Ottoman center (Constantinople) and in Palestine. It becomes clear that the path from Eastern Europe to Palestine was not linear; rather, it took multiple turns and was frequently abandoned.

I have used standard Library of Congress transliterations whenever possible. In Ladino, I opt for *Aki Yerushalayim* spelling. This project relies on an important memoir by Albert Kant, *Mémoires d'un Fermier Juif*. With the exception of Kant's memoir and a few other published sources, most of the sources used in this study consist of archival material that made its way to Jerusalem after the Shoah. Some material pertaining to the Ashkenazi community remains in the hands of private individuals in Istanbul. Fortunately, I was able to examine some of this material in the Ashkenazi Synagogue.[79] My hope is that in the future, this material will be archived and made accessible to scholars. In the meantime, this book should provide a starting point to anyone interested in Tevye's Ottoman daughters.

A note on Terminology

The names of the cities, nation-states, and empires that took shape in this time often took various forms depending on the people discussing them and their political perspective. I have chosen to use place names consistent with the sources that I use. Therefore, Constantinople refers to the capital of the Ottoman Empire until 1908. After the Young Turk Revolution, I refer to it as Istanbul, as did my sources. Smyrna is Izmir until 1923, and "Russia" refers to the Russian Empire prior to the 1917 Bolshevik Revolution.

---

79   In particular, I would like to thank Rabbi Mendy Chitrik for his assistance and generosity in allowing me to access materials in the Ashkenazi Synagogue on Yüksek Kaldırım in Istanbul in the Spring of 2015.

PART I:
CONSTANTINOPLE
1890-1923

Chapter 1

"LOS RUSOS" IN THE JEWISH ENTREPÔT

"The world is a mirror.
What you see in others is a reflection of yourself."

Baal Shem Tov

On December 7, 1891, *El Tiempo*, Constantinople's Ladino-language newspaper, published an article describing Russian migrants in the streets of the Galata neighborhood. The Russians were "humans abandoned in the middle of the street, without bread, without shelter, exposed to the rain and the elements."[1] The scene, the author continues, "had me think about the indifference among our brothers-in both blood and religion- which is the darkest of miseries." He goes on,

> It is time that we Jews of Constantinople should take upon ourselves the sad situation of our brothers. It is a scandal in Judaism that the 50,000 Jews of Constantinople allow these destitute Jews to die from hunger, to watch it happen to their coreligionists with their own eyes. We are responsible day after day in front of humanity.[2]

The author, likely *El Tiempo's* editor David Fresco, invokes the language of nineteenth century nationalism, of fraternal brotherhood of both "blood and religion" to deplore the Jewish community for having done nothing to assist the "poor Russian Jews."[3] The article is a call to action. A fund was formally

---

1   "Los Israelitas Rusos en Konstantinopla," *El Tiempo* December 7, 1891

2   Ibid.

3   Ibid.

established to assist the Russian migrants and the editors ask their readers to understand that they were "responsible…in front of humanity."

Yet what is perhaps most interesting is what follows the descriptions of the Russian Jews in the streets. The editors call upon the *Haham Başı*, Moshe Halévy, to do his part. They write that he "needs to go in front of the community and appeal to the humanitarian sentiments of the Jewish community of the capital and of the philanthropists in Europe. Just like the other causes of the past, we have notified the Alliance, but what follows is on us, on our community." The article continues, "What is at stake is our humanity, our honor, and the Jewish name. What a sad example of our state when we see our fellow Jews, these poor families, dragging in fear through the streets." The article is noticeably self-conscious; the editors point out that what is at stake for the Jewish community of Constantinople is not only judgment by humanity but "honor…and the Jewish name." But why would the Jewish name need to be protected, and from whom?

The 1890s capture a unique moment in Jewish Constantinople. In what must have looked like a Jewish *entrepôt*, or warehouse, Jews of the two great East European empires encountered each other, and they did so in the wake of a broader Jewish debate about participation in the nation states and empires in which they resided.[4] In 1891, the Jews of France were preparing to celebrate two hundred years since their emancipation vis-à-vis the French Revolution, a process that seemed to spread "West to East" across the European continent. Yet full legal emancipation, at least according to the Western European and American Jewries writing these histories of Jewish emancipation, seemed to elude the Jews of both the Ottoman and Russian Empires until their respective statehoods in 1917 and 1923.[5] In their examinations of the Ottoman Empire,

---

4   See Sarah Abrevaya Stein, *Making Jews Modern*.

5   For a definition of emancipation, I turn to the iconic scholarship of Pierre Birnbaum and Ira Katznelson in their classic *Paths of Emancipation*. They argue that emancipation is "Shorthand for access by Jews to the profound shifts in ideas and conditions wrought by the Enlightenment and its liberal offspring: religious toleration, secularization, scientific thought, and the apotheosization of reason, individualism, the law of contract, and choice. It entailed a shift in legal position, both for the collectivity and its individual members….Admission to citizenship, the central hallmark of legal emancipation, also implied access to state power and the control of capital, and it raised fresh questions about the status of community, culture, and minority rights." This definition of emancipation is intentionally broad and sweeping, as it intends to identify specific moments when Jews were emancipated across the European continent. In the Russian Jewish case, scholars have expended a considerable amount of scholarly devotion into demonstrating that Jews experienced modernity *despite* not having legal emancipation until the Bolshevik Revolution in 1917. See Pierre Birnbaum and Ira Katznelson, *Paths of Emancipation: Jews, States, and Citizenship* (Princeton: Princeton University Press, 1994), 14.

scholars have pointed, inconclusively, to various points in the nineteenth and twentieth century as the moment(s) of emancipation. The Tanzimat Reforms inaugurated changes in the legal status of non-Muslims beginning in 1839. Previously, the Ottoman Caliphate, which was responsible for implementing *Shari'a* (Islamic) Law, recognized religious minorities as their own *millet* groups that turned to their own religious courts for legal resolution. The Reform Decree of 1856, while it allowed entry into Ottoman civil positions regardless of confession, as Cohen points out, failed to mention Jews by name, referring only to "Christians and other non-Muslim communities" in the Ottoman Empire. The new citizenship law of 1869, thirty years after the first reform, granted to individuals rights and obligations that were derived directly from the Ottoman State, rather than the individual *millet*. By 1869, while the Ottoman State may have been responsible for *de jure* "legally" emancipating its Jews, the civil legal system did not replace the *millet* courts, and only added a new level of bureaucracy of the Ottoman courts.

Historian Aron Rodrigue has argued more definitively that Jews were not emancipated until Turkish Statehood in 1923. He points out that the Ottoman state neglected to implement any successful educational protocols for their *millet* groups. Some Jewish students did enroll in Ottoman schools, but the majority remained in schools of the Alliance or Hilfsverein. In addition to the previously mentioned Alliance, most "Westernization" processes in the Ottoman Empire were initiated by foreign groups, such as these foreign groups, rather than the Ottoman State. Thus, together with the poll tax and a lackluster overarching Ottoman identity, the Jewish community remained *de facto* differentiated from the Muslim majority until Turkish Statehood in 1923. I contend that Jews were never abruptly emancipated at a specific historical moment. The boundaries of emancipation are fluid—Ottoman Jews, as this chapter will soon demonstrate, certainly considered *themselves* emancipated, even when the Ottoman state did not. Therefore, this study asks us to think beyond understood moments of historical rupture, such as 1839 as the year of the Tanzimat Reforms, or the Young Turk Revolution in 1908, or Turkish Statehood in 1923. A deeper understanding of the many meanings of modernity, and Jews' experience of it, in Constantinople, helps us to further understand the meaning of the fluidity of emancipation. Yet despite their lack of legal citizenship, Ottoman Jews still proclaimed in the Ladino Press that the "Centenary" of Jewish emancipation in 1791 was the beginning of Jewish emancipation "on this continent" and was an occasion to be celebrated by all Jews of Europe.[6] What accounts for this apparent disconnect between Ottoman Jews' perceptions of themselves vis-à-vis the Ottoman State, and the Ottoman State's perception of its Jewish subjects?

Because censorship of the press was still status quo prior to the Young Turk Revolution in 1908, it becomes important to mine the pages of *El Tiempo* for hidden clues and messages that the editors were trying to communicate to their readership. By examining the issues of the paper as a whole body of work, and seeing what else was on the editors' agenda, we begin to understand that Ottoman Jews' interpretation of "emancipation" and the French Revolution, and how they applied to the Jews of the Ottoman Empire, were perhaps quite different than the interpretations by their coreligionists in Western Europe. We see this specifically when we read articles covering "The Centenary" in conjunction with three other kinds of articles that ran in the press—about Russian Jewish migrants in the streets of Constantinople, articles about foreign philanthropists coming to the aid of these migrants in Constantinople, and preparations for the "Fourth Centennial," a new civic holiday commemorating Sephardic Jews' arrival in the Ottoman Empire. We learn that Sephardic Jews' understandings of emancipation had little to do with what *did* happen, and more to do with what *did not* happen. In other words, when read alongside stories of Russian Jews' suffering and "expulsion" from Tsarist Russia, we learn that Ottoman Jews considered themselves emancipated—or at least protected and not actively persecuted. And, when read against articles about how Jewish citizens of Western Europe were coming to the assistance of their coreligionists in the Ottoman Empire, we can see that Ottoman Jews were quite noticeably self-conscious and writing in part to demonstrate to their doubting coreligionists that their lives in the Ottoman Empire mirrored the emancipated Jewish experience in Western Europe.[7]

This chapter is about discourses surrounding newly arrived Russian migrants and how they factored into a process of self-fashioning for multiple audiences, both vertically (to the Ottoman administration) and horizontally (to the Jewish communities in both the Ottoman Empire and in Western Europe). I use the term discourses in the Foucauldian sense, explained shortly,

6   6 October 1891, *El Tiempo*; "El Centenario de la Emancipacion de los Djudeos de Francia"

7   Sephardic Jews' calls for support for their Russian coreligionists might be an example of Ottoman Jews taking "citizenship" into their own hands. Julia Phillips Cohen, *Becoming Ottoman*, 5

and the discourses surrounding Russian migrants on the pages of *El Tiempo* were intertwined with multiple, complex narratives including those of Jewish emancipation, loyalty and patriotism to the Ottoman Empire, narratives that relied on Russian migrants to serve as their counter example.

In these discussions of Russian Jewish migrants, we can see the anxieties and the priorities of Ottoman (Sephardic) Jews in the early 1890s. Through Sephardic Jews' depictions of the Russian migrants, we can see them engaging in an act of "reversing the gaze" of Western European Jewry, a gaze that dismissed Sephardic Jews as "backward" and "oriental."[8] The gaze, of which discourse is absolutely fundamental to, largely assumed that Sephardic Jews, once the torchbearers of Judaism in the Medieval Era, had been largely subsumed in the Ottoman Empire. Alphons Sussnitski, for example, wrote as late as 1912 that despite their living in the "Glorious city of the Golden horn… The spiritual decline of Spanish Jewry in Turkey is a fact that cannot be denied."[9] Sussnitski's statement typified this gaze, and by setting out to help their Russian coreligionists, Ottoman Jews hoped to both demonstrate their loyalty to the Ottoman Empire and also their modernity and emancipation to their sometimes doubtful Western European coreligionists.[10] Additionally,

---

8   A very interesting volume was published in 2020 that describes the reception and (re)production of Orientalism as a process by which broad networks of Muslims and Jews from Western and Eastern Europe as well as the Levant and North Africa engaged in a scholarly discourse that constituted Orientalism "in a parallel and often intertwining process" with their Western European (Christian) counterparts. This presents a "more complex picture of Orientalism, in which all sides are engaged in reconfiguring religious beliefs, scholarly methods, and political commitments," and also, various identities (1-2). In other words, Orientalism was not just an ideological framework imposed by the "West" unto the "East" but was rather a multidirectional exchange. For more see Susanna Heschel and Umar Ryad (ed.) The Muslim Reception of European Orientalism: Reversing the Gaze (New York: Routledge, 2020). Unfortunately the volume does not specifically offer a discussion of Sephardic Jews in this process.

9   Alphons J. Sussnitski, "Die Wirtschaftliche Lage der Juden in Konstantinopel," *Allgemeine Zeitung des Judentums*, 5 January 1912. Retrieved online 27 January 2017.
    http://sammlungen.ub.uni-frankfurt.de/cm/periodical/titleinfo/3229015.

10   A discussion of Jewish emancipation always seems to go hand in hand with a discussion of modernity. The debate over emancipation becomes even more complex when we begin to consider the composite of identities and experiences each of these Jews brought into the entrepôt. Indeed, what we can witness is the experience of modernity despite full legal emancipation, a phenomenon that we also witness in the Russian Empire. Benjamin Nathans has demonstrated that Jews experienced modernity through "selective integration" and "despite relatively unfavorable conditions, the historical trajectory of Russian Jewry was profoundly shaped by aspirations for civic emancipation and social integration." In Constantinople, we witness similar modes of experiencing modernity, and we have the unique advantage of the entrepôt, the port city that allows us to glean insight vis-à-vis Sephardic and Ashkenazi Jews, Ottoman and Foreign subjects, and later, citizens. For the purposes of this chapter, we witness the debates and discourses that inform Jewish practices of modernity. As Sarah Abrevaya Stein puts it, it is the experience of "modernity as mechanism and manifestation." See Stein, *Making Jews Modern*, 5.

through these representations, Sephardic Jews were also typifying an irony that anthropologist Paul Rabinow has described: "there is no such thing as modernity, only claims to it."[11]

Yet in their claim to modernity, Sephardic engaged in the fashioning of subjects, rather than being the object of discourse. Foucault defines the active subject in two ways. The first is that "subject" as "subject to someone else by control and dependence," and the second is that the subject is "tied to his own identity by a conscience or self-knowledge."[12] We see this self-knowledge, a kind of self-consciousness reemerge as Sephardic Jews begin to define their subject: Russian Jews. Thus, this is a dynamic predicated on power: "power produces the very form of the subject; it produces what makes up the subject… the form the subject takes is, precisely, determined by power."[13]

Julia Phillips Cohen has suggested that Sephardic Jews' public performances of Ottoman citizenship were meant to prove Sephardic Jews' loyalty to the Empire and specifically to sultan Abdülhamid II in the wake of nationalist movements in the late nineteenth century. I would add that the discourses in the Jewish press leading up to events such as the "Fourth Centennial" were written to suggest foils and parallels of other Jewish experiences for Sephardic Jews in the Ottoman Empire to consider. The Ladino press cast Sephardic Jews' experiences in the Ottoman Empire as parallel to the emancipation of Western Jews (broadly) vis-à-vis the French Revolution, while Russian Jews faced the opposite experience of never having achieved emancipation in the Russian Empire, forcing them to live under "Muscovite Oppression" an experience that mirrored the biblical exodus story.[14] Similarly, coverage of Western European Jews' philanthropic activities in the Ottoman Empire may have been printed to suggest that Ottoman Jews should follow suit.

The convergence of Russian (Ashkenazi) and Sephardi Jews in Constantinople also mirror a convergence of two historiographies that have, until recently, been considered separately. The occlusion of both Russian and Ottoman Jewry from the "emancipationist" historiographical narrative of

---

11   Paul Rabinow, *Marking Time: On the Anthropology of the Contemporary* (Princeton: Princeton University Press, 2007).

12   Foucault, *The Hermeneutics of the Subject,* 331-332

13   Michel Foucault, *Power/Knowledge: Selected Interviews and Other Writings 1972-1977* (New York: Pantheon, 1980) 83

14   *El Tiempo,* February 1892

Russian Jewry perhaps led Sarah Abrevaya Stein to note that "in a number of important respects, Russian and Ottoman Jewries resembled one another... more than they did their peers in the nation-states of Western and Central Europe."[15] Because neither emancipated their subjects, she points out, there "was not one but many European Jewish modernities."[16] While scholars of Jewish history have treated both the Ottoman and Russian cases as *sui generis* cases, their nineteenth century coreligionists tended to point to both as foils for their own emancipated states of existence in Western Europe.

Perhaps, then, Ottoman Jewish experiences share in what Benjamin Nathans has pointed out in his seminal history of Jews in the late Russian Empire, that "Russian Jews were cast very early...as outsiders not just in Russia but in the pan-European saga of Jewish emancipation."[17] Historians of Russian Jewish History have paid most of their attention to identifying the inception of nationalist (Zionist) movements, or in the assimilationist participation of the Bolshevik Revolution. Nathans attributes this to an "othering" process of Russian Jewry, in which historians have argued that because Jews were "excluded from Western European Jewry's Faustian bargain of emancipation in return for assimilation...substantial numbers of Russian Jews were driven to pursue a different modernity."[18] The case of Russian migration to the Ottoman Empire affords us a unique opportunity to examine Russian and Ottoman

---

15   Sarah Abrevaya Stein, *Making Jews Modern*, 2

16   Stein, *Making Jews Modern*, 1-2. Adeep Khalid, a scholar of Central Asia and Islamic Studies, provides a good framework for understanding this often nebulous term: Modernity is not reducible to the inculcation of culturally specific norms or traits; nor is it synonymous with economic development....the modern condition transforms traditions (indeed, it makes it possible to conceive of tradition as tradition; it takes-and produces-numerous cultural forms and it inheres in (economic) underdevelopment as much as in development. In late nineteenth century Constantinople, Jews—Ottoman, German, Ashkenazi, and Sephardi—reproduced a discourse that "Brings with it new forms of organization of self and society, new forms of intellectual production, and new ways of imagining the world (and one's place within it)." Whether it was Sephardi Jews' embourgeoisement or cultural orientation toward the West, or German Jews' anxieties surrounding their "double minority" status (and how being associated with Russian prostitutes might jeopardize their place in the Ottoman Empire), modernity took on multiple meanings and multiple linguistic forms. Borrowing from Khalid's definition, I shy away from making judgments about the connection between the transformation of traditions, how it "takes and produces numerous cultural forms," and economic development. Nor do I understand modernity as teleological, as guiding Jewish history towards an inevitable rupture, such as national statehood. See Adeep Khalid, *The Politics of Muslim Cultural Reform: Jadidism in Central Asia* (Berkeley: University of California Press, 1999), 2.

17   Nathans, *Beyond the Pale*, 7 See also Olga Litvak, *Conscription and the Search for Modern Russian Jewry* (Bloomington, Indiana University Press, 2006) and Jeffrey Veidlinger, *Jewish Public Culture in the Late Russian Empire* (Bloomington: Indiana University Press, 2009).

18   Nathans, *Beyond the Pale,* 7

Jewries as they encountered each other in the late fin de siècle —specifically, how Russian Jews were described in relation to questions of emancipation and participation in the Ottoman Empire and how it reveals something both particular and universal to the history of Jews of the Ottoman Empire and more broadly. This is precisely what happens in the 1890s in Constantinople. When questions of emancipation are considered from the point of view of the Ottoman (Sephardic) Jews, we see that they understood themselves as part of emancipated, European Jewry, especially when viewed in comparison to the plight of Russian Jewry.

I would like to first contextualize the discourses surrounding Russian Jews with a brief depiction of Western European Jewish concerns about Jewish life in the Ottoman Empire, especially of the Alliance Israélite Universelle. I focus on narratives discussing Jewish emancipation (and, according to them, Ottoman Jews' exclusion from it) to underscore how the responses in the Ladino press were very much in conversation with these discourses. I then move to a discussion of how Russian Jews were constructed in the Ladino Press, and the significance of articles describing their arrival in Constantinople ran alongside articles of the "Centenary of the Emancipation of the Jews of France" as well as articles advocating for the new civic holiday commemorating the arrival of Jews' in the Ottoman Empire. I examine relevant issues of *El Tiempo* as an integrative unit, looking for hidden messages that the editors of *El Tiempo* may have been trying to relay to their readers past the watchful gaze of the Ottoman censors.

Russian Jews and Sephardi Jews in Constantinople

The Russian Famine of 1891-1892 and the cholera pandemic of 1892, accelerated Russian emigration from the Russian Empire, and in September of 1891, the provincial governor from Volhynia forcibly evacuated Jews to Podolia. Once they arrived, they were then sent to Odessa. On October 4, 1891, the provincial governor issued an order expelling 1,168 Russian Jews, ordering them to leave within forty-eight hours.[19] Some of these Jews carried documentation that afforded them dual status as Ottoman and as Russian subjects, but nearly as quickly as these Russian Jews arrived, the government

---

19   *Congressional Record* (Senate), February 15, 1892, vol. 33, pt. 2 (52nd Congress,. 1st session), 1132 (speech of Senator W.E. Chandler); *New York Sun*, February 12, 1892, opt. cite in Markel, *Quarentine*, 1997

ordered that Ottoman citizenship was required for moving on to Palestine. The result was that some Russian Jews were forced to continue on to Argentina or to North America (with the aid of the Jewish Colonization Association, as discussed in the previous chapter), or, to remain in increasingly dim conditions in Constantinople. While the Ottoman authorities cited cholera as an official reason, as discussed previously, increased immigration to Palestine likely threatened Abdülhamid's perceived status quo in Palestine.

Russian Jews thus arrived in Galata that year. Typhoid was also considered to be a problem, and passengers on the *SS Massilia,* which left Odessa for New York City, went into port in Constantinople. The United States required that all infected passengers be returned to the last port at the steam company's expense, so the company decided to remain in port for three months in the Ottoman capital. The socialist Yiddish newspaper *Arbeit Zeitung* described the neighborhood as a center of "sin, pestilence, and death."[20] The Jewish community notified Baron Maurice de Hirsch, who, in addition to coming to their aid and helping to establish the Jewish Colonization Association in subsequent years, began to write and publish extensively on the topic of Jewish migrants. Some of the articles were reprinted in *El Tiempo.* Just two months after "Los Israelitas Rusos en Konstantinopla" was published, the paper republished an article from the July 1891 issue of an American based magazine, *The Forum.*[21] The Baron Maurice de Hirsch published "My Views on Philanthropy," originally written for a broad, American audience, it describes the Baron de Hirsch's motivations in assisting Russian and East European Jews and his views on the Jewish experience in Europe more broadly. The editors of *El Tiempo* wrote an introduction to highlight the Baron de Hirsch's "noble sentiments and his love for his coreligionists." He wrote that Russian Jews [generally] are in "a deplorable state." Their day-to-day struggles are material, as they "struggle to find something to eat and something to wear every day." He writes "our brothers could die of hunger while we live in abundance." He argues "the Jews have undergone numerous difficulties and have been in a state of fear." Yet according to de Hirsch the Russian Jew can be saved, but it falls on the shoulders of those who are able to "cultivate" and "to educate the Russian Jews."

---

20   *Arbeit Zeitung* New York 12 February, 1892 opt. cite in Howard Markel, *Quarantine! East European Jewish Migration and the New York City Epidemics of 1892* (Baltimore: John Hopkins University Press, 1997).

21   Founded by Isaac Rice, *The Forum* ran from 1885-1950 and was published in New York.

Reading this article, one might notice parallels between the Baron de Hirsch's description of Russian Jews and the articles written by the editors of *El Tiempo*. Indeed, the language is strikingly similar – from descriptions of destitute Russians on the streets—to the emphasis on "cultivation" and "education" as methods of helping their coreligionists. The latter are consistent with the mission of the Alliance, a recipient of significant funding from the Baron de Hirsch. Like the editors of *El Tiempo* who claim the future of "humanity" and "Judaism" is at stake, he places responsibility squarely on other Jews, especially those who "live in abundance."

In a letter to the *North American Review*, in 1891, the Baron de Hirsch describes his philanthropic motivations, "Through this matter I have the certainty that he who frees thousands of his fellow-men from suffering and an oppressed existence, and helps them to become useful citizens, does a good work for all humanity," and that "The Alliance understands very well this sad situation of Jews in the said country…but it may not have the resources to do it all."[22] The Baron de Hirsch continues:

> For many centuries, the Jews experienced fear, innumerable difficulties and obstacles…*they have been nothing more than guests at the hotels of their country.* Therefore their ambition had to be in commerce…Because of the fear that they had, being forced to live in their communities, commerce was the only option available to them…yet there were a number of celebrated Israelites that became distinguished in the sciences, letters, and in medicine…Jews in those cases were able to demonstrate their various aptitudes…[23]

The Baron de Hirsch entered into an important global discourse about Jewish emancipation, about their participation in modern nation-states and empires, and the role that other Jews should play in the assistance of their coreligionists. The Alliance Israélite Universelle had been at work in the Ottoman Empire since 1860, setting up a system of schools in the Ottoman Empire in 1860, whose goal it was to educate and civilize the "Jews of the Orient."

The Alliance's mission of *civilisatrice* aimed to combat Ottoman Jewish "backwardness and superstition." This mission was tied to an expression of

---

22   Hirsch, Baron Maurice de, "My Views on Philanthropy," *North American Review* 153 (416) in *The Nineteenth Century in Print*, Cornell University Library and the Library of Congress (http://memory.loc.gov/ammem/ndlpcoop/moahtml/snchome.html)], July 1891.

23   Ibid.

French political and cultural expansionism, and, similar to French schools in colonial Algeria, were designed to "Westernize" and "moralize" the Jewish population by "installing the virtues of cleanliness, exactitude, obedience, politeness," and was "quite open about its mission to integrate into Western civilization those groups of Jews which historical or political events had left outside."[24] By doing so, the Parisian leaders of the Alliance believed that Jews, too, could achieve emancipation, as the French had in 1791.

Regeneration--economically, socially, and religiously--was the key to emancipation according to the Alliance. Schools were targeted towards the poor (with training in menial and agricultural labor) as well as religious leadership. Aided by local support throughout the Ottoman Empire, the values of the Alliance permeated up as well as down, up to rabbinic leadership, the head of the Jewish *millet*. The Chief Rabbis of Constantinople in the time periods analyzed here, Moshe Halévy and Haim Nahum (1872-1960), were both products of the Alliance (although Halévy would be deposed after the Young Turk Revolution in 1908 for his alleged allegiance to the old Ottoman regime). As discussed later in the book, Nahum's allegiance would remain to the Alliance and the Ottoman Empire despite growing support for Zionism among his constituents.

The Alliance system created a network of philanthropists, pupils, and teachers who in turn helped facilitate an internal cultural orientation towards Western Europe, and specifically, France. Enlightenment discourses informed the Alliance's mission of regeneration, and the "panacea" to societal ills was education.[25] By the time that Russian Jews began arriving in the Ottoman Empire, Western Jewry, and Ottoman Sephardic Jewry, now educated by the Alliance and appropriately Francophile, fixed their gaze towards the newest of their backwards coreligionists: Russian Jews. In other words, as the Alliance's *mission civilisatrice* routinized in the Ottoman Empire, Sephardic Jews underwent a cultural reorientation and looked towards the incoming Russian Jews as central to the question of Ottoman citizenship. As Rodrigue points out, the "fundamental fissure in the nineteenth century Jewish universe was not that between the European or the Middle Eastern Jew, or between the Ashkenazi and Sephardi," but "the rupture that prevailed was between the

---

24   Aron Rodrigue, *French Jews, Turkish Jews: The Alliance Israelite Universelle And The Politics of Jewish Schooling In Turkey, 1860-1925* (Bloomington: Indiana University Press, 1990), 75

25   Aron Rodrigue, *French Jews, Turkish Jews,*10-11

"enlightened"...and the rest of world Jewry still steeped in Jewish tradition and popular culture."[26] Constantinople became an entrepôt with which to view this Alliancist delineation of the Jewish worlds—only by the 1890s, we can see that Ottoman Jews engaged in their own delineation in their descriptions of Russian Jews in the city.

French Jews, Turkish Jews—and Russian Jews

El Tiempo was the primary Ladino language Newspaper of Constantinople. Founded in the 1870s, the newspaper was first edited by Merkado Fresco and Sami Alkabez and financed by Hayim Carmona. David Fresco (1853-1933) served as the editor for the timeframe of this study, and, in addition to his position as editor of *El Tiempo*, edited four other Ladino periodicals, published over nineteen books in Ladino, and as one author described him, "from the banks of the Bosporus to the River Danube and along the whole coastline of the Mediterranean Archipelago, there was no Jew better known in all the Orient."[27] Ladino newspapers in the Ottoman World created their own literary community, reprinting each other's articles. Often, they would edit the original article in order to emphasize a certain point, or reprint sections of articles from foreign newspapers, as the case with the Baron de Hirsch's article in *The Forum*.

While French was considered the educated man and woman's *lingua franca*, Hebrew was strictly the language of religion. Ottoman Jews were more likely to speak Ladino than Turkish, Greek, or Italian—and the specific linguistic orientations were reflected in the papers' evolution in the late nineteenth century. For example, after the Tanzimat Reforms (1839-1876) the editors of *El Tiempo* proclaimed that it was necessary for the readers to know the language of your country "because we find ourselves under an Ottoman government," and began to include articles in Turkish, written out in Hebrew letters.[28] By the 1890s, once an entire generation at least had been trained in the Alliance schools, the newspaper took a more Francophile turn. French stories and French language ran consistently through the periodicals, and even the Ladino used was a francophone version.[29] Nearly one in two Jewish

26   Rodrigue, *French Jews, Turkish Jews*, 13.

27   Stein "The Permeable Boundaries of Ottoman Jewries" in Joel Migdal, ed., *Boundaries and Belonging*, 57

28   Ibid.

29   Ibid., 59-60

residents of Constantinople subscribed to the newspaper by the First World War.[30] By the time Russian migrants began arriving in Constantinople, a generation of Ottoman Jews had been brought up in the cultural orientation of the Alliance. French hegemony, and specifically French Alliancist hegemony, had penetrated Sephardic Jewish culture and had become mainstream. We witness this in the language, culture, and orientation of Sephardic Jewry, and in the way that Russian Jews were described as their foils.

We can see the fissure that Rodrigue noticed quite clearly in the October issues of *El Tiempo*. On 6 October 1891, *El Tiempo* ran "The Centenary of the Emancipation of the Jews of France."[31] The article took up over an entire page of the issue and describes what Jewish life was like in the "high Middle Ages" (likely to point out a contrast between that and the "Golden Age" of Spanish Jews), when the "Jews suffered because of humiliating laws…were imprisoned likes lepers in a ghetto…were unable to have business relations with Christians, were unable to hold public office, and were considered to be a pariah."[32] The Jews were "unable to enjoy the natural laws of man" until the "French people proclaimed fidelity and equality among all of the French people."[33] It was the French Revolution" that "proclaimed Jews as French citizens, with civic and public rights." Importantly, "little by little, all of the countries of Europe and their frontiers began to fall [to emancipating their people] regardless of race or religion." The editors are pointing to the significance of the French Revolution to the Jews of Europe, at least as they understood it. Interestingly, the front page of the issue also ran a special on the Jewish holiday of *Sukkot*, a biblical holiday that commemorates the forty years that the Jews spent wandering in the desert before they were led into the Land of Israel—perhaps a reminder of the common motif of migration and diaspora in Jewish religious and cultural texts.

The editors conveniently leave out any mention of the Terror and the dark underbelly of the French Revolution and instead describe how the National Assembly had finally brought "liberty and equality to the Jews of France."[34] The editors make a very distinct point:

---

30   Ibid.

31   "El Centenario de la Emancipacion de los Djudeos de Francia," *El Tiempo*, 6 October 1891

32   "El Centenario de la Emancipation de los Djudeos de Francia" *El Tiempo* 6 October 1891

33   Ibid.

34   "El Centenario de la Emancipacion de los Djudeos de Francia," *El Tiempo*, 6 October 1891

The achievements of Jewish emancipation in France should not be celebrated in France alone, but rather should be celebrated among all the Jews of Europe, because on this day [September 27, 1791] the emancipation of the Jews on *this continent* also began.[35]

The article does not mention the legal state of Ottoman Jews, who had achieved some legal rights through the Tanzimat Reforms, but who were not fully legally emancipated until the Turkish Republic was formed in 1923.[36] At this point, censorship of the press was a reality that editors like David Fresco had to contend with. Editorial messages were conveyed more subtly. Rather than going into debates over citizenship (which did become widespread after the 1908 Young Turk Revolution, and which I discuss in chapter 4), Fresco rather aligns Ottoman Jews with emancipated French Jews as able to share in the celebrations of "freedom and equality… "*on this continent.*"

An article titled "The Russian Israelites in Constantinople" shares the issue with the "The Centenary of Jewish Emancipation."[37] The article describes the efforts of the Jewish communities in assisting these "Russian brothers" in "desperate need:" a committee of the Alliance Israélite Universelle with representatives from the Office of the Chief Rabbi, together with a committee of German Jews from Constantinople. The editors point out that is the responsibility of "Ottoman Jews" to aid their coreligionists, and that had it not been for the immediate generosity of the Baron de Hirsch, "who knows what would have become of them [the Russian Jews]."

Another article, "A Society of Interest," even shares the work of "respectable" Sephardic Jewish women from Galata and Pera who were doing their part to come to the assistance of Russian Jews in Galata.[38] Emilia Férnandez, the wife of Isaac Férnandez, the regional president of the Alliance, led the "Society" in its "benevolent effort of generosity" to create a fund to assist the "most misfortunate among the Russian migrants."[39] The members of the organization were also connected to the Alliance, and its members included Esther Cohen (wife of Dr. Elias Pasha Cohen, 1844-1900), Mrs. Isaac Molho (wife of the director of the House of Camondo), and Mrs. Weissman. The organization

35   "El Centenario de la Emancipacion de los Djudeos de Francia," *El Tiempo,* 6 October 1891 my emphasis

36   See Aron Rodrigue *French Jews, Turkish Jews.*

37   "Los Israelitas Rusos en Konstantinopla" *El Tiempo* October 6, 1891

38   "Una Sociedad Interesante" *El Tiempo* March 10, 1891

39   Ibid.

requested a membership fee of a minimum of 60 *kuruş*, which then in turn assisted Russian migrants with food, fuel, clothing, and sometimes even small loans. Membership was restricted to women, but the organization did accept major contributions, which were inscribed on a plaque in the organization's headquarters.[40]

The Ladino press' depictions of Russian Jews add another layer of complexity to the "enlightened versus unenlightened" delineations of the Alliance. They reveal a discourse largely informed by imperial categories that would begin to be more visible after the turn of the century, discussed in the next chapters. In other words, the case of Russian Jews in Constantinople quickly becomes a discourse that differentiates Russian Jews from the rest of either emancipated, Alliancist Sephardic Jews, or the emancipated German Jews (who were also Ashkenazi). Jews in the Ottoman Empire were governed by a system of Capitulations that placed foreign subjects under the jurisdiction of their consular—adding a national or imperial subcategory to the Jewish millet.[41]

Thus, Ottoman Jews understood themselves not only in relation to French Jews (and the Alliance), but also in relation to Russian Jews. Using the Balkans of Ottoman Europe as a case study, Milica Bakić-Hayden has argued for the existence of what she calls "nesting orientalisms."[42] This helps explain the Sephardic representations of Russian Jews, especially as the "designation as an "other" has been appropriated and manipulated by those who have themselves been designated as such in orientalist discourse."[43] Bakić-Hayden points out that these "nesting orientalisms" are particularly valuable when appropriated for nationalist discourses, as in the Yugoslav case. However, in the case of Ottoman Sephardic Jews, the desired political outcome was almost entirely opposite: it was to demonstrate their loyalty to the Ottoman Empire from the moment they arrived on its soil, yet also to demonstrate their emancipation, at least relative to their Russian other.

---

40   See Nazan Maksudyan "This Time Women As Well Got Involved In Politics!": Nineteenth Century Ottoman Women's Organizations and Political Agency," in Nazan Maksudyan (ed.) *Women and the City, Women in the City: a Gendered Perspective on Ottoman Urban History* (New York: Berghahn, 2014), 112.

41   See chapters 3 and 4. Michelle U. Campos also points out that in the "Muallim Naci dictionary of 1891, *millet* was solely a religious group, whereas a nation should be referred to by either *ümmet* (امت) or *kavim* (قوم), See Michelle U. Campos *Ottoman Brothers: Muslims, Christians, and Jews in Early Twentieth-Century Palestine* (Stanford: University Press, 2011), pp. 49-50.

42   Milica Bakić-Hayden "Nesting Orientalisms: The Case of Former Yugoslavia," *Slavic Review*, Vol. 54, No. 4 (Winter, 1995), pp. 917-931.

43   Bakić-Hayden, 922 and Usamma Makdisi, "Ottoman Orientalism," 774.

Every *other* has their *other,* and Ottoman Jews could easily point to Russian Jews forced onto the streets of Constantinople as examples. Usamma Makdisi's concept of "Ottoman Orientalism" is even more useful here, I think, than "nesting orientalisms," although both are closely related, because of his observation that "layers of adaptation, emulation, and resistance-in short, the Ottoman engagement with an internalization of an entrenched European discourse of Orientalism" ultimately created "myriad other Orientalisms."[44] Key to the difference between the two is Edward Said's understanding of power and knowledge central to Orientalism-- Ottomans formulated Orientalist discourses in order to create an ideological space of resistance to Western colonialism.[45] Makdisi looks at the case of Mt. Lebanon and differences "configured in religious, ethnic, and spatial terms," but the case of the Jewish millet adds even another level of complexity to this taxonomy that was essential to the "projection of Ottoman imperial identity in a multi-religious and ethnic empire."[46] We see this pattern quite clearly in the Jewish (Sephardic) *millet* in the Ottoman Empire, who had long been the subject of the Orientalist discourses of the Alliance and Western European Jewry more generally.

Therefore, when Ottoman Jews began advocating for a new civic holiday celebrating their arrival in the Ottoman Empire, it makes sense that they would do so, once again, in conjunction with articles, depicting the plight of Russian Jewry. Here, Russian Jews are depicted as pogrom victims while Ottoman Jews engaged in a discourse of self-designation as civically engaged imperial subjects.[47] The editors of *El Tiempo* set out on this agenda in early 1891. While Russian Jews' had trickled into Constantinople in previous years, *El Tiempo* begins to cover the increasing number of migrants early that year.

The articles concerning Russian Jews and the *fiesta* multiplied over a period of approximately eight months. In the 20th August 1891 issue of *El Tiempo*, two

---

44   Usamma Makdisi, "Ottoman Orientalism," 772

45   Usamma Makdisi, "Ottoman Orientalism," 772.

46   Ibid.

47   For more, please see Julia Phillips Cohen *Becoming Ottoman.* As Cohen points out, this Ottomanization occurred alongside the Ottomans' attempts to negotiate their image in the world through diplomacy and showcasing. For example, in 1892, the Chicago World's Fair, set to commemorate the Fourth Centennial of Columbus' maiden voyage and discovery of America, would feature special Ottoman booths. In 1890, the United States government appointed Dr. Cyrus Adler, an archeologist specializing in Semitic languages and civilizations to travel to several n cities in the Near and Middle East in order to "entice the Mohammadeans" to participate.

articles ran on consecutive pages that explicitly connect the cause of Russian Jews to the civic demonstrations of loyalty to the Empire. The first is an article titled "Los Immigrantes Israelitas en Konstantinopla," and the second, "La Fiesta de 1892."[48] The first article is a continued report that approximately 700 men and women have arrived fleeing violence as immigrants from Russia, and that they seek to stay in Istanbul indefinitely. The article notes that the immigrants are overwhelmingly poor, and those in the Jewish community that have the means have stepped in to assist the new immigrants. It also states that despite the Jewish community having provided "a certain security" to their Russian co-religionists, the Jewish community is unfortunately unable to help all the immigrants and their needs. They add that Jewish leaders have been appealing to "His Eminence," as well as the Baron de Hirsch, a well-known Jewish philanthropist, to step in and intervene for *los desperados,* or "the desperate." French and British Jews responded in support, and one German Jew even sent a sum of 300 Francs that were distributed among the needy. In that same article, the editors progress to the topic of the Fourth Centennial, *La Fiesta de 1892.* The article states that a formal petition is needed to be submitted to the imperial offices to commemorate the day officially, and that the Jewish community should submit such a petition first to the Grand Rabbinate to demonstrate support for the holiday. The Grand Rabbinate would then in turn submit a petition to the office of the Grand Vizier. The article is a kind of call for support, the editors of *El Tiempo* encouraging its readers to demonstrate on behalf of a celebration.

In the 4 November 1891 issue, the editors begin to call upon the Ottoman Jewish community of "50,000" (according to their count) to come to the aid of their Russian Jewish "brothers." The article describes how Russian Jews live in a state of fear, and yet "none of the 50,000 Jews of our community come to their aid or to dispense a lending hand, and none offer even a word of consolation to these poor Russian brothers."[49] The article reports that some 280 additional migrants have arrived and will depart the port for Marseilles.

The editors of *El Tiempo* state clearly that the Jews of Constantinople are fully able to help their fellow coreligionists, without the interventions of the Jews of Europe or even of the Ottoman Empire for help (although in other articles "His Eminence" is mentioned.) In fact the 4 January 1892 issue ran

---

48   *El Tiempo,* 20 August 1891

49   *El Tiempo,* 4 November 1891

another article, "The Russian Jews in Constantinople," calls into question the *Haham Başı*, Moshe Halévy, who has finally "done at least something to help our Russian brothers who die of hunger and in the cold."[50] The Grand Rabbi joined a committee of German Jews and the Alliance, but so far "since writing these lines" has given "0000000!" to the cause of Russian Jews. Indeed, what better indication of emancipation and modernity than the Jewish community of Constantinople's own ability to solve this crisis?

Another article published in mid-December of the same year more directly implicates the Jewish community in not sufficiently coming to the aid of the Russian Jews. In the article "Our Indifference Towards the Unfortunates: A Criminal Case," the editors accuse Sephardic Jews of "betraying their brothers in blood and in religion."[51] While they do nothing, "these Russian brothers have pains of hunger." The editors ask their readers to "imagine women, children on the street….[then] the heart begins to open."[52]

These articles are evocative of the issues at stake for the Sephardic community of Constantinople. They take great care to describe the destitute Russians, described as homeless on the streets, living in cold and in fear, clearly in great need of help, to not only help raise more funds in support of these Russian Jews but to also underscore the differences between Ottoman Jews and these Russian Jews. They have pains of hunger, they are described as women and children, infantilized and emasculated in their inability to help themselves. They are also, tellingly, described in gendered terms. This seems to be the apex of the articles, and in the months leading up to the *fiesta,* the articles seem to refocus on the connection between Russian Jews and the celebration.

Several months later, in March of 1892, just before the start of the Passover Holiday (commemorating the Jewish exodus from Egypt and into the Land of Israel), *El Tiempo* ran an article called "Por Nuestros Hermanos Rusos" (Regarding our Russian Brothers).[53] The article is both an opinion piece and another fundraising effort. The writers suggest to their readers that as they prepare to celebrate the "grand holiday, to remember the salvation of [their]

---

50   *El Tiempo,* 4 January 1892

51   *El Tiempo,* 24 December 1891

52   ibid.

53   "Por Nuestros Hermanos Rusos" *El Tiempo* 18 March, 1892

ancestors." They urge the readers to recognize that "more or less, everyone sacrifices at this time of year to adorn their homes, to purchase new clothes," and otherwise prepare for the Passover holiday, the "national holiday," (*fiesta nasional*). The article reminds its readers that while the holiday commemorates their forefather's own exodus that they should also "think a little bit about their poor Russian brothers." They explain to the readers that the poor Russians have been given safekeeping in the Ottoman Empire and that they had been persecuted in Russia simply because of their "Jewish trait." The poor Russians struggle for food, for bread, for clothing each and every day. "We cannot see our brothers die during this holiday…we should support them and celebrate with them our arrival and salvation."

The article goes on to state that three members of the Sephardic community, Moshe Halévy, Mr. Leon Ruventhal and Mr. Yosef Boton, as part of a delegation from the office of the Chief Rabbi, have created a fundraising initiative to support the new immigrants in their "very sad state." The mission of the drive is not only to make sure their everyday needs are met, but for them to also receive the necessary ritual requirements to keep kosher for Passover, such as unleavened bread (*matzah*). They warn that many "could die during the festival," that "our happiness during this festival also has a touch of sadness and conscience." They encourage community members to take in Russian Jews for their ritual holiday meals (Passover *seder*). The Passover *seder* is a holiday celebrated in Jewish homes, with a festival meal that recounts the story of the Jewish Exodus from Egypt and slavery. Celebrating the festival, according to Jewish law, involves not only following the Passover *seder* but maintaining a level of dietary observance throughout the festival's eight days, something that is nearly impossible if traveling, or not in one's one home. A few issues later, the results of the successful fundraiser were proudly published in the pages of *El Tiempo*, with donation amounts totaling over sixty thousand lira (approximately 350,000 British Pounds).[54] Publishing the amounts fundraised did two things; first, by displaying the success of the amounts already raised, it generated momentum for the fund. Second, it offered publicity for the good deeds already done.

Jewish communal leaders' willingness to connect the narrative of religious ritual and holiday to a contemporary social and political issue worked in their

54   *El Tiempo*, February 1892

favor in two ways. First, emphasizing a connection between the Passover narrative and the contemporary exodus of Jews from Russia was a rhetorical way to connect Sephardic Jews with their Russian coreligionists in order to strengthen Sephardic communal unity as well as imbue a perhaps increasingly obsolete holiday with renewed meaning. As Julia Phillips Cohen points out, the nineteenth century marked the beginning of these centennial celebrations- no national holiday existed in the eighteenth century- adding to the timelessness of the Sephardic arrival in the Ottoman Empire.[55] She also points out that by connecting the exodus story to modern emancipation, especially to the French model of revolution subsequent Jewish emancipation, was celebrated in synagogues. The French Chief Rabbi Zadoc Kahn proclaimed that the French Jews' "Exodus from Egypt....[in the French Revolution is] our modern Passover," was another trend imported from Europe and an example of what Eric Hobswam described as a "centenarian revolution".[56]

Additionally, it was a response to conversion rates among Sephardic and Russian Jews. Beginning in the 1820s, Protestant groups from Britain and the United States, informed by millenarian beliefs that the upcoming twentieth century would usher in the End of Days- a cataclysmic period in which Jews would play an important role, began pouring into the Ottoman Empire. Some interpreters point to specific books in the Bible that suggest that only after the second coming of Christ would Jews finally recognize the error of their ways, follow Christ, and return to the Land of Israel where the Kingdom of David and Solomon would be reestablished. Thus, these missionaries viewed Jewish converts as necessary actors in this apocalyptic process.

The Jews of the Ottoman Empire went on to celebrate the fourth centennial late that year. Similar celebrations sprung up around the world for the fifth centennial, with the largest in Turkey, to celebrate 500 years of coexistence in 1992.[57] Sephardic Jews marked 1892 with commemorative poetry, presentations, and, a special prayer during the first night of Passover.[58] Some Jewish communities in Western Europe even sent letters to the Ottoman administration, including the Jewish Committee of Britain on April 14,

---

55 Cohen, 48

56 Cohen, 46

57 Celebrations included scholarly conferences and publications celebration Jewish Turkish life, including one that I draw from in this monograph.

58 "Jews Celebrate Spanish Roots of Sephardic Expulsion," *Daily Press*, March 3, 2008.

1892, and the Jewish Committee of France, offering profuse thanks for "the protection and hospitality kindly offered by the Ottoman state 400 years ago, thus [rescuing the Jews] from the persecution and cruelty of Spain."[59]

Conclusion

In 1912, Alphons Sussnitski published an article for a German Jewish publication, *The Culture of the Jews.* The three-part article offers a history of Jewish life and culture in Constantinople. The author's conclusion, especially about the history of Sephardim in the Ottoman Empire, is quite striking:

> A certain change for the better can already be noticed in the situation of the Jewry of Constantinople. Since the beginning of a proper education, and especially through the education in the language of the country, the Jewish youths have undergone a slow change in this respect. Even though the Alliance schools provided their pupils with only a thin French varnish, many succeeded in making themselves a good position as a bank or state official.[60]

I intentionally chose this article, published a few decades after the period under investigation in this chapter, because it magnifies the kind of Orientalist gaze that the Sephardic Jews of the Ottoman Empire had been the subject of. The Alliance, by this point, had been at work for over half a century, and yet, although their situation had improved, "Jewish youths had undergone a slow change" and had "only a thin French varnish" to show for it.

Makdisi makes a bold observation about the nature of Ottoman Orientalism, that those who engaged in it helped to "de-Orientalize the empire by Orientalizing it."[61] Indeed, when Russian Jews started arriving in Constantinople, we see just how central the Russian *other* was to Sephardic Jews' self-designations in the Ottoman world. Yet another shift was on the horizon. At the turn of the century, Western European Jews began to pay attention to the growing number of Ashkenazi Jews' (in particular, Russian Jews') participation in the "white slave trade." The Jewish communities of Constantinople would come under scrutiny for allowing or facilitating the

---

59   Ibid, 146-147. This was especially interesting in light of the accusation that the Alliance Israelite Universelle, accused of Zionist conspiracy.

60   Sussnitski, "Die wirtschaftliche Lage der Juden in Konstantinopel"

61   Usamma Makdisi, "Ottoman Orientalism," 773

"trade," and Ashkenazim and Sephardim's reactions to this scrutiny reveal the priorities and anxieties of the dynamic Jewish millet in the city.

In the next few chapters, we will meet "Tevye's Ottoman Daughters," and the varied routes and paths their lives may have taken in Constantinople. We will meet their families, their rabbis, and take a closer look at the diversity and the new political priorities of the Ashkenazi community that greeted them at the turn of the century. The Ashkenazi community grew so quickly that the office of the (Sephardic) Chief Rabbi Moshe Halévy declared a new position of the *Baş Haham*, or "principal rabbi" of the Ashkenazi Jews. Sephardic Jews were so appalled by the move that David Fresco, the editor of *El Tiempo,* predicted a "schism…between Ashkenazim and Sephardim…that affects not only our community [in Constantinople] but the community of the entire Ottoman Empire,"[62] the very same community that had come together years prior to celebrate "The Fourth Centennial of Spanish Expulsion." As the white slave trade on the one hand, and the politics of Zionism on the other became to complicate perceptions of the Jewish communities of Constantinople,. The new *Baş Haham,* David Feivel Markus (1870-1944), a young Rabbi from Russia, came to Constantinople in 1900, reinvigorated Ashkenazi Jewry and engaged in ontological debates concerning Zionism, emancipation, and the role that Jews would play in the wake of the Young Turk Revolution. For the first time, the Ottoman state abandoned censorship laws, and the Zionist press exploded. With it came new ideas about citizenship, and former discourses in the Sephardic press boasting of brotherhood in "blood and religion"[63] quickly capitulated into a divisive polemic of "Ottoman Jews" and "Foreign Jews." Fresco warned his "Ottoman" coreligionists that "a few *European* Jews conceived of the project of building a Jewish state in Palestine."[64]

---

62   *El Tiempo,* 26 December 1910.

63   "Los Israelitas Rusos en Konstantinopla," *El Tiempo,* 7 December 1891.

64   David Fresco, *Le Sionisme* (Contantinople, 1909) 69-72, my emphasis.

Chapter 2

TEVYE'S OTTOMAN DAUGHTERS: ASHKENAZI JEWS, SEPHARDI JEWS, AND THE "WHITE SLAVE TRADE" IN CONSTANTINOPLE

As is the mother, so is her daughter.

Ezekiel 16:44

The history of the Association for the Assistance of the Elderly in Istanbul notes that "In 1915, two former prostitutes, Rozi and Fremond, purchased Or Chadash, colloquially known as the 'Pimp's Synagogue,' and turned it into a shelter for former prostitutes. Eventually this became an old-age home."[1] This remarkable anecdote is unfortunately the only part of Rozi and Fremond's story that has been transmitted in the organization's historical record. When I sought out additional sources concerning Rozi and Fremond and this incredible anecdote, I found nothing. Instead, what I did find, however, is that a considerable amount of material documenting Western European and North American Jews' anxieties over Russian Jews' involvement in the "white slave trade," to use the parlance of the time. Where I had hoped to find primary sources documenting the story of these extraordinary women (or others like them), I found, instead, material expressing Jewish communities' fears and anxieties. Indeed, the association of Russians, and Ashkenazi Jews more generally, with prostitution was so pervasive that even David Ben-Gurion, the future Prime Minister of Israel, was told by his host in Salonica not to

---

1   The authors elsewhere describe Rozi and Fremond as two "Jewish women from Russia who, because of poverty, were forced to settle in the red light district of Galata," which I interpret as an oblique reference to their status as former prostitutes. Aslan Yahni (ed.), *90 Yıl Kuruluşundan Bugüne İhtiyarlara Yardım Derneği* (Istanbul: İhtiyarlara Yardım Derneği, 2006), 29.

mention the fact that he was Ashkenazi for fear that he might be confused with a "white slaver."[2]

Belina Goldfeld offers a contrasting route of exit to that of Rozi and Fremond. She was born in Odessa in 1881.[3] Her father Mordecai, a tailor, became concerned about a new Russian Tsar, especially in the wake of the assassination of Alexander II and the May Laws of 1882. He crossed the Black Sea to Constantinople, where he felt that Jews were being treated reasonably well, and so applied for Ottoman citizenship. He brought his wife and unmarried children, including Belina and three boys, and his mother Miriam to Constantinople in 1891. They settled in the Galata neighborhood close to the Galata Tower. Belina eventually married a Jewish immigrant from Romania, Emmanuel Soroker, in 1910 or 1912. He went to work in the A. Mayer Department store in old Stamboul, owned by Ashkenazi Jews from Austria-Hungary.[4] Belina's three brothers all eventually moved to the United States or France. Her daughter, Klara, married an Ashkenazi Jew from Czernowitz and their children remain in Istanbul to this day.

As I set out to write the history of Tevye's Ottoman *daughter,* I found that it was nearly impossible to discern whether she followed the path of Rozi, of Belina, or someone in between. Why were the Ottoman and Turkish Jewish communities not forthcoming about Rozi and Fremond's past, and how can we understand the history of a marginalized, migrant community, especially if many members of the community worked in professions where it was unwise to leave a paper trail?

Despite an incomplete archive, the anecdote of Rozi and Fremond, however brief, attests that these two remarkable women existed, alongside many other Russian women whose stories may never be told.[5] Yet there is a startling contrast between the scarcity of sources about Rozi, Fremond, and Belina as individuals, and the abundance of sources about the anxieties that surrounded

---

2   David Ben-Gurion, *Zichronot* (Tel Aviv: Am Oved, 1971), 55.

3   Interview with Robert Schild, May 2015.

4   For more on western-style department stores and their multiethnic employees, see Yavuz Köse "Vertical Bazaars of Modernity: Western Department Stores and Their Staff in Istanbul (1889–1921)," *International Review of Social History* 54, no. S17 (December 2009): 91. For more information on Mayer and his department stores see Adelhad Mayer, Elmar Samsinger, *Fast wie Geschichten aus 1001 Nacht: die jüdischen Textilkaufleute Mayer zwischen Europa und dem Orient,* Mandelbaum Verlag, Wien, 2015 and Rıfat N.Bali, *Portraits From a Bygone İstanbul: Georg Mayer and Simon Brod,* Libra Kitap, İstanbul, 2012.

5   Emma Perez, "Queering the Borderlands: The Challenges of Excavating the Invisible and Unheard," *Frontiers: A Journal of Women Studies* 24 (2003): 122–31.

בס"ד

Ketubah (marriage contract) of Emmanuel Soroker and Belina Goldfeld,
signed by Rabbi David Markus, courtesy of Robert Schild

them as women. Why, in a city largely remembered as Sephardic, was there such an anxiety surrounding Ashkenazi prostitution in Constantinople? And what can these anxieties teach us about the relationship between Ashkenazi and Sephardi Jews in the final years of the Ottoman Empire?

Prostitution preoccupied both Ashkenazi Jews residing in Constantinople and Ashkenazi Jews in the wider European world, inspiring German-Jewish social worker Max Kreutzberger to call white slavery in Europe and North America the "public fear of the last decade."[6] Haskel Rabinowitz, a foreign correspondent for the *Tageblatt*, an Orthodox Yiddish newspaper founded in New York in 1885, wrote that so many Jews engaged in the Constantinople sex trade that they formed a third community, after the Sephardic and Ashkenazi Jews.[7] One Sephardic member of the Jewish community of Istanbul explained "There is a saying that comes down to us from those days...it's said especially with a Russian accent: first the wheat, then the treat!"[8]

Sephardic Jews in Constantinople, however, seemed largely to ignore the issue of prostitution until a perfect storm saw increasing numbers of Sephardic women in the trade combined with increasing political pressure from abroad. Beginning as early as 1890, Jewish philanthropists from Western Europe and England increasingly began to appeal to the *Haham Başı* Haim Nahum (1873–1960), the Sephardic Chief Rabbi of Constantinople, inviting him to conferences on combating prostitution. Well-to-do Western European Jewish women informed by the Victorian politics of social purity and intent on forestalling anti-Semitism, notably Bertha Pappenheim and Lady Constance Rothschild Battersea, targeted Constantinople, the critical link in the trafficking of women between the Russian Empire and the "New World." These European Jews blamed the flourishing of prostitution in Constantinople on the "backwardness" of Sephardic Jews.[9] Ashkenazi Jews of Constantinople, concerned with being associated with these "Oriental Jews," began to distance themselves from their Russian coreligionists, worrying that prostitution was "a black mark sullying the good reputation of our German community."[10]

---

6   Edward Bristow, *Prostitution and Prejudice: The Jewish Fight against White Slavery 1870–1939* (Clarendon: Oxford University Press, 1982), 44.

7   Bristow, *Prostitution and Prejudice*, 183–84

8   Rıfat N. Bali, *The Jews and Prostitution in Constantinople 1854–1922* (Istanbul: Isis, 2008), 25.

9   See for example Bertha Pappenheim, *Sisyphus-Arbeit: Reisebriefe aus den Jahren 1911 und 1912* (Leipzig: Paul E. Linder, 1924), 40–42

10   Letter from Aron Halévy to Alliance Paris, 3 January 1890 (AIU/Turkey).

This chapter argues that Russian Jews, and in particular Russian Jewish women, were at the center of a transnational discourse which refracted the various anxieties, priorities, and competing political aspirations of three major Jewish groups: Ashkenazi Jews in Constantinople, Sephardi Jews of the same city, and Jews of Western Europe. By examining both local and global sources, we can see how categories demarcating national difference among Jews such as "German," "Russian," and "Pole" emerged as Ashkenazi and Sephardi Jews came under the focus of Western European Jewish gaze. These categories were often highly gendered and connected to moral concepts and categories with biblical and Talmudic roots, such as *eishet chayil*, the "woman of valor" or "woman of virtue." These gendered moral categories were generated in a dialectic with their other, who are described as "lost girls" or women "lacking virtue." I use the term gaze in the Foucauldian sense—it is "not just the object that is constructed but also the knower," as Ashkenazi Jews in Constantinople were the object of the gaze but also, in their depiction of Russian Jews, the knower as well.[11] Examining the discourse on prostitution yields insight into both the idealized constructions of gender among Constantinople and Western European Jews, women included, and the subject of Russian Jewish pimps and prostitutes.

Paula Hyman, a pioneering scholar of gender and Jewish history, argued that constructions of Jewish gender are highly connected to the processes of migration. Jewish male migrants, responding to anti-Semitic tropes about the male Jewish body as effete, "represented Jewish women as responsible for the burdens of Jewishness they had to bear."[12] This coincided with Jewish embourgeoisement; that is, "their concern was heightened by their awareness that their own status and image were linked in the public imagination with the ... newcomers."[13] Therefore, "Jewish social workers, reformers, and philanthropists were particularly sensitive to the mores and image of women, for the entire group's honor could be called into question by disreputable conduct of its women."[14]

11   Claire O'Farrel, *Michel Foucault* (London: Sage, 2005).

12   Paula Hyman, *Gender and Assimilation in Modern Jewish History: The Roles and Representation of Women* (Seattle: University of Washington Press, 1995), 9.

13   Hyman, *Gender and Assimilation*, 106

14   Hyman, *Gender and Assimilation*, 106

Ashkenazi and Sephardi Jews alike took interest in prostitution when it came to be viewed as a problem among their specific Jewish subgroup. For Ashkenazim, Russian participation in the white slave trade in Constantinople likely occurred after the Crimean War (1853–56), but the number of participants multiplied in the fin-de-siècle. For Ottoman Sephardic Jews, the issue of prostitution did not become acute until the Balkan Wars of 1912–13 internally displaced many Ottoman subjects and Sephardic women increasingly came to be found in the brothels of Constantinople. Interestingly, in Salonica, Chief Rabbi Jacob Meir became the first Chief Rabbi to attempt to curtail Jewish participation in prostitution in 1908. He created a plan to expel them from Salonica, and, when the bid proved unsuccessful, forbade prostitutes to be buried in the Jewish synagogue.[15] Ultimately, both Ashkenazi and Sephardi Jews articulated their beliefs that this social vice reflected poorly on the state of Jews in the modern world more broadly.

Previous studies have dealt with prostitution in the Ottoman Empire in relation to the norms of gender and sexuality of Ottoman Muslims. Hülya Yildiz points out that Ottoman Muslim subjects were drawn to non-Muslim prostitutes in the brothels located on the European side of Constantinople. These were "peculiarly modern spaces" where an important ethnic and sexual other was constructed.[16] Malte Fuhrmann's inquiry into the marginalized subjects of the entertainment industries in the port city of Izmir alludes to but does not specifically interrogate Jewish prostitution.[17] He does however cite Donald Quataert's observation that the field of Ottoman Studies has been slow to find its subaltern turn due to an easily-accessible archive and the abundance of research that remains to be done on the Ottoman state.

The literature addressing Jewish philanthropists' response to white slavery and prostitution has been more descriptive than analytic. Lloyd P. Gartner's 1982 essay in the *Association for Jewish Studies Review*, for example, examines British sources and offers a purview of Anglo-Jewish responses, but suffers

---

15   Devin E. Naar '"The Mother of Israel" or "Sephardi Metropolis": Sephardim, Ashkenazim, and Romaniotes in Salonica?" *Jewish Social Studies , 22(1)*, 81-129.

16   Hülya Yıldız, "Limits of the Imaginable in the Early Turkish Novel: Non-Muslim Prostitutes and Their Ottoman Muslim Clients," *Texas Studies in Literature and Language* 54, no. 4 (Winter 2012), 533–34.

17   Malte Fuhrmann, "Down and Out on the Quays of İzmir: 'European' Musicians, Innkeepers, and Prostitutes in the Ottoman Port-Cities," *Mediterranean Historical Review* 24 (2009): 169–85.

from sensationalism.[18] Prostitution has been examined more broadly in the field of Jewish history, but most research examines prostitution in relation to particular states.[19]

This chapter seeks to understand the question of prostitution and white slavery in Constantinople as a lens through which to view how Ashkenazim and Sephardim, in Constantinople and abroad, understood their own place in the Ottoman Empire, in Europe more broadly, and in relation to their coreligionists. Rather than examining states' regulation of prostitution, as previous studies have done, my analysis here is lateral and done from an intracommunal vantage point. My sources—newspapers, correspondence, diary entries, and memoirs—help us to understand what was at stake for Jews in Constantinople and beyond. I begin to unravel the historical enigma: who were Tevye's Ottoman daughters?

The Oriental Port and its Orientations

Alfred Kant, a Russian Jewish farmer who lived on Tikfour Tchiflik[20] just outside of Panderma, often visited Constantinople during the First World War and through the Russian Civil War. In Constantinople he found a "reprieve" from "provincial life," especially in the Galata neighborhood, where newly arrived Russian émigrés awoke the city which had been "half-asleep in its Orientalism":

> There I could see the arrival of the first Russian émigrés who fled from the advancing victorious Bolshevik armies. All types of people were there: the rich, the poor, the lower-middle class, the aristocrats, those of the nobility and the military such as generals, officers and soldiers.... Many restaurants that prepared Russian specialties opened everywhere, but especially on the main

---

18   Lloyd P. Gartner, "Anglo-Jewry and the Jewish International Traffic in Prostitution, 1885-1914," *AJS Review* 7 (1982): 129–78.

19   For the Israeli state, see Deborah Bernstein, "Gender, Nationalism and Colonial Policy: Prostitution in the Jewish Settlement of Mandate Palestine, 1918–1948," *Women's History Review* 21, no. 1 (2012): 81–100. For Jewish prostitutes in the United Kingdome, see Lara Marks, "Jewish Women and Jewish Prostitution in the East End of London," *Jewish Quarterly* 34, no. 2 (1987): 6-10. For Jewish prostitutes in 1940s France, see Jim Dreyfus, "The Economic Aryanization of Brothels: An Illumination of Some Jewish Prostitution and Procurement in Occupied France, 1940-1944," *Revue des Etudes Juives* 162, no. 1-2 (2003): 219–46. For an overview of prostitution in Turkey, see Mark David Wyers: *Wicked Istanbul: The Regulation of Prostitution in the Early Turkish Republic* (Istanbul: Libra Kitap, 2013). For a study of prostitution in the Russian Empire and the Soviet Union, see Laurie Bernstein, *Sonia's Daughters : Prostitutes and Their Regulation in Imperial Russia* (Berkeley: University of California Press, 1995).

20   I have kept the spelling consistent with that of my sources. However, Tikfour Tchiflik is known as Tekfur Çiftliği in Turkish.

street of Péra, such as cafes, dance halls, etc. with their signs in Russian. The stairs that go from Tunel Square to Galata was completely cluttered with Russian vendors, who sold many different items in Russian.[21]

The historically cosmopolitan neighborhood of Galata, which lay adjacent to the Port of Constantinople and surrounded the Galata Tower, had originally been a Genoese colony but now swelled with these Russian émigrés. Many of these Russians were Jewish and, as a well-known Turkish anecdote summarized, the "Russian Jews in Constantinople now rubbed shoulders with the head of the White Army, who had set fire to their *shtetl* just a few years before."[22] While for Kant the neighborhood seemed to be experiencing a revitalization, offering an escape from agricultural life in the "uneducated and dull hole" of Tikfour Tchiflik, he also described the underbelly of the city that resulted from the Russians "leaving in haste" from "Southern Russia":

> Misery was rife among them, and prostitution spread in a terrible way. We saw decent women and young girls giving their bodies for a little money. We found them everywhere, on the sidewalks of the streets of Pera, in the Petit Champs Garden, in the Russian bakeries and multiple brothels of Constantinople.[23]

Pera and Galata were two principal Jewish neighborhoods connected to one another. Galata, the area near the Galata Tower, was closer to the port, and just up the hill was Pera (modern day Beyoğlu). Galata had become more international in the late nineteenth century and was the site of the new Tofre Begadim Synagogue, Or Chadash, whose name meant "new light," and the Ashkenazi Synagogue (rebuilt in 1900). Yet because of its proximity to the port, Galata also became the ideal local for a brothel. As Alphons Sussnitski noted in the German periodical *Allgemeine Zeitung des Judentums*,

> The development of Constantinople into a modern city ... and the accompanying increase in foreign traffic, with its debauched nightlife and its luxurious sensual pleasures, were yet another category on which the Ashkenazi Jews in the Turkish capital "had a lock": traffic in women. And these, too, organized themselves into their own separate community. I counted 92 members in their synagogue, whose president is a long-time member of the guild.[24]

---

21   Albert Kant, *Mémoires d'un Fermier Juif*, 96–97.

22   Interview with Robert Schild, Istanbul, 19 May 2015.

23   Kant, *Mémoires d'un Fermier Juif*, 105, 97.

24   Alphons J. Sussnitski, "Die Wirtschaftliche Lage der Juden in Konstantinopel," *Allgemeine Zeitung des Judentums*, 5 January 1912. Retrieved online 27 January 2017.
     http://sammlungen.ub.uni-frankfurt.de/cm/periodical/titleinfo/3229015.

In the nineteenth century, the port city of Constantinople was ripe for prostitution. The high traffic of steam ships and vessels passing through its waters lent itself to problems typical of a port city. It is estimated that approximately 10,000 freight vessels and 15,000 passenger steamships passed through the Bosporus by 1914.[25] The beginnings of Jewish involvement in prostitution were likely tied to the Crimean War (1853–56), as several Jewish soldiers who were taken prisoner first opened brothels on Yüksek Kaldırım Street (the same street as the Ashkenazi Synagogue) in the Galata quarter. According to a letter from Aron Halévy to the Alliance Israélite Universelle, "To these unhappy people [former soldiers from the Crimean War] there came several Jewish families from Romania, Hungary and Russia who fled from persecutions ... or wanted to save their children from the vigor of military service."[26] Many Ashkenazi women were lured by promises of eventual immigration to Palestine, favorable marriage matches, or high-paying jobs.

Constantinople served as a point of entry for Jews and others leaving the Russian Empire to the wider Mediterranean, Levant, Northern Africa, Asia and South America, which meant that many Russian women were either trafficked to or by their own accord made a stop in Constantinople, and some never made it to their intended destination. Sometimes Russian women who had departed from Odessa were trafficked at the port in Constantinople, lured by men working for pimps and madams.[27] According to a report from the Anti-White-Slavery Committee at Alexandria, the customary itinerary began in Russia, Romania, and sometimes Greece and Hungary, stopped along the way in Constantinople, and ended in "Alexandria, Cairo, or Port Sid, Bombay, Colombo, Singapore, Saigon, Hong Kong, and Shanghai."[28] Many more ended in the Jewish Colonization Association's colonies in Brazil and in Argentina. Some Jewish migrants began in the Russian cities of Bedzin, Soznowitz, Rokiciny, but many more came through Odessa.[29] The memoir of Mordechai

---

25   Rıfat N. Bali, *The Jews and Prostitution in Constantinople 1854–1922* (Istanbul: The Isis Press, 2008), 13. See also Edward J. Bristow, *Prostitution and Prejudice: The Jewish Fight against White Slavery 1870–1939*. (Clarendon: Oxford University Press, 1982).

26   Aron Halévy, "Les Israélites Polonais De Constantinople Leur établissement à Constantinople—leurs moeurs," 16 March 1890 (AIU/Tur 1C17)

27   Ibid.

28   Rapport du Comité Executif, Société Internationale Pour la Repression de la Traite des Blanches à Alexandrie (1907), p. 4 in 1C, 13, AIU/Alexandrie 1C-13

29   Bristow, Prostitution and Prejudice, 127.

Or Chadash Synagogue, contemporary views
(photographs by Alberto Mondiano)

Or Chadash Synagogue, contemporary views
(photographs by Alberto Mondiano)

Alpersohn, an early pioneer in the Jewish Colonization Association's colonies in the Pampas, describes the sight of Russian prostitutes in Buenos Aires upon his arrival in 1891: "Near the gates of the immigration house we met a few dozen elegantly dressed women and fat men in top hats. Through the gates they were talking with our wives and gave children chocolates and candy."[30] While the Jewish Colonization Association's colonies were not yet ready for the newly arrived immigrants, "some inevitably got caught up in the economy of commercial vice."[31]

Yet migration was not unidirectional. Russian Jews sometimes went to Constantinople, moved on to Buenos Aires, and then returned to Constantinople. For example, Gusta and Bercia Bleiberg, a married couple who were both involved in the business of prostitution, moved from Czernowitz to Constantinople in 1911.[32] By the end of the year, both decided to move to Buenos Aires for a few months, but returned to the Ottoman capital after they decided the climate of Buenos Aires did not agree with them. Kune Gross, Nessie Wechsler, and Baruch Blum also went to Buenos Aires, but they returned to Constantinople once they had saved up enough money and purchased Gusta Farer's brothel at 47 Yüksek Kaldırım in Galata, just down the street from the Ashkenazi Synagogue.[33] Approximately 80% of all female prostitutes who registered in Buenos Aires in 1911 were Jews from Russia, Romania, and Hungary.[34] By 1896, Russian officials at the port of Odessa claimed that trafficking of female prostitutes was impossible, but a police roundup of the traffickers in 1915 by Osman Bedri Bey demonstrates that this must not have been the case.[35]

In Constantinople, locals learned foreign languages to act as intermediaries and tour guides for disembarking visitors. Many would receive a commission from brothel owners for bringing in patrons at the port.[36] For example, Basil

---

30   Mordechai Alpersohn, *Dreissig Jahren in Argentina*, vol. 1 (Berlin, 1923). Ch. 2

31   Bristow, *Prostitution and Prejudice*, 117.

32   Ibid.

33   Bristow, *Prostitution and Prejudice*, 120–122.

34   Bristow, *Prostitution and Prejudice*, 117–119. According to Bristow, "prostitution in Buenos Aires was never a purely Jewish nor even a mostly Jewish business. The well-organized French ... took over first place before the war and the Italians came quickly into third place." See also Rıfat N. Bali, *Jews and Prostitution*, 20.

35   *First International Congress for the Suppression of the White Slave Traffic* (London, 1899), 25–26.

36   Bali, *Jews and Prostitution*, 13.

Zaharoff (born Basileios Zacharias Zacharoff, 1839–1946), the infamous Greek arms merchant who dealt indiscriminately with the Ottomans, Russians, and the British, first held a job as a "guide for the tourists to the Galata or Prostitution district of Constantinople, helping his clients to find the forbidden pleasures that went beyond the bounds of normal prostitution."[37]

The mostly Jewish neighborhood of Galata quickly became the area with the most concentrated number of brothels. Its proximity to the port and its synagogues—the Ashkenazi Synagogue and the newly built Tofre Begadim or Tailors' Synagogue constructed especially for new Russian immigrants arriving in the late nineteenth century—made it well-situated for the Jewish-owned brothels: it was convenient to live and work close to the house of prayer, which religious Jews would need to visit three times a day for daily prayers. Yet the brothel owners and pimps who lived in this Jewish neighborhood were soon prevented from praying at the Ashkenazi Synagogue or the Tailors' Synagogue. Instead, they would need to pray at Or Chadash, a synagogue originally opened by Russian migrants in the 1880s.[38] As Rafael Sadi recalls, the "Karaköy brothel and the Ashkenazi synagogue were practically right next door to one another." According to Sadi, the

> Ashkenazi Jews who ran the brothel had brought their capital when they came from Russia to Constantinople and established a place of people who kept all of the religious ordinances and who prayed three times a day without fail. That's the reason that they built the synagogue close to their establishments.[39]

A debate would ensue about the existence of Or Chadash, discussed below. Prior to Ottoman authorities shutting down the synagogue in 1915, the Sephardic community allowed it to remain open because the community boasted that none of the "inmates" were Sephardic and they were not breaking any laws or causing any problems.[40] According to a letter to the Jewish Colonization Association in London from Samuel Cohen, a Jewish British citizen who later served as an emissary and secretary to the Jewish Association for the Protection of Girls and Women, in twenty eight white slavery cases it

---

37   Ibid.

38   Other sources describe the migrants as Polish. It is likely that they came from the Polish parts of the Russian Empire.

39   Bali, *Jews and Prostitution*, 13.

40   Ibid.

handled in 1898, "Both traffickers and victims were members of our race from Poland, Russia, Galicia."[41]

Moral Vernaculars and the Transnational Debate over White Slavery

By 1910, white slavery had entered the popular lexicon in Western Europe and in North America, hastening Jewish responses that once began as mostly reconnaissance missions in the 1890s to becoming moralizing philanthropic missions as the rest of Europe and North America took notice of the white slave trade.[42] The Swiss and Danish National Committees for the Suppression of White Slavery created a silent film on the subject, and commercial filmmakers followed with *White Slave 2* and *White Slave 3*. There were plays on Broadway, plays in Yiddish, and books with titles such as *The Great War on White Slavery* or *Fighting for the Protection of Our Girls: Truthful and Chaste Account of the Hideous Trade of Buying and Selling Young Girls for Immoral Purposes*. In Max R.W. Kauffman's *House of Bondage*, by then in its fourteenth edition, the white slaver Max Crossman is described in anti-Semitic tropes, a deceptive "Hungarian" who pulls "large roll[s] of yellow bills" and tries to "Jew down" the innocent Violet.[43]

Still, Western European Jews debated whether or not they should become involved in combating the white slave trade at all. Some Jews argued that by admitting to its existence, they would legitimize anti-Semitic tropes that Jews dealt in finance and in flesh. As Bertha Pappenheim put it, "If we admit the existence of this traffic our enemies decry us; if we deny it they say we are trying to conceal it."[44]

The novelist and Territorialist Israel Zangwill (1864–1926) argued against intervention: "It is not possible for Jews to try and stamp out this evil; it is not possible for them to police the world."[45] In 1914, aware of both these debates, and having been hired by the Jewish Association for the Protection of Girls

41   Letter from Samuel Cohen to ICA London, 17 December 1899.

42   For example, Samuel Cohen's reports on behalf of the Jewish Association for the Protection of Girls and Women to Constantinople were written in the late 1890s. See Letter from Samuel Cohen to JCA London, 17 December 1899.

43   Reginald Wright Kauffman, *House of Bondage* (Mofat: New York, 1911), 22, 37, 146. See also Bristow, *Prostitution and Prejudice*, 40–41.

44   "The Burning Shame of a Terrible Scandal: Jewish Conference in London on the White Slave Traffic," *The Jewish Chronicle*, 23 April 1910.

45   Ibid.

and Women, Samuel Cohen countered the idea that suppressing the white slave trade would

> Cause a diffusion of the idea that the traffic is entirely in the hands of the Jews. This is a very unfortunate position to take up.... It is only when Jews show that they are not indifferent to this evil, and that they mean to fight it ... more energetically than others, that the prevalent idea of the extent of Jewish participation in the evil can be set right.[46]

Until 1912, the parties most interested in white slavery and prostitution in Constantinople were foreign Jewish philanthropists, in particular, well-to-do Jewish women of Western Europe. The organization with the greatest presence in Constantinople, the Jewish Association for the Protection of Girls and Women, worked to combat anti-Semitism and was also informed by the Victorian politics of social purity. William Coote (1863–1924) was a British social purity leader who traveled around Western Europe and North and South America in support of the new movement and was originally supported by the likes of Claude Montefiore and Samuel Cohen, secretary of the Jewish Association for the Protection of Girls and Women. In 1885, Louisa Montefiore de Rothschild's daughter, Lady Constance Rothschild Battersea, founded the Association, which provided relief efforts for former prostitutes but also put pressure on local leadership to eradicate prostitution. Not coincidentally, the Rothschilds were also major contributors to the Alliance Israélite Universelle.

The Jewish Association for the Protection of Girls and Women focused on Russian Jewish prostitutes in particular because they were "migratory prostitutes." As they understood it, they not only participated in an "immoral" profession but were also targeted by pimps and "slavers" because they were foreigners. As the later League of Nations put it, there was a "well-known incapacity of prostitutes particularly foreign prostitutes in a strange country, to manage their own affairs."[47] While many prostitutes and brothel keepers were actually quite successful, the Association worked to shift international opinion and helped pass two international agreements, in 1902 and in 1910, to have white slavery recognized as a juridical concept in international law, which was then advanced at the 1913 International Congress for the Suppression of

---

46 Samuel Cohen, "Report of an Inquiry Made in Constantinople on Behalf of the Jewish Association for the Protection of Girls and Women," in Bali, *Jews and Prostitution*, 74-75.

47 *League of Nations Report of the Special Body of Experts on the Extent of the International White Slave Traffic,* Part 2 (1927), 16.

White Slavery in London.[48] A Christian women's organization, the Association for the Protection of Young Girls, even formed a Jewish section, led by Eugene Simon, although her work was mainly in French port cities and in Paris.[49]

In 1910, the Jewish Association for the Protection of Girls and Women convened a conference in London to set the agenda for Jewish responses to white slavery, and they fixed their gaze on Constantinople. Pappenheim and Zangwill joined Baron Horace Gunzberg (1833–1909) of St. Petersburg, Sylvain Levi, president of the Alliance Israélite Universelle (1863–1935), and Paul Laskar, representing the Hilfsverein der Deutschen Juden (1857–1926), as well as Dr. Sigismond Sonnenfield of the Jewish Colonization Association. *The Jewish Telegraph* covered the conference and its articles were reprinted in Jewish papers from Detroit to Constantinople, including in *El Tiempo*.[50]

Lady Constance Battersea set the tone for the mission in her opening remarks: "The work behooved them to protect the individual as well as to protect society at large."[51] What was at stake here was not just the salvation of the individual women who had become (to use the Conference's terms) "tricked" and "deceived" into white slavery, but to save the "Jewish Race."[52] The salvation of the "Jewish Race" is both literal here and metaphorical: literal in the sense that there was a need to assist Russian Jews entrapped in the white slave trade, but also metaphorical, because Western European Jews' preservation was caught up in the reputations of Jews more broadly.

With these concerns in mind, several delegates from the London conference traveled to Constantinople between 1911 and 1914. Acting as emissaries to various Jewish communal organizations and included among the delegates were Bertha Pappenheim, Madame Eugene Simon, German officials from the Hilfsverein and the B'nai B'rith Organization, as well as Samuel Cohen from the Jewish Association for the Protection of Girls and Women.[53] What they described were Jewish women kept against their will in the brothels of Galata. Samuel Cohen wrote:

---

48   See International Bureau for the Suppression of Traffic in Women and Children, *Traffic in Women and Children: Past Achievements, Present Tasks* (London, 1949).

49   *Diaries of Lady Battersea,* 21 November 1901.

50   See, for example, *The Jewish Chronicle,* 23 April 1910.

51   Ibid.

52   Ibid.

53   Bristow, *Prostitution and Prejudice,* 276.

In Galata.... the inmates of the brothels show very markedly by their haggard and repressed manner that their life has no charm for them, and that they are kept there by some outside force, by some influence which they cannot shake off. Escape is almost useless even if it were possible, for to whom could these girls turn for sympathy? Others in the same district would be afraid to help them, and if they went further away nobody could understand their language.[54]

Cohen's description of helpless Jewish women as "inmates" who, lacking any agency, "are kept there ... by some influence which they cannot shake off," matches a theme that echoed throughout the 1910 conference. The speakers of the conference insisted that it was the "activity of the traffickers ... who cause the Jewish girls to become immoral."[55] Casting the blame on a few "bad seeds" that would undermine the reputation of Jews in Europe was an idea echoed by Ashkenazim in Constantinople, concerned with their own reputation and participation in broader German-Jewish identity.

German Jews and German Jews in Constantinople

Aron Halévy, the president of the Ashkenazi community, wrote a letter to the Alliance Israélite Universelle in Paris, France in 1890. In it, he describes the dire state of Ashkenazim in the Jewish neighborhood of Galata:

The brothels that are located in a place near to Yüksek Kaldırım [Ashkenazi Synagogue street] are full of Jewish girls who have been lost to the community.... These establishments, which go on one after another for a lengthy stretch of the street, *are a black mark sullying the good reputation of our German community....* If there is any comfort that can be had, it can be mentioned that one does not encounter prostitution among the young Sephardic girls, and the upright demeanor of the Sephardic girls who go to work at the Tobacco Régie to earn their living keeps the dandies and Lotharios from approaching them.[56]

The letter differentiates the various kinds of Jews living in Constantinople, affected by the brothels and prostitution prevalent in the neighborhood surrounding the Ashkenazi Synagogue. These Ashkenazi women, having been lured into prostitution, have been "lost to the community." Sephardic girls, by virtue of the fact that they had been born on Ottoman soil, were perceived to be immune to the trade run by "dandies and Lotharios." Even Halévy's use of the

---

54   Cohen, "Report of an Inquiry," 74.

55   *Jewish Telegram*, April 1910

56   Letter from Aron Halévy to Alliance Paris, 3 January 1890 (AIU/Turkey). My emphasis.

term Lothario is notable. It comes from the first part of *Don Quixote*, when Don Quixote and Sancho Panza encounter a man obsessed with testing the fidelity of his wife. Lothario is hired to seduce her in *The Impertinent Curious Man*.

Interestingly, designating the women in the brothels as "lost to the community" reflects upon Halévy's larger concern of the health and reputation of the Constantinople "German Jewish Community." This statement expresses Halévy's intention to make a distinction between German Jews and Ashkenazi Jews; "Ashkenazi" is a term that could include Russian Jews who might be enmeshed in the white slave trade. The designation as *German* Jews is a nod to the *Haskalah*, a historical period central to the "Paris-Berlin praxis" of enlightened, emancipated European Jewry.[57] After all, Constantinople's Ashkenazi community dedicated their rebuilt synagogue on Yüksek Kaldırım Street in 1900 to Francis Joseph I, Emperor of Austria-Hungary. At its dedication, with several Austro-Hungarian and French dignitaries in attendance, hymns were read, and "Dr. Adolph Rosenthal gave the opening speech in Turkish and German."[58] In doing so, they reaffirmed the importance of Austro-Hungary and German culture more broadly, and clearly demonstrated Ashkenazi Jews' cultural allegiances and orientation toward German Jewry.[59]

Bertha Pappenheim also noticed this trend of differentiating German Jews from other Jews of Constantinople. She recalled in her memoires a meeting and a tour with a "certain representative of the Ashkenazi community, a Mr. R.," noting that

> you have to get used to the fact that the Russians, Galicians and Romanians who are registered with the characteristic names (*Kosenamen*) of the Poles in Germany, here in the Orient play themselves off as "German Jews" and disparage the Spanish [Jews] as backward and incapable of possessing culture.[60]

---

57   Jonathan Frankel, "Assimilation and the Jews in Nineteenth-Century Europe: Towards a New Historiography?" in Jonathan Frankel and Steven Zipperstein, eds., *Assimilation and Community: The Jews in Nineteenth Century Europe* (Cambridge: Cambridge University Press, 1992).

58   Ibid., 65.

59   Devi Mays has suggested that this could be read as a shifting of political alliances. I believe this is more of a cultural alliance with German Jewry as representations of modernity, assimilation, and the Haskalah.

60   Pappenheim, *Sisyphus-Arbeit*, 73–74.

The interiors of the Ashkenazi Synagogue in Galata
(Photograph by Alberto Mondiano)

Interestingly, Pappenheim noticed that the Ashkenazi Jews not only identified as German Jews, but also differentiated themselves from Sephardic Jews. Benjamin Sperer (1921-2022), the son of second-generation Russian Jewish migrants, commented in his memoir that "the Sephardim...clung to their Spanish heritage," the "Ashkenazim collectively labeled "*lehlis*"...by the Sephardim, continued to live out the culture of Central Europe."[61] He recalled that the

> Ashkenazim spoke Yiddish or German with each other, sent their children to the German school in Istanbul, flocked to visit Yiddish theater groups, and even conducted their religious services in Hebrew and German. The Haggadah at the Seder table was recited as "Der Auszug aus Aegypten."[62]

We see this pattern, the *other* engaged in its own *other*, among Sephardic Jews, especially in their depictions of Russian Jews in the 1890s. In the next decades, the trend spread to Ashkenazi, or in this case "German Jews," who then found it necessary to self-designate as distinct from their Russian coreligionists.

Women of Virtue, Women of Valor: Sephardi and Ashkenazi Jewish Women in Constantinople, the Alliance, and Combating Immorality

The 1910 London Conference agreed that poverty and lack of education, in addition to pimps deceiving innocent Jewish women through false marriages and other promises, were the root of "immorality."[63] The civilizing premise of the Alliance coincided with Victorian ideals of morality and education. For Victorians, self-cultivation meant education and adherence to moral codes of chastity and purity. As Jews became emancipated legally, and elite Jews became acculturated and integrated into bourgeois society, the question of the education and civilization of their coreligionists became more apparent. The system of schools and the Alliance more generally "emerged as the very distillation of all the ideological and political forces that had created the emancipated, acculturated social and intellectual elite of modern French Jewry."[64] In Germany the idea of *Bildung*, or education in the form of personal

---

61   Benjamin Sperer, *Under Turkish Skies* (Istanbul: Libra Kitap, 2017), 15

62   Sperer, *Under Turkish Skies*, 15-16

63   *Jewish Telegraph*, April 1910

64   Aron Rodrigue, *French Jews Turkish Jews*, xii.

cultivation and improvement, informed many of the Jewish assistance agencies and philanthropists active in the Ottoman Empire, including the Hilfsverein der Deutschen Juden.

Thus, along with political emancipation came a certain set of moral codes and behaviors, many of which the Alliance worked to transmit to the Jews of the Ottoman Empire. Central to the Alliance's *mission civilisatrice* was its idea of "moralizing."[65] Teachers were "missionaries of progress" and, according to instructions sent in 1903,

> Education consists of both intellectual and moral education.... The virtues that one seeks to inspire in the child are love of country, love of all men, love and respect of parents... nobility of sentiment, love of the public good, the spirit of solidarity.[66]

Jewish organizations at work in Constantinople were concerned with prostitution because it threatened to undermine the embourgeoisement, informed by the Victorian era, that Jews of Western Europe had achieved. In the language of the Alliance, the mission was to "rail constantly against the vices of the local population."[67] Constantinople is described by local and visiting Ashkenazi Jews as a city rife with immorality, including both participation in prostitution and also the Sephardic community's lack of response and apparent indifference to it.

Therefore, it made some sense for the local Ashkenazi community to petition the Alliance Central Committee in Paris. Aron Halévy, the local leader of the Constantinople Ashkenazi Community, appealed to the moralizing mission of the organization when he described the Galata quarter:

> A few of the serious Poles look disparagingly at this impudence that would compel some of their co-racialists to open a "shop" on Yüksek Kaldırım. In the opinion of the [brothel owners], nothing could be more intelligent than to earn a living from the fruits of an extremely practical trade.[68]

---

65   Ibid., 72.

66   Ibid.

67   Ibid.

68   Letter from Aron Halévy to Alliance, 7 January 1890 (Turkey 1C1), as quoted in Bristow, *Prostitution and Prejudice*, 87.

In this letter, Halévy does not explicitly state that the Ashkenazi brothel owners and their disapproving coreligionists are Jews, instead calling them "Poles." It is also possible that he was referring to them as Poles, or, if Ladino had entered his lexicon, as *lehlis,* a pejorative of the Hebrew word *melukhlakh* (dirty).[69] We know they were Jewish because the "shop" to which he refers to was adjacent to Or Chadash. Halévy also describes them as having knowledge of Jewish scriptures.[70] According to Halévy, having knowledge of Jewish law and scripture does not preclude acting immorally, and, according to these "co-racialists," earning a living from prostitution was simply an expedient choice. Only a complete lack of morals, according to Halévy, could cause one to justify such a profession.

> In reference to the women in the brothels and their pimps, Halévy is more direct:
>
> When you attempt to speak with them [Jewish pimps] on the subject of the women's virtue, they look at you with disbelief and say: these are not virtuous women such as those mentioned in the Holy Scriptures. All of these women are of doubtful morality, and find it an irresistible pleasure to taste the forbidden fruit. Or, an even more repulsive explanation: the husbands of these women are simply obtaining benefit from the lust and passion stirring in their spouses.[71]

We can glean from this important statement a conception of gender and femininity that is rooted in the concept of *eishet chayil,* the "virtuous woman" or "woman of valor" found in Proverbs 31. This Proverb, traditionally sung in observant Jewish families before the Sabbath evening dinner to the women of the household, asks, "A capable wife, who can find? ... The heart of her husband trusts in her.... Strength and dignity are her clothing.... She looks well to the way of her household."[72] The idea of this "woman of valor" goes back to the text of Proverbs 14:1: "the wise woman builds her house, the foolish one tears it down." In the context of Mandate Palestine, women's sexual purity

---

69   David M. Bunis, *Voices from Jewish Salonika* (Jerusalem, 1999), 62–63; Sarah Bunin Benor, "Lexical Othering in Judezmo: How Ottoman Sephardim Refer to Non-Jews," in *Languages and Literatures of Sephardic and Oriental Jews: proceeding of the sixth International Congress for Research on the Sephardi and Oriental Jewish Heritage,* ed. David M. Bunis (Jerusalem, 2009), 65–85. For the case in Salonica see Devin E. Naar, "The 'Mother of Israel' or the 'Sephardi Metropolis'? Sephardim, Ashkenazim, and Romaniotes in Salonica," *Jewish Social Studies* 22, no. 1 (2016): 81–129.

70   Ibid.

71   Letter from Aron Halévy to Alliance, 12 March 1890 (Turkey 1C1), as quoted in Bristow, *Prostitution and Prejudice,* 87

72   Bernhard W. Anderson, Bruce M. Metzger, and Roland E. Murphy, *The New Oxford Annotated Bible with the Apocryphal/Deuterocanonical Books* (New York: Oxford University Press, 1991).

came to represent the transmission of the Jewish nation state, and prostitution, especially sex with non-Jews, threatened the ideological underpinnings of Jewish statehood.[73] In this context, however, women who are not "women of valor" or are "lost to the community" refer to the biblical concepts of gender that had been frequently reiterated in rabbinic and in response literature. Halévy's description of prostitutes is also highly sexualized, describing them as desiring a "taste of the forbidden fruit." Far worse, however, is that men are obtaining benefit from "the lust and passion stirring in their spouses."

In 1911, Bertha Pappenheim described the Constantinople Sephardic Community's lack of response as fundamentally a moral problem. She wrote in her diaries during a visit to Galata in 1911:

> I am frustrated that the "sexuality" here has not given rise to any *moral outrage*. I still must hear and see and compare and observe here before reaching any conclusions, but one thing is clear to me: one cannot simply sit on one's hands![74]

Many of the reformers tackling the issue of prostitution invoked notions of morality, which are not easily delineated from the orientalist discourses that she engaged in. Pappenheim suggested that the Jewish prostitutes in Galata *should* invoke a response among her coreligionists, but they do not. This lack of a moral compass, as Pappenheim understood it, is directly connected with what she saw as a "moral defect ... that ... derives from living together with the Turks, or—what appears to me as more probable—a hereditary mindset among the oriental Jews."[75] This is a common trope in the depiction of Sephardic Jews in the Ottoman Empire by Ashkenazi Jews. They claim that Sephardic Jews, once at the forefront of medieval Jewish life, have been subsumed by or lost in "the Orient." Alphons Sussnitski wrote in 1912: "The spiritual decline of Spanish Jewry in Turkey is a fact that cannot be denied."[76] The Sephardic community's lack of response only added to this immorality.

Samuel Cohen's later descriptions of the Galata quarter similarly paint Jewish Constantinople as immoral and "licentious":

---

73 Deborah Bernstein, "Gender, Nationalism and Colonial Policy: Prostitution in the Jewish Settlement of Mandate Palestine, 1918–1948," *Women's History Review* 21, no. 1 (2012): 81–100.

74 Pappenheim, *Sisyphus-Arbeit*, 8 April 1911. My emphasis.

75 Pappenheim, *Sisyphus-Arbeit* , 40–42.

76 Ibid.

Everything appears as free and licentious as possible. There are no hindrances and no difficulties from the authorities. Except for the fact that a policeman is placed in a kind of sentry box in one or two places, there is not the slightest supervision. The streets themselves are nightly crowded with men of all nationalities, with a large preponderance of sailors. The inmates of the houses appeared to me to be mainly Russian and Polish Jewesses, though there were many others.... There are also churches, schools, and synagogues in this district, but until recently no attempt was made to bring about any improvements. It must be remembered that the majority of the people who reside in Galata are not Mohammedans, but Greeks and Jews, and most of the principal business houses are within a few minutes' walk of these streets.[77]

In addition to describing the multicultural fabric of the city, Cohen points out the contradictions of the neighborhood, with "churches, schools, and synagogues" alongside the brothels in the Galata district. The juxtaposition is used as a device to prove the prevalence of "licentiousness" in spite of the prevalence of what should be a moral lighthouse: the synagogue. Cohen continues, and appeals to the heart strings of his employers by pointing to the youngest victims of prostitution: "In this district ... there are other houses with numbers of children, and these children are running about the streets where the immoral houses are and thus being bred in evil from their babyhood. What an effect this must have on them as they grow older!"[78]

The same year that Halévy wrote his letter, the Ashkenazi community of Constantinople managed to close down the synagogue. However, *Haham Başı* Moshe Levy "soon thereafter allow[ed] these families to reopen their house of worship on the condition that it would be surrounded on all sides by a high wall."[79] In 1910, Rabbi David Markus unsuccessfully attempted to buy Or Chadash synagogue.

Why did the Sephardic Chief Rabbi allow the synagogue to be reopened? While the specific reasons are unknown, the Sephardic community's hesitation to oppose prostitution at least suggests that prostitution was not their primary concern in turn of the century Ottoman Constantinople. By the time that Haim Nahum took the office of Chief Rabbi in 1908, he faced a multitude of communal problems, especially with the Ashkenazi community. Bertha

77   Cohen, "Report of an Inquiry," opt. cite., Rıfat N. Bali, *Jews and Prostitution*

78   Ibid.

79   Ibid., 29.

Pappenheim describes Chief Rabbi Haim Nahum (whom she otherwise calls "sympathetic to the cause of white slavery") as fundamentally incapable of doing anything about it.

> He knows all manner of things, but certainly not enough, and therefore I do not believe that he has the necessary power to do anything. He knows for example … that in Constantinople there is an entire synagogue of white slavers, in which women's rooms purchase for their pimps the "Eliyahus," the honors and the blessings during the religious services and Torah readings and such; he should have the power to prevent this "House of God" and yet he does not![80]

Some Ottoman citizens argued that it was morally permissible to visit prostitutes that were outside of their religion, and it was also technically legal in the Ottoman Empire. Samuel Cohen, sent to Constantinople by the Jewish Association for the Protection of Girls and Women, noted in 1914 that the Ottoman authorities did not involve themselves in the matters of brothels as it

> Does not concern them as long as the inmates of the brothels do not belong to the Mohammedan faith.... Their argument is that if other nations and other religions permit women to act as prostitutes in their own country, why should they be permitted from doing so in Turkey.[81]

In fact, following the Treaty of Berlin in 1878, each consulate maintained jurisdiction over their subjects, and since many Russians retained their Russian passports or forged Russian documents, it was nearly impossible to punish them.[82] The problems presented by the Ashkenazi community, combined with the assumption that white slavery was a problem only among the Ashkenazi, prevented Haim Nahum from taking any measures against it.

Sephardic Jews, armed with the moralizing tools and rhetoric of the Alliance Israélite Universelle, became more seriously concerned with prostitution after more Sephardic women fell into the trade after the Balkan Wars in 1912–1913. The Jewish Chronicle reported that at least six hundred women and children arrived in Constantinople from the town of Kirk Kilise "in a state of complete destitution," and "a number of children have reached this city [Constantinople] without their parents, whom they lost during the panic which

---

80   Pappenheim, *Sisyphus-Arbeit*, 8 April 1911.

81   Bristow, *Prostitution and Prejudice*, 183

82   Ibid.

prevailed at the train station."[83] By the Wars' end, Constantinople's Ashkenazi and Sephardi Jews, despite being engaged in quite serious intracommunal and politically motivated debates, came together under the Ashkenazi-led B'nai B'rith organization to target prostitution in the capitol. Rather than articulating concerns about the safety and well being of the victims of the white slave trade, it was argued that the prevalence of this vice reflected the poor moral health of the Jewish nation.[84] The issue was similar to others that the B'nai B'rith organization was tackling. By 1912, eradicating the white slave trade was an issue that could bring together both Ashkenazi and Sephardi Jews at a time of extreme intracommunal religious tension (see Chapter 4). By 1913, prostitution and the white slave trade became an existential threat to Ottoman Jewry writ large, one in which Ashkenazi and Sephardi Jews united and were "obligated in order to eradicate the filth and damned stain and save this generation."[85]

The Balkan Wars and the Filth of Galata

With the exception of one article in 1905, it does not appear that *El Tiempo* reported any incidents of white slavery until 1912, when *El Tiempo* published an article entitled "Misfortune of Russian Jews." In it, Russian women are described as being so destitute and uneducated that they are easily "tricked" (presumably by white slavers or perhaps landlords), but prostitution or white slavery is never mentioned by name. The article refers more generally to a "crisis among the Jewish community."[86] While the authors do not differentiate between Ashkenazi and Sephardi Jewish communities, they imply that it is a crisis among the *entire* community. It seems that the editors were attempting to garner support for those Russian Jews whom they saw were in need— migrants who had fled *pogroms* and "Muscovite violence"—and prostitutes did not constitute the needy, as previous chapters have established. Some scholars have argued that the broad disinterest among Sephardic Jews was due to the industry not specifically involving Sephardic women.[87] It seems probable that the editors of *El Tiempo* intentionally left out the stories of pimps and

---

83   "Jews and the War: Jewish Refugees in Constantinople" November 8, 1912, *The Jewish Chronicle*

84   There were some exceptions to this rule, including "Drama de la Familia," *El Tiempo* 17 April, 1912

85   "Kontra el Abominable Komercio de Las Blankas," *El Tiempo*, 22 October 1913.

86   "La Disfortuna de los Djudeos de Rusia," *El Tiempo*, 18 May 1905.

87   See Bali, *Jews and Prostitution*.

prostitutes because such figures were not the focus of philanthropy, and also because they wanted to obscure the prevalence of prostitution.

The Jewish Association for the Protection of Girls and Women made several appeals to local Jewish agencies, and the archives of the Jewish Colonization Association and the office of the Chief Rabbi preserve several incoming petitions. One invitation from Claude Montefiore and Arthur R. Murro of the Gentlemen's Committee appealed to the Chief Rabbi that it was not only "in the Jews' interest, but it is also the Jews' duty to combat this evil, because as we have seen, [it is] the only way to stop the anti-Jewish propaganda."[88] The Chief Rabbi was invited on several occasions to attend the Jewish International Conference in London in 1910 but never accepted the invitation.[89] He did submit a list of pimps and procurers then active in the capital to the Ottoman Interior Ministry.[90]

The Balkan Wars of 1912–13 changed the face of prostitution in Galata. The Wars created thousands of internally displaced people, and Sephardic Jews migrated from parts of the Aegean to Constantinople. After 1913, Sephardic women were found in larger numbers in the brothels of Galata.[91] Haskel Rabinowitz reported that at least 200 Sephardic families became involved in prostitution, with all family members performing a role in the exchange.[92] The prostitution problem, once an issue largely ignored by the Sephardic community, was now of immediate interest.

In 1913, the Grand Lodge of the B'nai B'rith organization formed an International Committee to combat the White Slave Trade. The Ambassador Henry Morgenthau became its ambassador, and Dr. Israel Auerbach (1878-1956), a German-born Jewish educator, arrived as the Hilfsverein's representative in Constantinople in 1908 and became the organization's secretary. The outbreak of World War I cut short the activities of the International Committee. Working on behalf of the World Zionist Organization, Auerbach went on to co-found the B'nai B'rith Lodge with Rabbi David Markus and Joseph Niego (see Chapter 3). One of the principle agenda items was the intracommunal effort to eradicate the

---

88   Letter from Claude Montefiore and Arthur R. Moro, Jewish Association for the Protection of Girls and Women Gentleman Committee to Rabbi Haim Nahum, 28 September 1908 (CAHJP HM2/8643).

89   Ibid.

90   *Emmanuel*, 30 September 1910; *Jewish Tribune*, 30 September 1910.

91   See Cohen, "Report of an Inquiry," opt. cite., Rıfat N. Bali, *The Jews and Prositution*

92   *New York Tageblatt*, 27 December 1911.

white slave trade in Constantinople. It was at this time that *El Tiempo* also began reporting on the white slave trade, and in 1913, it published a call for a collaborative response between Sephardic and Ashkenazic Jewish communities. That same year, discussions in the Ladino and new Jewish presses that had sprung up in Constantinople began to make a clearer connection between morality, honor, and the nation. Their language is reminiscent of the language of the *mission civilisatrice* of the Alliance, and it also invokes nationalist rhetoric, which makes sense given the post-1908 context (the connection to Jewish nationalism will be explored in greater detail in Chapter 3).

In the 16 July 1913 issue of *El Tiempo*, the editors reported on "El kongreso internacional por la suppression del komersio de las blankas" that took place that month in London. In attendance were the Chief Rabbi of England, the Archbishop of Canterbury, and the Cardinal of Westminster Abbey. The editors of *El Tiempo* reprinted the speech of Rabbi Joseph Hertz because it had caused a "sensation among the delegates" due to its "frankness, its passion, and above all the Rabbi publicly declared that it is the country of Russia that encourages prostitution and forces its Jewish daughters to dishonor themselves and sends them into the abyss."[93] The Russian delegate, for his part, advised the other delegates that the Chief Rabbi was "ill-informed" and objected to the accusation that "Russia gave these Jewish women no choice but to take the 'yellow ticket' to cross its borders."[94] The focus of the coverage was on the public declaration of Russia's role in the white slave trade, not on the cities or populations that participated in it.

Calls for the Chief Rabbi to intervene also began around this time. An article entitled "A Family Drama," republished from Smyrna on 17 April 1913, tells the story of a woman from Aydın who had been trafficked into prostitution. The paper points to the "indifference of the Jewish communities" and asks Rabbi Nahum to intervene in Constantinople.[95] Another article published on 1 August 1913 described Rabbi Nahum's intervention on behalf of two young Russian Jewish girls who had been trafficked aboard a ship bound for Marseilles that was in port in Constantinople.[96] The young girls were returned

---

93   "El Kongreso Internacional Por la suppression del Komersio de las Blankas," *El Tiempo*, 16 July 1913.

94   Ibid.

95   "Drama de la Familia," *El Tiempo*, 17 April 1912.

96   "El Gran Rabino Nahum Salva Dela Perdisyon Dos Jovenes Israelitas", "El *Tiempo*, 1 August 1913.

to Constantinople, and the trafficker, a Vitali Puego, was arrested in Marseilles after Chief Rabbi Nahum communicated via telegraph to the Chief Rabbi of Marseilles.[97]

A year later, *El Tiempo* reproduced an article that had been published by the Ashkenazi community on the Jewish holiday of Yom Kippur, the Day of Atonement, in 1913.[98] The original article was published in both "Yiddish and Judeo-Spanish," addressed to "Hermanos y hermanas," their brothers and sisters.[99] While the article contained little commentary by the editors of *El Tiempo*, the article's title ("Kontra el abominable komercio de las blankas," "against the abominable white slave trade") and the reprinting of the article in its entirety suggest that the editors agreed with it and supported the Ashkenazi community.

The Ashkenazi community used Yom Kippur, the holy Day of Atonement and a day of "reflection where Jews ask their forgiveness of God," as an opportunity to reflect primarily on the moral health of Constantinople's Jews who were bystanders to the white slave trade, and only briefly alluded to the moral health of the pimps and prostitutes themselves.[100] They indicted the entire "Jewish community of Turkey for [their] indifference towards what is happening internally." The Jews of Turkey have been "preoccupied with providing bread," and have met [prostitution] with "minimal protest," and have become "disinterested in their material and intellectual questions, or in questions of morality." They have also not been interested in the "national education of the city nor of the misery of the city." "Never in the life of the city," they continue, "has there been this kind of exploitation.... The commerce of flesh takes a toll on the city, the disgrace of the Galata neighborhood is rife with this leprosy [prostitution]." To see these "miseries should inspire us, but instead it has destroyed all of our understandings of morality, of noble sentiments, and the honor of the nation, and of the city of Constantinople.... These are the indirect effects of prostitution."

This vice was regarded as affecting not only the morality and the health of the nation, but also the honorable families whose children walk and play in the

---

97 Ibid.

98 "Kontra el Abominable Komercio de Las Blankas," *El Tiempo,* 22 October 1913.

99 Ibid.

100 Ibid.

"dirty streets of Galata." They are the "unintended victims of this dishonor." In other words, not only were the Ashkenazim concerned with the moral health of the prostitutes and those involved in the white slave trade, but they were also concerned with the moral well-being of the Jewish community itself. By ignoring the white slave trade, the Jews of Constantinople were suffering and the integrity of Ottoman Jewry was at stake.

Unique to the Ashkenazi community, which otherwise was at odds with the Chief Rabbi and the *meclis-i cismani,*was a call for unity among their coreligionists. They asked their Sephardi and Ashkenazi brothers and sisters to find some "noble sentiment in their hearts" that "we are obligated to fight the damned stain if we want to preserve and save this generation [of Jews]." They called upon their coreligionists to unite all the societies, organizations, and sects in Constantinople for the "good of the public and the future of the community," and that "they should stop at nothing to win this sacred fight." They concluded with a call to their "brothers and sisters to protect their morality, to abolish this dirty stain! Long live the power of the Jewish family!"[101]

The invocations of family ("the Jewish family," "brothers and sisters") and nation ("honor of the nation," "national education") were powerful, especially since the article was printed by a "Society of well known Ashkenazi Jews," as the editors of *El Tiempo* stated in the beginning of the article, and the article concludes that these Jews were in fact "radical and nationalist."[102] Again, the emphasis was not on the individual prostitutes but rather on the collective health of the Jewish community of Constantinople. The language this group of Ashkenazi Jews used in order to discuss the white slave trade reflected its larger values and aspirations—and, by the Ladino press's effort to publish it-- reflects the values of the Sephardic community as well.

The End of Or Chadash and the New Ashkenazi Leadership

The Ottoman police did nothing about the brothels because many of the men and women were subjects of foreign consulates and, because of the Capitulations, the police had no jurisdiction over them. Or Chadash Synagogue was finally shut down in 1915 when the Prefect of Police, Osman Bedri Bey, took advantage of the Ottoman Empire's entry into the First

---

101 Ibid.
102 Ibid.

World War and the freeze on the Capitulations and rounded up some 176 individuals. Henry Morgenthau reported to the United States that the majority of those arrested, one hundred and two out of one hundred and twenty seven, were Russian, while twenty-four were Romanian and 6 were Greek. The head pimp, who went by the Ottomanized name Michael Pasha, was actually a Michael Moses Salamovitz, claimed to be a Russian spy, and was the president of the "pimps' synagogue."[103] He was a Russian subject and was deported. Also in 1915, as mentioned at the beginning of this chapter, the two former prostitutes Rozi and Fremond purchased the Tofre Begadim/ Schneidertempel, the second Ashkenazi synagogue in the Galata quarter, which served as an assistance house for former prostitutes.[104]

The debates over Russian Jews and prostitution in Constantinople overlapped with what had become another politicized debate: the debate over Russian Jews and Zionism. While one segment of Russian Jewry became the centrifuge for debates over larger Jewish life in Europe, Ashkenazi Jews simultaneously began to come to the fore of communal debates and leadership in Constantinople. In the next chapter, we will follow the story of how Ashkenazi Jews moved from the outskirts of Constantinople Jewish life to its center. They built new synagogues, schools, and institutions in the city and began to participate and chip away at Sephardic hegemony, effectively transforming the face of Ottoman and Turkish Jewry.

---

103 See *Traite des Blanches*, July 1901,

104 Aslan Yahni (ed.), *90 Yıl Kuruluşundan Bugüne İhtiyarlara Yardım Derneği* (Istanbul: İhtiyarlara Yardım Derneği, 2006), 29.

Chapter 3

"THE NATIONAL AWAKENING?" ASHKENAZI JEWS IN CONSTANTINOPLE

In 1936, the Istanbul lodge of B'nai B'rith ("people of the covenant") hosted a series of lectures by one of its founders, Rabbi Dr. David Feivel Markus (1870–1944), giving Rabbi Markus the opportunity to reminisce on his decades of service there. Markus had come to Constantinople in 1900 to serve as headmaster at the Goldschmidt School, a school for Ashkenazi Jews, and became one of the most influential members of the Jewish community of the late Ottoman Empire and early Turkish Republic. In 1911, a group of influential Ashkenazi and Sephardi Jews had established the B'nai B'rith lodge as an organization to bridge the gap between Ashkenazi and Sephardi Jews, which had become a "crisis" according to its founding members.[1] In his 1936 lecture at the Istanbul lodge, *Trois Mille Ans d'Histoire Juive* (three thousand years of Jewish History), Markus spoke about the entire course of Jewish history from the Maccabees to the *Haskalah* (the Jewish Enlightenment) to the Hebrew revival of Eliezer Ben Yehudah. But it was his comments about a new "national awakening" that were particularly relevant for the Sephardic and Ashkenazic Jews in the audience who were celebrating both the "silver anniversary" of the Lodge and the "bar mitzvah" of thirteen years of Turkish statehood.

---

1   *Bulletin de la Grande Loge de District XI et de la Loge de Constantinople, No. 678 (1913)*, 119. According to one document, the lodge's mission was to "inspire a large Jewish solidarity movement, encourage private initiatives, and to shake local indifference and to organize relief [to Jews in Constantinople] in a methodical and rational way."

According to Markus and his historical teleology, the ongoing national awakening was not a deviation from the course of three thousand years of Jewish history but rather its fulfillment. All of the "epochs" that had preceded a Jewish state in Palestine are links in the chain of Zionist history. Markus asserted that renewed interest in the Hebrew language was

> Only a means to awaken, to fortify, to preserve national sentiment; the awakening of the Hebrew language is a consequence, a result of national sentiment [that has] already [been] awoken, a continuation of historical Jewish life, a development that does not move away from the center but rather moves closer. As we will see later, new energies will be brought from the Orient to the Occident. Oriental and occidental Jews will meet again to reconcile and to openly declare their attachment to one same and singular people.[2]

The discussion of a "same and singular people," a classic image of the essentialized nation, worked particularly well for an audience recovering from nearly forty years of intra-communal conflict in Ottoman and now Turkish lands (see below). Markus predicted that nationalist sentiment would intensify as a "development that does not move away from the center but rather moves closer," and "oriental" Jews would finally play a key role in the fulfillment of three thousand years of Jewish history.

Yet who were these "oriental" Jews whom Markus, an Ashkenazi Ottoman Jew, addressed in 1936, and why did Markus address them in such nationalist terms? In the years since his arrival, Markus had witnessed a transformation of the Jewish community from one that was largely Sephardic and Alliancist in political orientation to one with a significant Ashkenazi minority population as Jews from Russia flocked to the Ottoman capital. With this diversity came a wide range of political opinions and aspirations, and, in particular, multiple and competing claims to the legacy of the Committee of Union and Progress. Beginning in 1912, Markus became a discreet yet vital centrifuge for the intra-communal debates and politics between Istanbul's Ashkenazi and Sephardi Jews.

Under Markus's watch, Ashkenazi Jews would for the first time play a *visible* political and civil role in the Ottoman and Turkish Jewish milieu of

---

2   *Trois mille ans d'Histoire juive: cycle de conférences tenues par Mr. Le Dr. D. F. Markus à la Béné Bérith d'Istanbul au cours du premier trimestre de l'année 1936* (Istanbul: Société Anonyme de Papeterie et de l'imprimerie, 1936). My thanks to Christina Sztajnkrycer for her help in translating this passage.

Constantinople. As Markus foresaw, "Oriental and Occidental Jews" did in fact "meet again to reconcile and to openly declare their attachment to one same and singular people," although not in full measure until 1948 and the creation of the State of Israel. [3] While this chapter is about Ashkenazi Jews' visibility, it also seeks to complicate Markus's teleology and his argument for the inevitability of Jewish national statehood.

The ascension of Ashkenazim in the Jewish social fabric of early twentieth-century Istanbul occurred concurrently with the growing popularity of Zionism on the one hand, and on the other the decline of the office of the Chief Rabbi, which had been the principal site of official interaction between the Sublime Porte and Istanbul's Jews.[4] After the Young Turk Revolution in 1908, Istanbul's Ashkenazim and Sephardim found themselves in a bitter dispute over questions of Zionism and a possible Jewish homeland in Palestine, which seemed in many cases to devolve into a polemic based on national difference.[5] Yet despite its intensification after 1908, this polemic was not new. As previous chapters have demonstrated, Ashkenazim, and in particular Russian Jews, had often been accused of being morally or politically subversive. In earlier Sephardic representations, Russian Jews were seen as victims of Tsarist oppression who needed Sephardic Jews' help, in contrast to the Sephardic experience in the Ottoman Empire largely represented as a "romance between Jews and empire."[6] In later representations, however, Ashkenazi and Russian Jews evolved into "foreign Jews" or "Jews with foreign nationality" who could undermine both Sephardic hegemony in the Ottoman capital and their position as the "privileged millet."

This chapter will examine Jewish communal life, politics, and leadership in Constantinople during the aftermath of Russian emigration to the Ottoman capital between 1890 and 1923 by focusing on the history of the *Haham Başı* and the *Baş Haham*, the Chief Rabbi and the position of "Principal Rabbi"

---

3   Ibid.

4   I refer to Constantinople in this chapter as Istanbul to reflect my sources.

5   There were many visions of Jewish life in Palestine among Sephardic Jews and Ashkenazi Jews, and independent statehood was neither typical nor popular, at least while the Ottoman Empire was still intact. Even the foreign Zionists that came to Constantinople after 1908 declared their commitment to preserving the territorial integrity of the Empire. Thus, it would be more correct to speak of Zionisms versus the singular Zionism.

6   See Julia Phillips Cohen, *Becoming Ottomans: Sephardi Jews and Ottoman Citizenship in the Modern Era* (New York: Oxford University Press, 2014).

proclaimed by Rabbi Moshe Halévy in 1890. In the latter half of this critical period—the Constitutional Era and beyond—the Young Turk Revolution of 1908 transformed discussions about modernity and emancipation into a debate between Zionists and anti-Zionists that, similar to discussions in previous decades, largely fell out along national lines. In these debates, Ottoman Ashkenazim, and especially Rabbi Markus, promoted Zionist politics through various institutions Markus helped found, most notably the B'nai B'rith Lodge 648. Nationalist discourses also featured prominently in the Jewish press of Constantinople, which rapidly expanded after the Young Turk Revolution lifted censorship laws and allowed a new Zionist press to emerge. As the discussion below will show, however, the Ladino press took a dimmer view, describing Russian Jews as either Zionists or, even worse, "Jews of Foreign Nationality," as they became the discursive subject revealing the anxieties and aspirations of Ottoman Jews on the brink of Turkish statehood.

Michelle U. Campos's 2011 monograph *Ottoman Brothers: Muslims, Christians, and Jews in Early Twentieth Century Palestine* has significantly furthered our understanding of these critical years in the Ottoman Empire and by so doing has called into question the inevitability of Jewish nationalism.[7] Campos examines the years after the Young Turk Revolution and the history of what she calls "civic Ottomanism" in Palestine and in Istanbul to elucidate what other political geographies were possible in the early twentieth century. Campos's emphasis is on the *intra*-communal debates among Ottoman Christians, Muslims, and Jews. While she does discuss the anti-Zionism of Sephardic Jews and, in particular, David Fresco's dismissal of Zionism as a product imported by newly arrived Ashkenazi immigrants, this chapter aims to shed additional light on the *inter*-communal discussions that Ashkenazi and Sephardi Jews in Istanbul were having.[8] Ashkenazi Jews did not suddenly

---

7   Michelle U. Campos, *Ottoman Brothers: Muslims, Christians, and Jews in Early Twentieth Century Palestine* (Stanford: Stanford University Press, 2011).

8   See, for example, "The Turkish Press and Zionism," *Ha-Herut*, 21 January 1910, as cited in Campos, *Ottoman Brothers*, 197. According to the article, reprinted in the newspaper *Liberty*, while Ottoman Jews were trustworthy, "foreign Jews refused to integrate into Ottoman society, did not serve in the army, and caused problems with locals." See also Esther Benbassa, "Zionism and the Politics of Coalitions in the Ottoman Jewish Communities in the Early Twentieth Century," in *Ottoman and Turkish Jewry: Community and Leadership*, ed. Aron Rodrigue (Bloomington: Indiana University Press, 1992): 225–51. Benbassa, writing primarily from the vantage point of Haim Nahum, argues that the rise of Zionism in post-1908 Constantinople was largely a strategic and political struggle between Ashkenazim and Sephardim.

arrive in the Ottoman Empire after the Young Turk Revolution (although their numbers certainly increased); rather, they had been engaged in at least a thirty-year negotiation with their coreligionists. While the polemics became more visible and politicized after 1908, as the previous chapters have demonstrated, they were not novel. And yet despite these polemics, Ashkenazi and Sephardi Jews made several attempts to forge communal and ultimately political alliances, including the B'nai B'rith lodge, which suggests that the Ashkenazi and Sephardi political divide was far more porous than has been assumed.

When Albert Kant left his farm, Tikfour Tchiflik, for the safety of Constantinople during the First World War, he arrived in a city flooded with even more Russian migrants who had escaped the Bolshevik Revolution (see Chapter 4). In a way, this chapter foreshadows the next, and I will demonstrate how conversations with these migrants impressed upon him new ideas about a possible life in Palestine. If Kant can be taken as a representative of ordinary Russian Jewish migrants on a personal level, this chapter examines the overarching communal and political context and explores how, once again, discourses about the "other"—this time conceptualized as the politically subversive "Zionist"—circulated in the late Ottoman period. In this case, Zionism became a kind of nationalism that functioned as both "cause and effect," as Rogers Brubaker argues.[9] The press and titular nationals played a mutually constitutive role in developing *and* representing nationalist ideas. This chapter traces the story of how Ashkenazi Jews became more visible and began to disrupt Sephardic hegemony in the key communal institutions of early twentieth-century Constantinople and Istanbul.

---

9   Brubaker, *Nationalism Reframed*, 4–5. Brubaker describes central European states undergoing a process of "nationalizing nationalisms" in the twentieth century, a concept that I find useful for describing an opaque triangulation between the Jewish press, Jewish communal leaders (titular nationals), and the Jews of Constantinople. However, Brubaker uses the term to describe states and introduces another term, "transborder nationalisms," to counter "nationalizing nationalisms" as a process that "asserts states' rights, indeed their obligation, to monitor the condition, promote the welfare, support the activities and institutions, asses the rights, and protect the interests of 'their' ethnonational kin in other states. Such claims are typically made when the ethnonational kin in question are seen as threatened by the nationalizing policies and practices of the state in which they live."

Two Chief Rabbis and Two Communities?
Moshe Halévy and the *Baş Haham*

In 1890, the United States government appointed Dr. Cyrus Adler, an archeologist specializing in Semitic languages and civilizations, to travel to several cities in the Near and Middle East in order to "entice the Mohammadeans" to participate in the upcoming Chicago World's Fair, set for 1892, to commemorate the fourth centennial of Columbus's maiden voyage to America. After being granted a leave of absence from Johns Hopkins, Professor Adler embarked on his grand tour of the Levant, Egypt, Tunisia, and Constantinople. He spent most of his time with the Jewish communities of these cities, and he described his first impressions of the Chief Rabbi, the *Haham Başı*, who lived in a "very commodious house, almost a palace, up on the Asiatic side of the Bosporus."[10] "We proceeded there in splendor," Adler writes, "and found the rabbi in state, surrounded by a sort of cohort of rabbis, with guards and soldiers stationed at the entrance. The Rabbi held out his ring to be kissed." Dr. Adler and the Chief Rabbi, Moshe Halévy (1827–1910), spoke on many topics and the Rabbi "deplored the fact that the Ashkenazim ... were different communities, and wished there could be one Chief Rabbi in the various cities instead of two."

The existing Ashkenazi community, composed mostly of well-to-do German and Austrian Jews, had their own communal institutions but still answered to the *Haham Başı*, who had been Sephardic ever since the Ottoman Empire proclaimed the new position in 1835.[11] The Ottoman Porte established the office in Constantinople to act as an interlocutor between it and all the Empire's Jews (with the exception of the Karaites) just on the eve of the first *Tanzimat* Reforms in 1839. By handling all religious matters, including marriage, divorce, and civil disputes, the office of the *Haham Başı* served as more than just the Jewish community's representative to the Ottoman administration or an intermediary between the Ottoman State and its Jewish subjects. Moshe Halévy was the Chief Rabbi for nearly three decades, from 1873 to 1908. Born in Bursa, Halévy was the last Chief Rabbi to be appointed

---

10   Cyrus Adler, *I Have Considered the Days* (Philadelphia: Jewish Publication Society of America, 1941) 91-92.

11   Avigdor Levy, "The Appointment of a Chief Rabbi in 1835" *The Jews of the Ottoman Empire* (Princeton: Princeton University Press, 1994), 425–39.

to the position.[12] The influx of Russian migrants beginning in the late 1880s placed more pressure on a Chief Rabbi who was already politically unpopular. By 1890, the Ashkenazi and Sephardi Jews were engaged in an early power struggle over intra-communal issues such as the *gabela,* or meat tax, exacerbated by a butcher's strike in Edirne and in Smyrna. In 1890, Halévy enacted an agreement in Istanbul establishing the rights and duties of Ashkenazim under the Chief Rabbinate in order to ameliorate the situation, although it did not make distinctions between nationalities within the Jewish *millet.*

Like other religious *millets* in the Ottoman Empire, the administration did not distinguish among ethnic or national divisions. Despite the existence of at least five types of Jews in the Empire with different customs and traditions (Russian, German/Ashkenazi, Sephardic, Italian, and Karaite), a Sephardic Chief Rabbi had jurisdiction over all civil matters involving the Empire's Jews. The Muslim *millet* was also not differentiated according to ethnic or national difference. For example, Arab Muslims in Lebanon were governed by the same *sheikh ul islam,* a Grand Mufti, as were Muslim Serbs. *Sunni, shi'a,* and *shi'ite* Muslims all constituted the Muslim *millet* that was privileged by the right to hold *waqf* (religious trusts) and by the power of the *sheikh ul islam* to confirm the sultan. In other words, the Ottoman Empire governed less according to nation than according to confession.[13] In this, it had something else in common with the Russian Empire.[14]

The 1890 agreement concerning the Ashkenazim was published in *El Tiempo* on 30 June 1890: "The Convention: An Agreement between the Chief Rabbi and the Community of the Ashkenazim: Between the Chief Rabbi and Misters Leon Ruventhald, Friedman, and Meyefayr."[15] The article appeared on the third page of the issue, which might suggest that the paper's editor, David Fresco, did not find the agreement worthy of the front page, or that he wanted to bury it behind reports from beyond the borders of the Ottoman Empire. Halévy had excommunicated Fresco in 1885 for his harsh critiques of the Chief Rabbi, including his lack of action on behalf of Russian Jews (see

---

12   D Gershon Lewental, "Levi (Ha-Levi), Moshe," in *Encyclopedia of Jews in the Islamic World Online,* ed. Norman A. Stillman (Brill: 2010).

13   Jewish intra-communal tensions in comparison to other Ottoman *millets* also governed by single appointed (and eventually elected) religious leaders would be a fruitful project for future research.

14   Robert Crews, *For Prophet and Tsar,* 2006

15   "Una Convension," *El Tiempo,* 30 June 1890.

Chapter 3), so Fresco may have been reluctant to promote any achievements of the Chief Rabbi.

For the first time in Ottoman history, the agreement established an official Jewish religious leadership defined by nationality and recognized by the Sublime Porte. The agreement stated in its opening line that there was no distinction among the various nationalities of Ashkenazi Jews in Constantinople and that the agreement was simply between the Ashkenazim and the Chief Rabbi (perhaps implying that the Chief Rabbi was and should be Sephardic). There are ten points to the agreement, all having to do with communal affairs, jurisdictions, authority, and precedence in communal organization and structure. The first and most important point is that the "Chief Rabbi has authorized there to be put in place a Rabbi of the Ashkenazi Israelites" as well as a "committee of Ashkenazim."[16] This agreement thus established what became known as a *Baş Haham* (Principal Rabbi) of the Ashkenazim.[17] Other points of the agreement stated that the committee must be comprised of "all of the different synagogues" in Constantinople, and that the "Ottomans and Ashkenazi Israelites have the same attributes." If there were any disagreements, then the Chief Rabbi had the final say in matters of communal affairs, and the "Convention" also granted the Ashkenazim a sum of at least six million liras to be used specifically for the Ashkenazi community. The agreement also documents that three distinct Jewish communities—Karaites, Ashkenazim, and Jews—had been discussed at a Military Commission of the Chamber of the Ottoman Empire, a meeting in which Halévy had vocalized his support for Jewish military service. The fact that Halévy distinguishes between "Ashkenazim" and "Jews" is a statement of who he and his advisors believe are his constituents are and who he believes constitute the Jewish community of the Ottoman Empire writ large.[18]

For the first time, an official organ of the Ottoman Imperial administration recognized the existence of more than one community of Jews. This recognition that the Ashkenazi community needed its own rabbinic representation (from multiple synagogues) demonstrates an awareness on the part of the office of the Chief Rabbi that perhaps the customs (*minhagim*) not only differed according

---

16   Ibid.

17   *El Tiempo*, 30 June 1890.

18   Ibid.

to Ashkenazi and Sephardi Jews, but also that those differences needed to be represented in an official capacity. The Ashkenazi community responded not by simply building a new Ashkenazi synagogue, but also by deciding to find a new rabbi who could serve as the Chief Rabbi of the Ashkenazim: the *Baş Haham*.

For this reason, in 1894 the German Jewish community of Constantinople decided to bring in a foreign rabbi, one who could both lead the growing Ashkenazi community and serve as an intermediary between the Ashkenazi and the Sephardi community. First, they set out to build a synagogue to accommodate the growing Jewish community of largely Russian migrants. The Beit Knesset Tofre Begadim, or the Tailor's Synagogue, opened its doors for services on September 8, 1894. The permission for the synagogue was given by the Association for Ashkenazi Tailors headed by Mayer Schoenmann a German Jew (from the Austro-Hungarian Empire) and the tailor of sultan Abdülhamid. The new synagogue was built not only to accommodate the wave of Ashkenazi immigrants needing a new place to worship, but also because "the rich would rather go to the Yüksek Kaldırım Synagogue," according to one document.[19] Interestingly, when the Tofre Begadim Synagogue was founded in 1894, its Viennese Jewish patrons dedicated it to the Emperor of Austria-Hungary, Francis Joseph I.[20] The Tofre Begadim was a place of worship and a relief society, and it aided many incoming immigrants upon their arrival to Constantinople. By 1912, more formal institutions operated out of the synagogue, including *Lechem v'Bassarl'Anayim* (Meat and Bread for the Poor) provided hot soup, meat and bread for the needy, especially on Shabbat, and *Ruchama* (Comfort), which assisted pregnant women and young mothers.

By 1900, the Ashkenazi Jewish Community rebuilt its synagogue on Yüksek Kaldırım (the original synagogue on that spot had earlier burned down). For the opening of the new synagogue, just before the Rosh Hashanah and Yom Kippur holidays, the Ashkenazi community invited foreign dignitaries, including the Austro-Hungarian Ambassador Baron de Kalaci, the Sephardic Chief Rabbi Moshe Halévy, and the French Ambassador H. Fournier (who

---

19   Robert Schild et al., *A Hundred Year Old Synagogue* (Istanbul: Galata Ashkenazi Cultural Association, 2000).

20   Ibid.

unfortunately was unable to attend).[21] At the opening ceremony, the "building was covered in oriental carpets.... A magical choir performed the hymn *a tovu ohalekha ya'akov, mishk'notekha yisra'el* [How great are your tents, O Jacob, your dwelling places, O Israel]"—a hymn traditionally sung expressing reverence for houses of worship—and "the *sefer torah* [Torah Scrolls] were put in their places with prayers by the procession headed by the Chief Rabbi Mose Halévy [*sic*].... Cantor Vladovski lighted the "continuality oil lamp," expressing reverence for the Chief Rabbi and, therefore, the Ottoman Empire. After reading hymns, "Dr. Adolph Rosenthal gave the opening speech in Turkish and German," reaffirming the importance of both empires.[22] Thus the Ashkenazim had at least three synagogues by 1890: the Ashkenazi Synagogue on Yüksek Kaldırım, the new "Tailor's Synagogue," and, of course, Or Chadash, the "pimp's synagogue" (see Chapter 3). In 1900, the search for a new rabbi was complete, and the Ashkenazi leadership hired the aforementioned Rabbi David Markus to lead the congregation.

Rabbi Markus, the *Baş Haham*, and the B'nai Brith Lodge

Born the son of a poor tailor in Novgorod in 1870, David Markus fell in love with and married his cousin Sarah Hina Berkman when they were nineteen and fifteen years old, respectively. He graduated from a yeshiva in Lomza, Poland, and he and Sarah immigrated to the Netherlands. Markus then decided to pursue the study of the Talmud in Germany while his wife stayed behind in Amsterdam and supported her husband by working in a cigarette factory. He continued his studies and earned his doctorate in philosophy in 1901 under the supervision of Benno Erdmann, a neo-Kantian philosopher and psychologist. Fluent in German, Yiddish, Russian, Polish, French, Turkish, Latin, Ancient Greek, and Spanish, Markus was well positioned to serve a diverse Ashkenazi community. In 1904, Markus was invited by the German Ashkenazi community to become the Principal Rabbi of Istanbul's Ashkenazim and serve as the head of the Jewish School.[23]

Markus arrived in Istanbul to a "fractured community" where "religion was not popular among the youth," and "Christian missionaries were

---

21   Erdal Frayman et al, *A Hundred Year Old Synagogue in Yüksek Kaldırım* .

22   Ibid, 65.

23   Sarah Zaides interview with Leah Weinstein Yahya and Robert Schild, May 2015.

trying to convert the Jews to Christianity."[24] To instill religious values, he instituted mandatory Shabbat services in the school, and delivered "effective and instructive speeches [d'rash], to annihilate the destructive ideas of the missionaries and to attract Jews to their own faith." Markus and other Ashkenazi leaders were particularly worried that many Russian Jews would abandon religious practices and many of his efforts were directed toward religious revival.

Yet his contemporaries and descendants describe him as being "far from a religious fanatic." They describe him instead as "tolerant" and "rational," someone who was committed to the Jewish community with the "highest morals and commendable character ..., not lured by opulence or wealth."[25] Markus seemed like the perfect choice for the German Jewish community of Constantinople: a Rabbi from Eastern Europe, "culturally Russian, but German educated."[26]

Benjamin Sperer also recalled this syncretism of Russian and German traditions among the Ashkenazim of the city. Himself the grandson of Russian migrants who arrived to Yüksek Kaldırım, the "main artery of Ashkenazi Jews," Sperer recalls that in addition to religious services being conducted in Hebrew and in German, the haggadah at the Passover seder table "was recited as "der auszug aus Aegypten.""[27] Sperer's father Samuel Sperer, or "Shmulik," worked for an Austrian department store in Constantinople, traveling often to Vienna. From Benjamin Sperer's descriptions of Vienna as "one of Europe's centers of cultural activities and of everything that made life pleasant and elegant," citing "Wiener Schnitzel to Sachertorte" to "operas and operettas to symphony concerts," it is clear that the Sperers perceived themselves as culturally oriented towards Vienna.[28]

Markus was ideologically at odds with the mission civilisatrice of the Alliance Israélite Universelle and especially the politics of Moshe Halévy.

---

24 Erdal Frayman et al, A Hundred Year Old Synagogue in Yüksek Kaldırım , 69

25 Ibid. – note footnote is not correct. Find source.

26 In addition to the Tofre Begadim Synagogue and Rabbi Markus's efforts, the Ashkenazim set up the following institutions: Lehem v Basar L'anayim (Meat and Bread for the Poor, established 1912), provided hot soup, meat, and bread for the needy, especially on Shabbat; Ruchama (also 1912), a foundation to help pregnant women and infants.

27 Benjamin Sperer, Under Turkish Skies (Istanbul: Libra Books, 2017), 16

28 Sperer, Under Turkish Skies, 17

Halévy was through and through a product of the Alliance and was on close terms with the Ottoman administration and with sultan Abdülhamid II in particular. Halévy supported the study of the Turkish language (which the Ottomans also favored) and reacted positively when Abdülhamid extended military service to Jews. Crucially, Halévy was also not a Zionist. During the festivities of the Fourth Centennial Celebration, it was Halévy who presented the sultan with a Turkish translation of a Hebrew prayer read in synagogues throughout the Empire. When Theodor Herzl visited Constantinople in 1902, he asked Halévy to arrange a meeting so that he could press the sultan to allow greater Jewish emigration to Palestine. This meeting distressed Halévy— apparently so much so that he fell ill immediately afterward—and he made several attempts to secure another meeting with the sultan to reaffirm his and the Ottoman Jews' loyalty to the Ottoman Empire.[29]

While Markus originally was brought to Constantinople to serve as the *Baş Haham* and the head of the Goldschmidt School, he quickly retired from Goldschmidt to pursue a loftier goal: making Jewish education available to the entire Jewish population, not just the "German Jews" from Austria-Hungary.[30] He established a small Talmud Torah and, after enlisting the help of the Hilfsverein der Deutschen Juden, a German educational and aid organization much like the Alliance, established three more schools and one high school. Nahum refused to grant funds for Markus's high school, so Markus raised the funds through the auspices of B'nai B'rith and the Bergel Fund, named after Mr. S. Bergel of Berlin. The Jewish Colonization Association's *Caisse de Petits Prêts* later helped fund the organization, under Joseph Niego's stewardship.[31] The school, first called Midrash Yavne, was later renamed the B'nai B'rith High School and still stands in Istanbul today.[32]

It is unclear at what point Rabbi Markus became a Zionist. While he supported Zionist institutions, his lectures and sermons did not invoke a specific political ideology by name, as doing so would have undermined his objective to ameliorate intra-communal tensions. Rabbi Markus was interested

---

29   Julia Phillips Cohen, "Fresco, David," in: *Encyclopedia of Jews in the Islamic World*, Executive Editor Norman A. Stillman. Consulted online 03 May 2017. First published online: 2010.

30   Frayman et al., *Hundred Year Old Synagogue*, 71.

31   "B'nai Brith's Silver Jubilee: The Lodge's Fine Work," March 27, 1936 *The Jewish Chronicle*

32   "Ulus Özel Musevi Okulları Tarihçesi," accessed 7 October 2010, http://www.uoml.k12.tr/content/view/247/220/.

in religious reinvigoration, but by 1908, he began to be more interested in fostering unity between Sephardi and Ashkenazi Jews and promoting the Zionist movement through the institutions he founded and supported. A telling example of Markus's institution-building was his foundation of a B'nai B'rith lodge in 1911 under the auspices of then-late *frère* (brother) Siegmund Bergel and R. Lévy, with Joseph Niego as President.[33] The Grand Lodge XI was the overarching organization of B'nai B'rith in the Ottoman Empire, whose nineteen member lodges in 1913 were scattered all over the Ottoman world, including the Balkans, from Adrianople to Jerusalem and from Sophia to Salonica. Constantinople's Lodge No. 678 was the largest of all.[34] The lodge's primary goal of bringing Ashkenazim and Sephardim closer continued until 1938, when the Turkish Republic passed a law prohibiting the activities of foreign associations. According to Esther Benbassa, while the B'nai B'rith movement is the oldest "secular Jewish organization" in the United States, in the Ottoman Empire, it became primarily an "opinion group"—which must be taken as something of an overstatement in light of the amount of aid the organization distributed, particularly in its early years, when its members came to the aid of earthquake victims in Gallipoli and Çorlu and in aiding Jewish and Muslim migrants of the Balkan Wars of 1912–1913.[35]

In 1911, Joseph Niego delivered a speech explaining the politics and aims of the lodge, which was reprinted in the *Bulletin* two years later, in 1913. Niego, a Sephardic Jew from Edirne, had studied at Mikveh Israel in Palestine and was the Chief Agronome for the Jewish Colonization Association in Constantinople. He began his speech with an often-cited quote from Leviticus: *ahavta lereacha kamocha* ("love thy neighbor as thyself"), which he called the "true motto of our sublime religion."[36] He stated that the union between Sephardim and Ashkenazim is the union between the "immigrants from Spain, the ancestors of the likes of Ibn Gabirol ... and Maimonides ..., and the representatives of

---

33   *Bulletin de la Grande Loge de District XI et de la Loge de Constantinople, No. 678* (1913), 105.

34   Ibid., 102–103.

35   See Esther Benbassa, "Associational Strategies in Ottoman Jewish Society in the Nineteenth and Twentieth Centuries," in *The Jews of the Ottoman Empire*, ed. Avigdor Levy (Princeton: Darwin, 1994), For the B'nai B'rith's disaster relief and philanthropic activities, see "Rapport du Israel Auerback: Delegue de la Grande Loge No. XI aux lieux du désastsre cause por tremblement de terre du 9 Aout 1912" and "Rapport de la Commission de secours aux éprouvés israélites de la guerre balkanique lu dans la séance extraordinaire du 30 Janvier 1913" in *Le Bulletin de la Grande Loge de district Xi et de la Loge de Constantinople, No. 678*.

36   *Bulletin de la Grande Loge de District XI et de la Loge de Constantinople, No. 678* (1913), 109.

Western modernity."[37] "The time has come," Niego continued, to "combine the scruples and self-esteem and the fiery Castilian pride [of the Sephardim] with the spirit of enterprise, endurance to prosecution, as Ashkenazim bring with them the cultivated circles of the places in Europe in which they have lived."[38] Niego lamented that in Cairo and in the United States, Sephardi and Ashkenazi Jews had established separate B'nai B'rith lodges, but "fortunately we do not fall into the same error."[39] On the issue of Zionism, Niego insisted that the B'nai B'rith lodge would not "take sides for Zionism but also will not condemn [it].... We will give access in our midst to the many supporters of this movement and with it their worth and respectable representatives."[40] Joseph Niego appears to have been the mouthpiece for Markus and the Zionist cause—however subtle—at the Lodge.

Markus's politics emerge more clearly in his correspondence with the Central Zionist Bureau in Berlin beginning in 1912, to be discussed below, which took place in the wake of the Young Turk Revolution and the changed political climate of 1908–1911 that allowed for open public debate about Zionism, a contest that has often been described as a debate between Ashkenazim and Sephardim.

Young Turks, "Young Jews," and the Inheritors of the 1908 Revolution

In 1908, the Young Turks seized power in Constantinople through a peaceful coup d'état, ending seventy-six years of Hamidian Rule and ushering in the Second Constitutional Period. The Young Turks restored the 1876 constitution and instituted an electoral system subject to the Ottoman Parliament.[41] The critical years between 1908 and 1911 were also pivotal years in the history of Ottomanism as it increasingly gave way to a preference for a Turkish nationalist regime with a strong central government.[42] The controversy over Zionism and the office of the Chief Rabbi was a debate not just over Jewish national statehood, but also between conflicting visions of the role that Ottoman Jewry would play in the post-1908 empire.

37   *Bulletin de la Grande Loge de District XI et de la Loge de Constantinople*, 112–13.

38   *Bulletin de la Grande Loge de District XI et de la Loge de Constantinople*,, 112.

39   Ibid.

40   *Bulletin de la Grande Loge de District XI et de la Loge de Constantinople*, 113.

41   Hasan Kayalı, "Elections and the Electoral Process in the Ottoman Empire, 1876-1919", *International Journal of Middle East Studies* 27.3 (1995): 265–86.

42   Ibid.

Six months after the Young Turk Revolution, Ottoman Jews elected a young Sephardic Rabbi from Smyrna, Haim Nahum, to the position of *Haham Başı*. While the Alliance was wary of becoming entangled in the communal politics of the Chief Rabbi, the Alliance had groomed Nahum for the position.[43] Nahum had been born into an impoverished family in Manisa, Turkey, before moving with his grandfather to Tiberias, where he learned the Qur'an in Arabic and the Talmud in Hebrew. After returning to Anatolia, he enrolled in an Ottoman *lycée*, won a scholarship through the Alliance, and traveled to Paris to study at the Rabbinical Seminary there. Nahum returned to Turkey in 1897 and taught at the Alliance Rabbinical Seminary in Istanbul.[44]

Nahum corresponded with Jacques Bigart (1855–1934), the Secretary of the Alliance Israélite Universelle in Paris, and it became evident, as Rodrigue notes, that the Alliance had "earmarked [Nahum] as future Chief Rabbi of the Ottoman Empire."[45] Nahum also maintained a post as a secretary of the administrative council of the Istanbul community. After the Hamidian regime, to which Halévy maintained close ties, was overthrown in 1908, a strategy to elect Nahum as the next *Haham Başı* emerged.

As the Chief Rabbi, Moshe Halévy had had jurisdiction over all civil matters involving the Empire's Jews for over thirty-five years, but he had served without a formal appointment. He was controlled by several Jewish notables that were nicknamed *banda preta* (the black camarilla) by critics, including Abraham Galanté.[46] The election of Halévy's successor was contentious, not least because Nahum ran against his father-in-law, Abraham Danon. Although German Orthodox communities accused Nahum of being too secular, Nahum nevertheless prevailed and was elected Chief Rabbi on January 24, 1909.[47] Bigart wrote a telling letter of congratulations: "Your Victory is so fine and so complete…. Your success is that of the liberal circles, in the French meaning of the term."[48] At least in the words of Bigart, the Young Turk Revolution

43   Esther Benbassa, *A Sephardic Chief Rabbi in Politics, 1892–1923*, trans Miriam Kochan (Tuscaloosa: University of Alabama Press, 1995).

44   Ibid., 123. See also Aron Rodrigue, *French Jews, Turkish Jews: The Alliance Israélite Universelle and the Politics of Jewish Schooling in Turkey, 1860–1925* (Bloomington: Indiana University Press, 1990).

45   Ibid., 123.

46   Ibid., 122–23. See also Benbassa, *Sephardic Chief Rabbi in Politics*, 56.

47   Ibid., 123. See also Benbassa, *Sephardic Chief Rabbi in Politics*, 101–102.

48   Ibid.

fulfilled the spirit of the Alliance, from whose schools "numerous generations have drawn the sentiments of gratitude, devotion, and affection for Turkey," so that one could say that "the Turkish revolution is like a triumph of our ideas, so moderate but so liberal."[49]

The Committee of Union and Progress and the New Jewish Press

After the Committee of Union and Progress (CUP) abandoned censorship in favor of modernization, Westernization, and secularism, Victor Jacobsohn opened an office of the World Zionist Organization, at first using the Anglo-Levantine Banking Company in Constantinople as a front before the Zionists began operating openly in 1914 as the Histadrut Tziyonit Otomanit. During these years, the Jewish press teemed with Zionist thought. The Jewish newspapers *Le Jeune Turc, L'Aurore,* and *Hamevasser* joined *El Tiempo* as censorship laws eased during the Second Constitutional Era. Previous discussions of Jewish emancipation and life in the Ottoman Empire between 1890–1908 had focused on the roles of Russian Jewish migrants and established communal boundaries in national terms such as "German," "Sephardic," and "Russian" Jews. After the Young Turk Revolution, these typologies took on a new political meaning: a polemics of Zionism and, for the purposes of this study, anti-Zionism that was predicated on these previously established communal boundaries (or in some cases, lack thereof). By 1908, questions surrounding Zionism emphasized the contrast between "foreign nationalities" versus "Ottoman Jews." The debate over the political fate of the Jews of the Ottoman Empire was in fact a debate as to which political idea would become the inheritor of the Young Turk Revolution.

The newspaper *Le Jeune Turc* was published in Istanbul from 1908 until 1919 with the journalists Vladimir Jabotinsky, Sami Hochberg, and Celâl Nuri as editors. The predecessor of *Le Jeune Turc, Le Courrier d'Orient,* was actually owned by a well-known anti-Semite, Ebüzziya Tevfik. Hochberg, Jacobsohn, and David Wolffsohn purchased the paper in 1909 and transformed it into a Zionist paper, promoting Ottomanism, the politics of the Committee of Union and Progress, and Turkish language and culture. Their vision of Zionism promoted in *Le Jeune Turc* was one of Jewish settlement in Palestine that was

---

49   Ibid., 125.

not separatist but rather intended to benefit the Ottoman Empire that would maintain the Empire's territorial integrity, a popular belief prior to 1911.[50]

The Zionist, Hebrew-language newspaper *Hamevasser* had a brief but important appearance in Constantinople from 1910–1911. Printed in the Ottoman capital and distributed throughout Bulgaria, Greece, Tunisia, and Morocco, the newspaper saw itself as the organ of the Hebrew national revival movement in the Ottoman Empire and as the link between the Jews of the Ottoman Empire and the Jews of Western Europe. Nevertheless, *Hamevasser* almost entirely avoided the debates between Zionists and non-Zionists that preoccupied *L'Aurore* and *El Tiempo*. The reason for the neutrality of *Hamevasser* is two-fold. Remaining impartial was likely a strategic decision on the editor's part in order to avoid conflict and to maintain the newspaper's focus on the goal of recruiting Ottoman Jewry to cause of Jewish nationalism. It is also probable that mutual intelligibility prevailed between the readers of *El Tiempo* and *L'Aurore*: those who in 1910 spoke and read Ladino had likely been educated by the Alliance and therefore spoke and read in French.

Hamevasser, whose editors Vladimir Jabotinsky, Nahum Sokolow, and Victor Jacobsohn at other times held editorial positions with *Le. Jeune Turc* and *L'Aurore*, maintained similarly nationalist yet pro-Ottoman positions, arguing that "the Ottomans would welcome the Zionist movement's policy of establishing Jewish settlements in Palestine because of their contribution to advancing the economy of the empire."[51] In other words, they made what was a familiar argument that one could *of course* be both. To further illustrate this point, *Hamevasser* also ran an article on the close, "brotherly" connection between Judaism and Islam as attested by the series of forty questions and responses supposedly posed to the Prophet Muhammad by Jews from Yemen and Mecca.[52] Like *El Tiempo, L'Aurore,* and *Le Jeune Turc, Hamevasser* also was in favor of Ottoman military service for Ottoman Jews, the adoption of Hebrew as a first language, and the use of Turkish as a second language in Turkish-speaking areas or Arabic as a second language in the Levant

50   *Hamevasser* also argued that Jewish settlement and development of Palestine would be economically beneficial for the Ottoman Empire and did not advocate political separatism. See *Hamevasser,* 1.3, 43–45 and 7, 100–102.

51   Aryeh Shmuelevitz, "Zionism, Jews and Muslims in the Ottoman Empire as Reflected in the Weekly *Hamevasser*," in *Jews, Muslims and Mass Media: Mediating the "Other"*, ed. Tudor Parfitt and Yulia Egorova (New York: Routledge, 2004).

52   *Hamevasser* 2.35–36.

and other Arabic-speaking regions. The editors of *Hamevasser* argued that Turkish was the "language of the homeland," while Hebrew was the "Jewish national language, the language of tradition," while also recommended French as the "international means of communication" and Arabic as the "vehicle for business [in Palestine and the Levant]."[53]

L'Aurore began publication in Constantinople on the day following the proclamation of the Ottoman Constitution in 1908 under the leadership of Lucien Sciuto (1868–1947). The first issue opened with a quote by Theodor Herzl, the father of Zionism, boldly on its front page. Sciuto published *L'Aurore* in Istanbul from 1908 to 1920 and then in Cairo from 1924 to 1931.[54] Sciuto promoted both Ottomanism and Zionism, seeing them as complimentary movements, and published articles by prominent Zionist such as Nahum Sokolow (1859–1936), Victor Jacobsohn, Vladimir Jabotinsky (1880–1940), Abraham Elmaleh (1876–1967), and David Isaac Florentin (1874–1941). In 1909, the World Zionist Organization began subsidizing *L'Aurore*, and by 1910, the newspaper had a circulation of about fifteen hundred. Sciuto faced financial challenges and ended up selling the newspaper to none other than the Chief Rabbi Haim Nahum, despite the World Zionist Organization's attempts to stop it. After the sale, the WZO focused its attention on the creation of *La Nation* in October 1919.

Born to a religious family in Salonica, Sciuto was a student of the Alliance Israélite Universelle until the age of fourteen. He worked at the Zionist *Journal de Salonique*, eventually serving as its assistant editor before moving to Istanbul in 1899. Sciuto wrote thousands of polemics and articles during his career, especially on the subject of Zionism, freedom of speech, and freedom of the press. He wrote for a Turkish-language journal, *Le Tanin*, and, after the sale of *L'Aurore* and the occupation of Istanbul, moved to Palestine, where he worked briefly as an insurance agent for the German La Victoria Insurance Company. In 1924, Sciuto moved to Cairo and revived *L'Aurore*, whose pages

---

53   Shmuelevitz, "Zionism, Jews and Muslims in the Ottoman Empire as Reflected in the Hamevasser" in Tudor Parfitt et. al *Jews, Muslims, and the Mass Media: Mediating the Other* (New York: Routledge, 2005). A promising topic for future research would be to identify the discursive differences among the three Zionist newspapers of Istanbul from 1908–1917. The line between "homeland" (the Ottoman Empire) and a Jewish "nation" is thin and ought to be explored.

54   D Gershon Lewental, "L'Aurore (Istanbul)," in *Encyclopedia of Jews in the Islamic World Online*, ed. Norman A. Stillman (Brill: 2010).

were filled with critiques of Egyptian Jewish elites who had assimilated into the upper echelons of Egyptian society.[55]

Sciuto's passion for both the Young Turk Revolution and Zionism is evident in an issue celebrating the revolution's first anniversary, also the first anniversary of the paper's publication. On July 23, the front page of *L'Aurore* proudly proclaimed: "Long Live Constitutional Turkey." It devoted the first half of its page to the anniversary of the Revolution:

> On this day there is an aureole of golden sun in Turkey: we can feel the incomparably beautiful joy, the heartbeat of a multiple of a great people.... This day is indescribable, how we felt a year ago the elation of how, under one great fraternal flag, thirty years of hatred was abolished.

The article continues:

> The important event was commemorated by programs in our Jewish clubs, proof of our ardent, elated patriotism, and proves who we are and what we want: a great Turkey.... With our hearts reenergized by the patriotic ceremony, with voices and tears made more penetrating and sincere, we can now cry out in joy to drown out our enemies inside and outside, and our sublime cry of all the Ottoman people will be united into one Bronze seal upon our Constitutional Turkey.[56]

The language of the article is striking because it invokes pan-ethnic nationalism ("the heartbeat of a multiple of a great people ... under one great fraternal flag") as a proven remedy for "thirty years of hatred." It is unclear if Sciuto was referring to the thirty years of hatred among Sephardi and Ashkenazi Jews or among all the ethnic minorities of the Ottoman Empire; the answer is likely both. The article specifically emphasizes that Jewish clubs had commemorated the anniversary, thus proving their "patriotism." Similar to honoring the sultan in the Fourth Centennial Celebrations, Jewish clubs' commemorations of the Young Turk Revolution were a symbol of patriotism

---

55   D Gershon Lewental, "Sciuto, Lucien," in *Encyclopedia of Jews in the Islamic World Online*, ed. Norman A. Stillman (Brill: 2010). See also Esther Benbassa, *Ha-Yahadut ha-ʿOthmanit beyn Hitmaʿarevut le-Ṣiyyonut, 1908–1920*, trans. Meʾir Yisraʾel (Jerusalem: Merkaz Zalman Shazar, 1996); Abraham Elmaleh, "ḤaluṢe ha-ʿIttonut ha-Yehudit ba-Mizraḥ uve-Ṣefon Afriqa," *Mizraḥu-Maʿarav* 4 (1930): 207–11, 286–94; "Lucien Sciuto journaliste, écrivain et poète," *La Boz de Türkiye*, April 1, 1947, 210–11, May 1, 1947, 246–47, May 15, 1947, 262–63, June 1, 1947, 277–78; Abraham Galanté "Comment fut fondé L'Aurore," *La Boz de Türkiye*, June 15, 1947, 297–98; *Histoire des Juifs de Turquie* 2 (Istanbul: The Isis Press, 1985), 111–12; Juda Romano, "Lucien Sciuto Murio," *La Boz de Türkiye* , March 1, 1947, 199.

56   *L'Aurore*, 23 July 1909.

and citizenship. Immediately below Sciuto's front page-editorial, the following article, "Theodor Herzl, The Young Jew," identified its author (Sciuto again) in bold type. Sciuto's message was clear: not only were Zionism and the Young Turk Revolution compatible, but Zionist Jews were *the most patriotic* of all Ottoman Jews.

The Ladino press disagreed with Sciuto. To prove the point, editors of the Ladino periodicals pointed to the divisions between Ashkenazim and Sephardim, between the *Haham Başı* and the *Baş Haham*, and between the *Haham Başı* and the *meclis-i usmani* to sound the alarm that Ottoman Jewry faced a schism over the politics *du jour*: Zionism.

Ottoman Brothers? *El Tiempo* Predicts a Schism

An important discursive shift occurred within the pages of *El Tiempo* in the years 1890–1910. When the first wave of Russian immigrants arrived in Constantinople, *El Tiempo* depicted Russian Jews as brothers and relatives who were in great need of the Sephardic community's support. But by the last months of 1910, it became clear that the Russians and other "non-Ottoman" Ashkenazim threatened not only the status quo of the Ottoman Jewish community but also the community's supposedly privileged position in the Ottoman Empire. Nahum shared in Fresco's anxieties, stating in his letters that the Zionists were easily finding "new recruits among the coreligionists from Russia."[57]

One issue that sparked controversy was an Ashkenazi dispute about the sharing of revenue from the *gabela*, a tax on kosher meat that they received directly from the Chief Rabbinate. The controversy over distribution of the proceeds was discussed in both *El Tiempo* and in the Zionist periodicals.[58] Other disputed issues included the formation of a *histadrut ha-rabanim* or collective council of rabbis, and the establishment of a *beit hamidrash* or house of study. Both were promoted in the Zionist press as signs of the awakening orthodox religious movement.[59]

It was the disagreement over the *gabela*, however, that finally spurred David Fresco to publish an article on December 26, 1910, entitled "Ashkenazim

---

57   Benbassa, *Sephardic Chief Rabbi in Politics,* 119.

58   Articles on this topic appeared in *El Tiempo* on 6 January 1911, 1 June 1911, 5 June 1911, and 9 August 1911.

59   See Esther Benbassa, "Zionism and the Politics of Coalition," pg. 234

and Sephardim: The Sephardic and Ashkenazic Communities and the Chief Rabbi, Preparations for an Assault Against Ottoman Judaism." In this article, Fresco predicted a "schism, a separation between the Ashkenazi and Sephardi Jews" that not only "affects our community but the community of the entire Ottoman Empire."[60] Fresco noted that, to an unprecedented degree, the entire Empire was at stake.

In this article, Fresco looks back to a time when cultural differences did not contribute to cultural division. According to Fresco, while the "communities of Israel, those of Spain and Portugal and those of various other parts of the world, have had different customs and beliefs, not in any epoch did anyone pay any attention to these differences." Fresco states that the "Ashkenazim and Sephardim were always congenial, like members of a single family," and describes the Ashkenazim in Constantinople as a "colony of Jewish brothers, the most observant of whom are made up of mostly Romanian and Russians who have conserved their nationality." Fresco's reference to "nationality" illustrates the changing status of that category during these years. In the context of the late-nineteenth century Ottoman Empire subject to the Capitulations—the years of early Russian migration—mention of foreign nationality might have alluded to pimps or others seeking to avoid the law of the Sublime Porte. For Fresco in the years after the Young Turk Revolution, however, the Russian Jews were quite literally "colonies" within the Ottoman Empire (although these colonies might threaten to undermine their coreligionists). Fresco's description of the Russians as brothers and "members of a single family" is consistent with his practice in earlier decades (see Chapter 3). He draws on classic tropes of nationalism, romanticizing years of peaceful coexistence between Sephardi and Ashkenazi Jews.

Yet Fresco expresses fear of an imminent division of the Ottoman Jews based on nationality and religious observance. Fresco's observation that the most religiously observant Jews were Romanian and Russian Jews who had conserved their nationality might imply that Ottoman subjecthood (and presumably loyalty towards the Empire) should be accompanied by a secularism consistent with not only the Sephardi community but also the Young Turk Revolution writ large.

---

60   *El Tiempo*, 26 December 1910.

Later in the essay, Fresco mentions the "Jews who call themselves Ashkenazi but have adopted Ottoman nationality, and recognize that there are no religious or political differences that separate them from their Ottoman brothers that call themselves Sephardic." Thus Fresco concedes that there are some Ashkenazim who have "Ottoman nationality," just like "some of their respective languages are different than the indigenous [Ottoman] Jews.... They have lived in distinct communities." He continues that the Ashkenazim have become an "amalgamation of the members of the family of Israel." Notably, there is "only one political difference that impedes Sephardic and Ashkenazic Jews" in being part of the same religious group: "the Jews of foreign nationality simply cannot submit to the authority of the Chief Rabbi of Turkey for these civic and political reasons." Indeed, the issue at stake for Fresco is that some had chosen to maintain and *elevate* their national and religious differences, particularly in their unwillingness to submit to the Chief Rabbi. The election of the Chief Rabbi in 1908 had invoked the spirit and the reforms of the Young Turks, so to refuse to grant power to the elected religious leader of the *millet* was presumably an affront to the leaders of the revolution.

A year prior to the publication of the essay, Fresco had published *Le Sionisme,* a critique of Zionism. The pamphlet is important for understanding the evolution of Fresco's treatment of Ashkenazi and Sephardi Jews, and in particular his position on the importance of "Ottoman Jews" (in implied contrast to non-Ottoman Jews). Fresco begins by offering his version of the history of Zionism:

> Nearly fifteen years ago, following frequent persecutions against our coreligionists in Russia and Romania, a few *European* Jews conceived of the project of building a Jewish state in Palestine and transporting our unfortunate brothers persecuted in other countries.[61]

Fresco emphasizes that it was just a few *European* Jews who had conceived of Zionism in the context of the persecution of their "brothers" who were persecuted in *pogroms* in Eastern Europe. Fresco continues that the Zionist movement, which has "to date not achieved any results and will lead to no good," ultimately accomplishes nothing except that it "inspires in Jews a great distrust for progress, causes an estrangement from other peoples, and awakens religious and racial fanaticism." Fresco, truly a product of the Alliance, invokes

---

61   Fresco, *Le Sionisme*, 69–72 (emphasis added).

enlightenment and progress, which are at odds with extreme ideology and religiosity. He then appeals directly to the reader:

> Ottoman Jew, listen to me closely: that which Zionism demands of you is in no way compatible with what your religion or your conscience asks of you. I speak to you in the language of reason—the language of logic. Do not let yourself be led astray by a few wretches who have let themselves be taken in or by imposters who seek to deceive you.

Again, Fresco speaks of "reason" and "logic" being fundamentally at odds with Zionism. Fresco also sees Zionism as corrupted by "imposters," indecent individuals who exploit other Jews. Fresco even alleges that there are "dishonest individuals" who "exploit the idea [of Zionism] for personal profit ... [and work] to exalt spirits, excite imaginations, and awaken religious passions."

In Fresco's view, Ottoman Jewry was obligated to defend itself against Zionism. Otherwise, instead of a youth who would "work in earnest to uplift Ottoman Jewry ... [in order to] make rapid progress," the Zionists would turn the youth of Turkey toward their cause. Fresco again appeals to his reader:

> Ottoman Jew, can you gauge the immensity of disaster that will befall the Jews in this country if our compatriots, and particularly our Muslim compatriots, who constitute the majority, become convinced that the Ottoman Jew is not attached to his country, that he runs toward another ideal, that he dreams of the creation of a Jewish state to the detriment of Ottoman national unity?

Perhaps for the first time, Fresco points out how the Zionist promise could offend Ottoman Jews' specifically *Muslim* compatriots. Much as Fresco's writings in the 1890s were concerned largely with maintaining the "model *millet*" status of the Jews of the Ottoman Empire, he now observes that the Jews, in their newly (and truly) emancipated state, were still in a precarious position. Fresco continues that he is

> Convinced that the Ottoman Jew maintains an unwavering loyalty to his fatherland.... I am convinced that nothing in the world would undermine this loyalty—that the Ottoman Jew prefers Turkey to the most civilized countries. Ottoman Jew, I know that you do not need my lessons of moral honesty and patriotism, but even so I believe in my duty to warn you so that you do not let yourself be deceived by the appearance of an idea presented to you in the best light...an idea which will be ... the cause of your undoing should you adhere to it.

Fresco's invocation of "moral honesty and patriotism" draws upon a language of nationalism and "unwavering loyalty" to the "fatherland." While for Sciuto and *L'Aurore*, Zionist statehood might be the fulfillment of patriotism to the Ottoman Empire, for Fresco it clearly undermines it. In Fresco's polemics, we see a visible anxiety, an unspoken *what if*, should Fresco's readers chose Zionism.

The Agreement of 1912 and the Politics of Two Chief Rabbis

In 1912, an agreement was signed between the Ashkenazi community and the *meclis-i cismani* without the knowledge of the *Haham Başı*, granting autonomy and the establishment of a Principal Rabbi for the Ashkenazi Community.[62] The document did not recognize the various nationalities within the Ashkenazi community, and in many ways was a reiteration of the 1890 agreement. In response, Nahum chose to resign from his post. Esther Benbassa has argued that Nahum's resignation was "out of proportion" and that the resignation occurred more out of a "matter of principle than the signing of the agreement itself or the content of the agreement."[63] The Minister of Justice and Religion, followed by the Council of Ministers, refused to accept Nahum's resignation and refused to approve the conduct of the *meclis-i cismani*. In 1912, a "Ladino Committee" responded to the document, issuing a public notice in Ladino, which argued that the 1912 agreement was invalid and that the Ashkenazi organizations should resume their work.[64] Debate ensued in March of 1912, and Nahum asked the Ottoman government to step in to invalidate the vote. The agreement was annulled and the Ottomans affirmed the position of the Chief Rabbi. The *meclis-i cismani* resigned, Rabbi Markus included.

The document recognized the multiple communities and cites at least three, including "Ashkenazi and Italian"; the Italian community, which

---

62   Apparently, there was a deep misconception among the Ashkenazi community that Haim Nahum was paid by the Alliance, when in fact he was paid by the Jewish community. Markus notes that Nahum did "obtain his position because of this organization and its followers." See Letter from Markus et al. to Central Zionist Bureau, February 20, 1912 (CZA Z3/44).

63   Bigart responded to this resignation: "There must be motives, motives which the public is not in a position to appreciate behind this serious decision of Mr. Nahum, motives which must be inspired solely by the resolutions of the *meclis-i cismâni*." AAIU, School Register 23, Jacques Bigart to A. Benveniste, 7 February 1912. Opt cite., in Benbassa, *A Sephardic Chief Rabbi in Politics*, 237

64   *El Tiempo*, 15 March 1912.

had been present in Istanbul since the fifteenth century and had created their own synagogue in 1862 in the Şişli quarter, is mentioned as a distinct entity. The document described the historical roles of the *Haham Başı* and explained how and why the organization received its funding from both Ottoman administrators and through various taxes on such things as kosher meat, marriage, and even divorce. These funds were distributed to the three communities. The document then outlined a new committee that would be formed (with representatives from the Jewish Colonization Association farms as well), including Hasköy, Haydarpaşa, and Ortaköy. Delegates would have to "maintain the financial ... moral and material states ... of our population. The council will be able to fulfill its mission to the advantage of the public, will be able to reorganize communal life, social organizations, intellectual life, while the Chief Rabbi will be able to manage and steer the community towards progres.[65]

Rabbi David Markus was in close contact with the Zionist Central Bureau in Berlin over the situation with Nahum. Several letters exchanged between Rabbi Markus, Israel Auerbach, and Victor Jacobsohn discuss Markus's involvement and a plan to oust Rabbi Haim Nahum, despite the fact that the Council of Ministers "denied the demission of Nahum." Markus wrote that the goal was to "win the majority of the *meclis*."[66] Part of the issue with the original agreement was that the rabbis and other religious leaders on the *meclis* council had been progressives, and likely Zionist sympathizers, since the Young Turk Revolution.[67] On February 28, 1912, Markus, Auerbach, Neufach, and Jacobsohn, sent a letter to the Zionist Central Bureau, stating that they had been "unable to come to an agreement with the Chief Rabbi Haim Nahum" and that they "plan on doing what they can to convince Nahum to take a favorable stance on the issue of Zionism." They mention that the "drastically changed situation in Salonica," likely referring to the Balkan Wars and the annexation of Salonica to Greece in 1913, may work in their favor.[68]

In another letter to the Zionist Central Bureau on March 25, 1912, the same writers make clear that they shared the agenda of the Zionist bureau.

---

65   "Llamada al Publico," CAHJP ICA/TUR 1-110.

66   Letter from Rabbi David Markus to Zionist Central Bureau, 20 February 1912 (CZA).

67   Opt cite., in Benbassa, *A Sephardic Chief Rabbi in Politics,* 237237. Benbassa argues that this had been the case until the election of the new *meclis-i cismânî* in April 1911.

68   Letter from Rabbi David Markus et al. to ZCB, March 25, 1912 CZA Z3/44

Concerning the conflict between the Ashkenazim and Rabbi Nahum, they write:

> You can rest completely convinced, esteemed Gentlemen, that all our efforts are focused on working in your interest, i.e. primarily keeping in place the *cismani*. We are working towards that with all means, which, depending on the necessities of the day, need to be lenient at one time, and more forceful another time. This explains the occasionally harsh tone in the "Aurora." Dr. Jacobsohn, who went through this with us for weeks and followed the same tactic, will confirm this necessity. We believe we have consistently stuck to the guidelines we developed together with Dr. Jacobsohn.[69]

Jacobsohn was of course the head of the Anglo-Levantine Banking Company, or the Zionist branch in Constantinople. It is clear from this letter that he was recruiting and working with other leaders of the Ashkenazi community; these leaders in turn supported the publications of *L'Aurore*, which were admittedly highly political and contained an "occasionally harsh tone." The writers observe that

> These are no longer the times we were living in a year ago, especially regarding the changed situation in Salonica and Smyrna. Beside, it seems to us that it needs to be taken as established once and for all that the chief rabbi has already done everything he could and will do everything he can against Zionism, regardless if the "Aurora" and the "Welt" happen to use more powerful words today. We know that Dr. Jacobsohn agrees with us on this issue as well. Nahum can only be convinced to change his mind, if he sees a power in us and fears our strength. And we have demonstrated this strength to him, for one thing through the "Aurora," secondly through our victory in the [illegible].[70]

Here again, the authors point out the changed geopolitical context once Salonica became part of Greece in 1913. Despite Markus not appearing in *L'Aurore*, his influence is evident in the text.

Despite being a Zionist, Markus remained relatively demure in his publications and public addresses in the period under consideration. It is likely that his desire for unity among his congregants took priority and he did not want to be outwardly divisive. In the B'nai B'rith *Bulletin*, the leaders of the lodge claim that the lodge played a "considerable role in being the peacemaker between Sephardi and Ashkenazi Jews.... She [the B'nai B'rith lodge] was able

69   Letter to EAC Berlin, March 25, 1912 CZA Z3/44

70   Ibid.

to exercise power and balance a discussion of complex and multiple interests that were unleashed in the [Jewish] press."[71] The Lodge claimed to observe "strict neutrality," even as its leaders were actually writing to the Zionist Central Bureau. It is likely for this reason that Joseph Niego delivered nearly all (if not all) political remarks known to have been made at the Lodge. As discomfiting as the thought may be, the message may have been more salient coming from a Sephardic Jew. Markus even wrote letters to Nahum as late as 1913, asking for counsel on several cases among his congregants.[72]

The First World War and the End of Haim Nahum's Post

World War I profoundly impacted the economic, political, and social fabric of all of those living in Europe and North America. The Jewish populations of these regions fared no differently -- and to add to wartime complexities, we must recall that the Ottomans and the Russians became foes yet again as Central Powers vs. Entente. The final years of the First World War and the Bolshevik Revolution brought even more refugees to the Capitol -- although some refugees entered with difficulty and had to be housed in specific areas.[73] By 1922, it was reported that nearly 2,000 recently arrived Russian Jews, and many orphans, were living in the capitol, joining some additional 80,000 other Jews living on foreign aid (and some 150,000 refugees from other parts of Europe).[74] At this point, the concentration of Yiddish speaking Jews was high enough at one point to generate an audience for Sholom Brin (1889-) and his theater troupe. Brin, originally born in Yaffo, and educated in Lithuania, began performing in Yiddish theater troops during the twilight years of the Russian Empire.[75] He belonged to the Jewish Labor Bundt, and participated in several performances in Ukraine, especially in Crimea. It was there that he founded the Mendele Theatre Troupe. The members collectively lived through six pogroms from 1918-1920, losing many members, until finally, prompted by pogroms and also a proclamation by General Pyotr Wrangel

---

71   *Bulletin*, 119.

72   CAHJP HM2/9070.1.

73   See Devi Mays, *Forging Ties, Forging Passports: Migration and the Modern Sephardi Diaspora* (Stanford: Stanford University Press, 2020), 114

74   "80 Mil Sufrientes Djudios en Konstantinopla," *La Amerika* January 13, 1922

75   "Leḳsiḳon Fun Yidishn Ṭeaṭer: Yiddish Book Center." *Leḳsiḳon Fun Yidishn Ṭeaṭer | Yiddish Book Center*, https://www.yiddishbookcenter.org/collections/yiddish-books/spb-nybc201090/zylbercweig-zalmen-mestel-leksikon-fun-yidishn-teater-vol-2.

(1878-1928), the commanding general of the Imperial Russian Army, that forbid performances in Yiddish, some surviving members of the Mendele troop finally arrived in Constantinople. Here, they ran the Mendele Theater for approximately one year before they appealed to the Joint Distribution Committee in the United States through the Jewish Emigrant Aid Society. In their appeal, they explained that "the Sefardic [sic] Jews do not understand Yiddish; the wealthy Ashkenazim do not care for Jewish art; and as for the immigrated Ashkenazim, they are too poor to support a Jewish theatre." The troop consisted of thirty two adults and three children, and their appeal was ultimately to aid in their emigration to the United States. [76] This appeal was left unanswered, and the members of the troop eventually made their way to Vienna, where members of the troop fell ill with Typhus while performing at the Hotel Sofia.

In response, foreign aid organizations, including the Joint Distribution Committee and the American Red Cross, began operating in the City.[77] The Joint sent an envoy of board members to report back for the organization, tasked with assessing the state of affairs and how American Jewish funds were being used to support the refugees. The correspondances reveal much about the state of the refugees in Constantinople, and also, about the priorities and concerns that motivated the organizations tasked with helping them. One important correspondence is that between Jacques Maguite, a representative of the JDC, and the New York offices of the JDC. He wrote to the New York offices of the Joint on July 7 in 1920, explaining that the pogroms had worsened the refugee situation:

> The Jewish populace usually moved from villages and small towns into cities of different states where their life apparently seemed to be less dangerous. From these cities they later moved on to the ports on the Black Sea. The political situation on one side was anti-Semitic, and on the other side the high prices for objects of real necessity and food products reacted negatively on the refugees' [sic] physically as well as morally.[78]

76   Letter from Yiddish Theater Troop to Joint Distribution Committee, 8/28/1920
      Reference Code: NY AR191921 / 4 / 42 / 2 / 288.2
      In Folder: Turkey, Cultural and religious, 1919-1921

77   See Oscar Handlin, *A Continuing Task* (New York: Random House, 1964) and Devi Mays, *Forging Ties, Forging Passports: Migration and the Modern Sephardi Diaspora* (Stanford: Stanford University Press, 2020), especially chapter 3.

78   Ibid.

The first group of refugees arrived in Constantinople from Sebastopol on a small freighter called *The Khodinetz*. Many of the refugees made their way to "The American Hotel" in Pera where they were given a small stipend by the Joint. Maguite writes:

> Constantinople is one of these Eastern ports where corruption always reigned. Lately, through the immigration of enormous numbers of refugees from Russia, and the presence of the Allied-Army, same has over-gone every imagination of corruption, and as a result, the remaining girl refugees who were obliged to live in this hotel became victims of the Traders of White Live Goods, who, have free entrance to the Hotel. In spite of the interruption with Russia, many refugees have left said country and went to Constantinople, and naturally came to the Jewish community for help. [79]

He continues, that "the latest refugees immediately become objects of protection under the Jewish community in Constantinople the majority of who are so-called "Espanols" whereas the remaining few are of German or Austrian origin who do not understand the German Jew [ibid.]"[80]

The JDC deployed American Jewish representatives to report back to their local communities to help generate support at home. Julius Savitsky, a social worker and Executive Secretary for Chicago Joint Relief Committee described in a letter to Henry J. Bernheim, who had appealed to the Joint to an appropriated budget to assist Jewish refugees in Turkey.[81] Savitsky described a trip that he took to Turkey in August of 1921 to assess the situation there: "When I had reached the Turkish Capital, I had found many hundreds of Jewish refugees [from Russia] in such horrible plight, of which I did not see anywhere in the Countries which I had visited."[82] Savitsky continues that while he thinks the situation is so dire that only a local representative could fulfill the work of the Joint, he recommends a local Sephardic Jewish leader. He describes Mr. Morris Abraham as "a Sefarde [sic] but [someone who is] also popular among the Ashkenazim as well, and would meet the approval of the Zionists and non-Zionists alike.

---

79   Letter from Mr. Jacques Maguite to Joint Distribution Committee, July 7, 1920, ID 238751, in Records of the American Joint Distribution Committee, Turkey: Subject Matter: Turkey, Refugees, and Emigrants

80   Ibid.

81   February 13, 1920 "The Joint Distribution Committee", *The Jewish Monitor*, Dallas, Tx

82   Letter from Joint Distribution Committee of the American Funds for Jewish War Sufferers to Mr. Henry J. Bernheim, ID 238819, February 10, 1921, Records of the American Jewish Joint Distribution Committee, Turkey, Refugees and Emigrants, 1919-1921

Indeed, the First World War exacerbated tensions between Zionists and "Alliancists" -- tensions that often presented themselves in these communal organizations meant to ameliorate the situation of wartime Jewry. Nahum wrote a letter to the JDC insisting that tensions were calm and under control ("unanimity and perfect harmony has prevailed among the members"), but it quickly became obvious that the communities were disorganized and fractured.[83] By 1920, the JDC's activities even attempted to unify the communities through their plan of action for the distribution of funds, to one central committee, in an effort to bring together the 3 communities "the Sephardim, the Ashkenazim, and the Refugees."[84] However, things did not go so smoothly, and became fractured along politicized lines (Zionists, for example, wanted priority to be given to pioneers, over refugees in the city).[85]

Back in 1918, while Nahum was on a mission in Europe at the request of the Ottoman authorities, the Jewish community joined together to form a new council. Esther Benbassa sees this step as a Zionist initiative to replace the chief rabbinate. While this was not the first time Haim Nahum's authority was questioned in response to his ardent anti-Zionism, a political power struggle ensued as the "prewar Zionist agitation vigorously resumed and took the form of open demonstrations within the population."[86] Organizations allied with Zionism that sprang up at this time include the Hilfsverein der Deutschen Juden, B'nai B'rith, and the Maccabi.

Nahum describes the "campaign carried on against [him]" during his absence the previous year in his letters to the Alliance. He writes:

> This is what happened in Constantinople during my absence: the day after my departure, Monsieur Niego, president of the B'nai B'rith lodge, threw the first poisoned dart that would stir up the population: "The Chief Rabbi has left without warning the official bodies of the nation, he has done wrong, he has done very wrong." The rumor ran through the town like wildfire, reaching all the associations.... There was soon no public or private society where the chief rabbi's case was not judged a hanging matter. Monsieur Niego made himself the standard-bearer for the same group that held the famous campaign against me

---

83   Translation Letter from H. Nahoum to Grand Rabbinat of Turkey at Constantinople, ID 23841, Records of the American Jewish Joint Distribution Committee, Turkey, Administration, 1919-1921

84   Letter from Julius Savitsky to Mr. James H. Becker, November 8, 1920, Item 238431, Records of the American Jewish Joint Distribution Committee, Turkey, Administration, 1919-1921

85   Ibid.

86   Benbassa, *A Sephardic Chief Rabbi in Politics*, 176.

in 1912 and whose members, then as now, are Dr. D. Marcus, Dr. Ii Auerbach, Hilfsverein representative in Constantinople, Monsieur Abramovich, president of the Maccabi Society, N. Rousso (nephew of Monsieur Daoud Rousso, well known ICA lawyer), then president of the central consistory ..., president of the Zionist Federation and my bitter enemy. What Monsieur Niego and his colleagues aimed to do was to hoist on the central consistory (*meclis-i cismani*) outside of any law and simply by revolution, the formation of a self-styled national council, of which he would assume the presidency. He then planned to convene a national assembly to get himself delegated as the representative of the Jews of Turkey to Jewish Congress in London and Paris. [87]

Nahum was accused of deserting the Jews without notifying any Ottoman officials and also of being an "Ententist, since the Entente is the Turk's enemy." Nahum argues that the "consequence of this is blackmail: to bring my name into disrepute with the present government, with the Armenian and Greek elements persecuted by the Turks, and with the powers of the Entente." He also claims that the "Chief Rabbi is an Alliancist, consequently an anti-Zionist, and his journey can only damage the cause of Zionism.... The consequence: to discredit me as an individual and England and all world Jewry." Nahum states that he bears the responsibility for

> 400,00 Jews in the Empire ... that rendered greater services to Zionism in my obscurity than the most fervent of them, and that, thanks to the policy I followed, I prevented the Jews of Turkey and Palestine from sharing the fate of the Armenians and Greeks (and the Greek papers themselves have proclaimed this loud and clear).

Nahum's claims echo those of the previous Chief Rabbi, Moshe Halévy, in attributing the special protection for the Jews of the Ottoman Empire to their privileged position with the sultan or with the Ottoman administration. This point is especially significant in the context of the 1915 Armenian genocide, in which Ottoman Jews bore witness to the slaughter of another Ottoman ethnic and religious minority group.[88]

When intra-communal tensions came to a head after the First World War, Nahum wrote to the President of the Alliance Israélite Universelle, describing the actions of the primarily Ashkenazi Zionists against him:

---

87   Nahum, letter to Bigart, 27 April 1919, opt. cite in Benbassa, *A Sephardic Chief Rabbi in Politics*, 176.

88   Turkish Jewish responses to the Armenian Genocide comprise another promising topic for further study.

There were subsidized public speeches inciting the poor and ignorant masses in the Bolshevik manner, making them believe that the chief rabbi was the cause of all their poverty, that one word from him to the government, had he so wished, and their husbands, brothers, and sons would have stayed at home and would not have died like dogs in the war, that he offered his flock as a sacrifice to the country ..., that if he had so desired, a word from him and the Jews would long since have had Palestine and Jerusalem.[89]

The letter concisely expresses the anxieties surrounding Russian Jews by the end of the decade. Where they had been viewed prior to the Young Turk Revolution as an essential counterpart to Sephardic identity, Russian Jews could now be tethered to the ultimate wartime and ideological enemy: Revolutionary Russia. The "poor and ignorant masses" were eager, according to Nahum, to blame him for losing Jerusalem, the ultimate prize.

In 1919, Férnandez, Salem, and Taranto formed a defense organization comprised of some two to three hundred members.[90] Nahum was invited within a few days and their primary goal was to "work for the reawakening of Jewish national feeling, while conserving the Jews' rights and duties in the countries they inhabit, of which they wished to regard themselves as citizens."[91] That same year, the two Ashkenazi communities, the "foreign" and the Ottoman, merged on the first of January and formed a Provisional Executive Committee of Ashkenazi Jews. Its president was none other than Rabbi David Markus. The Committee issued a *Manifesto* in which the members expressed support for the Jewish cause in Palestine as well as for the Jewish National Council, the main organization supporting the *Yishuv* in British Mandate Palestine. Benbassa sees these steps as arising from the need of the Ashkenazi community to free itself from Sephardi guardianship.[92]

The newly aligned Ashkenazi community prepared for the return of Nahum, who had been away on assignment for the Ottoman authorities since1918. But a few years later, in 1920, Rabbi Haim Nahum resigned from his position and moved to Paris. While in Paris, he served the Turkish government and attended conferences surrounding the Treaty of Lausanne. In 1925, Nahum

---

89   Nahum letter to Bigart, 27 April 1919, opt. cite., in Benbassa, *A Chief Rabbi in Politics*, 176.

90   Nahum, letter to Monsieur le Président, 27 April, 1919, opt. cite., in Benbassa, *A Chief Rabbi in Politics*, 178.

91   Ibid.

92   Benbassa, *A Chief Rabbi in Politics*, 240–41.

moved to Egypt, where he was elected to the position of Chief Rabbi and confirmed by King Fuad I.[93] It was not until the British Mandate period in Palestine that an Ashkenazi Chief Rabbi (*Haham Başı*) was established in former Ottoman lands.

Conclusion

In the March 27, 1936 issue of *The Jewish Chronicle*, founded in London and the oldest continually running Jewish newspaper, an article appeared in praise of the "fine work" of the B'nai Brith Lodge of Istanbul, and in particular, of its founding members, Joseph Niego and Rabbi David Markus. The article highlighted in particular the partnership between the Lodge and the Jewish Colonization Assocation's *Caisse de Petits Prêts*, or small loan's fund, which worked to provide funds to "combat mendicancy." Thanks to the fund, which granted funds specifically to "small traders and artisans…not a Jewish beggar can be found on the streets of Istanbul," and this partnership resulted in "these splendid social results."[94]

On the occasion of Rabbi Markus' birthday, *Hamevasser* described him as a "Peacekeeper."[95] A few years later, *La Boz de Türkiye* published a warm and laudatory piece about the retirement of Rabbi Markus from the Jewish School of Istanbul on 15 March 1941.[96] The article describes Markus as a "striking figure of Turkish Judaism who has received his retirement after years of directing with remarkable competency …, who gave nearly twenty years of his heart and soul to the development of the school, who considered it his mission in life." The article enthuses that Markus would be leaving the school "in a state of moral excellence."[97] Obituaries published in Sephardic newspapers described him in similar warm tones. *La Boz* described his death as if "a star has disappeared in the sky of Oriental Judaism. A light has been

---

93 Between his time in Paris and Cairo, Nahum also visited the Sephardic community of Seattle. Nancy Blase, Arlene Cohen and Eugene Normand, "Treasure from the Jewish Archives," *Nizkor: Newsletter of the Washington State Jewish Historical Society* (spring 2013), as cited in "Rabbi Nahum's Visit to Seattle," *Sephardic Bikur Holim*, http://www.sbhseattle.org/rabbi-nahums-visit-to-seattle/.

94 "B'nai B'rith Silver Jubilee: Istanbul Lodge's Fine Work," March 27, 1936 *The Jewish Chronicle*

95 Joseph Schechtman, *The Life and Times of Vladimir Jabotinsky* (Silver Spring: Eshel Books, 1986), 155–57.

96 "El Lyceo Judeo y el Dr. Marcus," *La Boz de Türkiye,* 3 March 1941.

97 Ibid.

extinguished in the Jewish community of Istanbul, an eclipse has obscured the horizon of the Ashkenazi community of our city."[98]

The descriptions in the 1940s are a far cry from those of twenty years prior. After the beginning of World War I and the eventual dismemberment of the Ottoman Empire, Sephardi and Russian Jews living in places like Istanbul, Tikfour Tchiflik, or Or Yehuda had a choice to make. Would they remain in the place that had become a *kibbutz galuyot* and participate in the secular vision of Turkish Statehood, or would they follow Tevye's other daughters to Palestine, North America, or Western Europe?

---

[98]   "El Rev. Rabino Dr. David Marcus Murio, *La Boz de Türkiye,* 15 January 1944. Rabbi Markus became one of the most famous figures among the Ashkenazi Jews of Turkey. See also Aksel Erbahar, "David Feivel Markus," in *Encyclopedia of Jews in the Islamic World Online,* ed. Norman A. Stillman (Brill: 2010). According to Erbahar, Markus aided German Jews before his death in 1944 by facilitating Turkish visas for them. Although this detail is recorded only by Erbahar and may reflect Turkish national pride, my hope is that future research will substantiate the account and provide further context for it.

PART II:
THE OTTOMAN BORDERLANDS
1890-1923

Entrance to Ashkenazi Cemetery in Arnavutköy (Ulus) and views

Photos of Grave of Rabbi Dr. David Markus in the
Ashkenazi Cemetery

Chapter 4

A NURSERY GROUND FOR PALESTINE?
"JEWISH AGRICULTURALISTS" IN THE
OTTOMAN BORDERLANDS

Love work, loath mastery over others,
and avoid intimacy with the government

Pirkei Avot 10:1

When Albert Kant first looked upon Tikfour Tchiflik, the agricultural farm where his family had purchased land in 1913 just outside of Panderma (now Bandırma), it was wintertime. "Everything was gloomy and dirty," he recalled in his memoir, and the "idea of living there did not enchant me."[1] Kant had been born in Kiliya, just outside of Odessa in the Russian Empire, and a fear of *pogrom* violence there prompted his family to move to the Ottoman borderlands because of its "close proximity to the historic homeland of the Jewish People in Palestine."[2] Despite less-than-favorable first impressions, Kant remained in Tikfour Tchiflik for thirty years and first heard of the ideas of Theodor Herzl and later of the Balfour Declaration of 1917 from friends in Constantinople.[3] Though the Zionist ideas of those friends "ignited [his]

---

[1] Albert Kant, *Mémoires d'un Fermier Juif en Turquie* (Istanbul: Libra Kitap, 2013) 65.

[2] Ibid. This is how Kant recounts it in his memoir, and while it is important to be aware of the constructed nature of this and all memoire, due to the proximity of Kiliya to the site of the Kishinev Pogrom, I find Kant's story plausible. For more see:

[3] Ibid, 90-91. The Balfour Declaration was a letter dated 2 November, 1917 from Arthur Balfour to Lord Walter Rothschild, declaring the intention to create a "the establishment of a national home in Palestine for for the Jewish people."

passion," Kant remained in Turkey, unable to leave his farm behind, until, "little by little, [his] original kernel of Zionism went away."[4]

Approximately 250 kilometers away, in another agricultural colony called Or Yehuda (the "Light of Judah"), lived the Goldenbergs, another Russian Jewish family. Alfred Goldenberg (1907-1999) was just a few years younger than Albert and was born in the agricultural colony approximately one hundred kilometers outside of Smyrna (Izmir). His parents emigrated from Moldavia and Bessarabia in the Russian Empire, the site of the 1903 Kishinev Pogrom, to the new agricultural colony established by the Baron Maurice de Hirsch's Jewish Colonization Association in 1900. Alfred's father, Joseph Goldenberg, became the head of school at Or Yehuda. Alfred Goldenberg recalls his childhood on the farm:

> Everything was vast and new. The same company that built Turkish Railways built a station to serve the agricultural school...until then the train had passed Smyrna near the farm, but did not stop there. The new stop was named Tchiflik [the stop]. The JCA began building the school in the form of a large rectangular three-story building. On the ground floor were the dining room and kitchen, first floor classrooms and the chapel on the second floor dormitory... The JCA hosted farm families from Russia, Romania, and Bulgaria, driven from these countries by anti-Semitism. Each family received a flat similar to ours and a plot of cultivable land. There were families by the names of Soria, Alkalay, Abakou, Dehovna, and soon it was necessary to create two elementary school classes for the children of the farmers.[5]

Other projects sprung up around Or Yehuda, also owned by either the Jewish Colonization Association or their proxies (usually other members of the Association), including the Kant's plot on Tikfour Tchiflik, which was run by immigrants from Russia, Romania, and parts of the Aegean.[6] Goldenberg and his sisters later attended the Alliance school in Izmir, having been told that they had learned "all there is to learn at Or Yehuda."[7] Joseph Niego (1863-1945), the head *agronome* of the Jewish Colonization Association (JCA) and former headmaster of Mikveh Israel, an agricultural school outside of Jaffa in Ottoman Palestine, arranged for Goldenberg and his sisters to stay

---

4   Albert Kant, *Mémoires*, 91.

5   *Les Cahiers de l'AIU*, Tuesday, 1 December, 1998, pg. 31

6   Please see chapter one, as well as Justin McCarthy, "Jewish Population in the Late Ottoman Period" in Avigdor Levy's *The Jews of the Ottoman Empire* (Princeton: Princeton University Press, 1994), 375-397.

7   Ibid.

with the Benaroya family of Smyrna. After completing his education at the Alliance Israélite Universelle School in Paris along with his sister, Goldenberg became a teacher in the Alliance schools in Morocco.[8]

Teachers and Students of Or Yehuda, 1909.
CAHJP ICA/Tur 369-42

8   Ibid.

Façade of the agricultural school of Or Yehuda,
undated photograph, CAHJP ICA/Tur 369-42

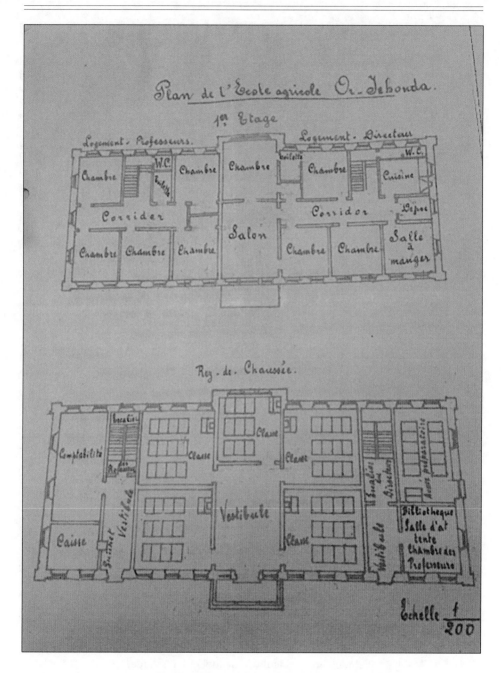

Architectural plans for the agricultural school of Or Yehuda,
CAHJP ICA/Tur 369-42

Façade of the agricultural school of Or Yehuda,
undated photograph, CAHJP ICA/Tur 369-42

Families like Kant and those that Goldenberg describes left Russia in response to *pogrom* violence, constituting one of the largest exoduses in Jewish history.[9] Approximately 2.7 million Jews left the Russian Empire prior to the Bolshevik Revolution,[10] and of those, thousands arrived in Constantinople aided by the JCA, a new organization founded in 1894 by the wealthy Viennese Jew, the Baron Maurice de Hirsch, in the cities of New York, London, Constantinople, and St. Petersburg. Many of these immigrants left Russia having convinced the Tsarist authorities they were headed to Argentina for new colonies on the plains of Patagonia, proposing a solution for the "Jewish Question," at least as the Russian Empire understood it.[11] However, some of these immigrants had no intention of ever traversing the Atlantic. Instead, they intended to make *aliyah* to the Land of Israel (*eretz yisrael)* or to become agriculturalists on settlements like Or Yehuda in Western Anatolia, just a relative stone's throw away from the Land of Israel. The JCA provided financing, partial or whole, for the majority Russian, Romanian, and Ottoman Jewish farmers.[12] Some farmers moved on to Palestine when it became feasible; others, disheartened by the trials of farming or of the confusing information coming from Palestine, abandoned the hope of *aliyah* and pursued opportunities in the Ottoman capital of Constantinople, in other major cities of Europe, or in North America.

Albert Kant and Alfred Goldenberg found themselves in one of the many borderlands of the Ottoman Empire at a critical juncture in history for two of the last great empires in Eastern Europe. As Omer Bartov and Eric Weitz point out in the introduction to their volume *Shatterzone of Empires,* borderlands are not only "places of interaction," but they are "spaces-in-between, where identities are often malleable and control of the territory and population is

---

9   Scholars derive this number from multiple censuses of the Russian Empire and the Soviet Union, notably 1897 and 1926. For the 1897 census, see Table 3 in Andreas Kappeler, *The Russian Empire: A Multiethnic History* (Essex: Pearson Education, 2001). In the Soviet case, see Lionel Kochan, *The Jews in Soviet Russia since 1917* (London: Oxford University Press, 1972).

10   Benjamin Nathans, *Beyond the Pale: the Jewish Encounter in Late Imperial Russia* (Los Angeles: University of California Press, 2002), 4-5.

11   For more on the nature of the "Jewish Question" in the Russian Empire, please see John Klier, *Russia Gathers Her Jews: the Origins of the "Jewish Question" in Russia, 1772-1825* (DeKalb: Northern Illinois University Press, 1986).

12   Theodor Norman, *An Outstretched Arm: A History of the Jewish Colonization Association* (Routledge: London, 1985).

subject to dispute."[13] As borderlands "are geographically or culturally distant from the seat of power…[they] become sites for all sorts of political, military, and economic projects."[14] This chapter tells the story of early Zionist dreamers who chose to stay close to the biblical Land of Israel and ended up in these borderlands, awaiting a shift in political currents. It is the story of how Kant and his companions lived, worked, dreamed, and even fell in love in these volatile lands. These borderlands were sites of exceptional religious and ethnic diversity, and Kant and his companions encountered Armenians, Circassians, and Greeks in the site of major population exchanges, wars in the Balkans (1912-1913), and internal migrations just as the Turkish nation was conceptualized and formed.[15] Yet, what Kant's memoire tells us is that, despite the importance of his farm in the Ottoman borderlands, it was his experiences there, along with critical conversations and encounters with Zionists, friends, and lovers in Constantinople that significantly impacted his ideological affiliations and identity.

This chapter explores a critical point in time where decisions to follow through with *aliyah* were made or unmade. It is the story of these migrants' benefactors, of the nature of their debates over what they believed to be the future of Russian Jewry, of the way in which the early inception of the Jewish Colonization Association reified paternalistic and Orientalist discourses about the nature of the "Jewish Question." It is also about the way in which the Association's representatives transformed the mission and goals of the organization as Zionism gained traction in Europe and Constantinople. The protagonists of this chapter are many and varied, from philanthropists like the Baron Maurice de Hirsch, who first conceptualized and financed these agricultural projects to local Jewish leaders like Joseph Niego to everyday Russian farmers like Albert Kant and Alfred Goldenberg. They constitute the "colonizers, intellectuals, ideologues, locals and newcomers," that we

---

13   Omer Bartov and Eric D. Weitz, *Shatterzone of Empires: Coexistence and Violence in the German, Habsburg, Russian, and Ottoman Borderlands* (Bloomington: Indiana University Press, 2013), 3-5.

14   Ibid.

15   On the larger immigration patterns of Western Anatolia, population exchanges between Greece and Turkey, and the modern Turkish State, see Reşat Kasaba, *A Moveable Empire: Ottoman Nomads, Migrants, and Refugees* (Seattle: University of Washington Press, 2011), 123-139. A discussion of Kant and Goldberg's encounter with ethnic minorities is discussed in chapter four, "Memoire and Memory: Tevye's Ottoman Daughters."

frequently see in the borderlands of history.[16] This chapter is about Russian subjects like Kant and Goldenberg, who worked toward Ottoman citizenship, only to take an altogether different route of emancipation.[17] In the words of the First Deputy of the JCA, Colonel Albert E.W. Goldsmidt, these colonies were supposed to be "a nursery ground for Palestine," but instead became an important starting point for participation in Ottoman society on the eve of Turkish statehood.[18]

Previous studies have dealt with Or Yehuda and other settlements in Western Anatolia as anecdotal blips in the histories of Jewish social or educational experiments or as curious footnotes to the history of the Jews of Turkey written about in the correspondences of the Alliance Israélite Universelle.[19] Others have argued that Territorialist projects constitute proof that the Second Aliyah (1904-1914) was not as ideologically motivated as dominant Jewish historiography has demonstrated.[20] Contemporaries deemed these colonies failures because the colonies as such did not endure beyond the establishment of the Republic of Turkey and the Treaty of Lausanne in 1923.[21] In the history of Zionism, stories of these settlements, and those in Cyprus, are left out all together or are subverted to a conversation with hubs of Zionist

---

16   Bartov et. al., *Shatterzone of Empires*, 3.

17   See chapter two for an explanation of emancipation among Ottoman Jewry, "Los Rusos in the Jewish Entrepôt."

18   Grunwald, from David Joslin, *A Century of Banking in Latin America; to Commemorate the Centenary in 1962 of the Bank of London & South America Limited* (London, New York: Oxford University Press, 1963) 81.

19   Research for this chapter was conducted using several archival collections, but I was the first scholar to access the newly catalogued ICA/Turkey collection at the Central Archives for the History of the Jewish People in Jerusalem, Israel in the spring of 2015. My utmost gratitude goes to Yochai Ben-Gedalia, Hadassah Assouline, and, most of all, archivist Denise Rein for painstakingly cataloguing and preparing the materials for me. Previous mentions of the settlements in Turkey can be found in Jewish histories of Izmir, Salonica, and Istanbul. See, for example, Aron Rodrigue, *French Jews, Turkish Jews: The Alliance Israélite Universelle and the Politics of Jewish Schooling in Turkey, 1860-1925* (Indiana: Indiana University Press, 1990).

20   See Gur Alroey, *An Unpromising Land: Jewish Migration to Palestine in the Early Twentieth Century* (Stanford: Stanford University Press, 2014). Additionally, Theodor Norman wrote a history of the JCA in 1985 sponsored by the same organization, of which a few pages are dedicated to colonies outside of Argentina and Brazil including Or Yehuda. See Theodor Norman, *An Outstretched Arm: A History of the Jewish Colonization Association* (London: Routledge, 1985).

21   Joseph Niego mentions in his memoir that JCA achieved "minimal success in Turkey." See Joseph Niego, *Cinquante Années de Travail dans les Oeuvres Juives: Allocutions et Conférences, Bulletin publié à l'occasion du soixante-dixième anniversaire du Frère Grand Président J. Niégo, sous les auspices du District XI de la Béné-Bérith, avec une préface de J. Shaki* (Istanbul: Babok & Fils, 1933), 21.

activity in cities like Berlin and Jerusalem.[22] I argue that, by placing these sites in the center of our analysis as important sites where Jewish identity and politics were being fashioned and refashioned, we can broaden our understanding of Jewish geography and of the interactions between multiple Jewish cultures (both Ashkenazi and Sephardi), which will lead to an understanding of how the road to Zionism was neither linear nor inevitable.

Thus, this chapter seeks to disaggregate the experiences of Russian and Ottoman Jewry in the twilight years of the Russian and Ottoman Empire from any singular experience. Routes of exit for Tevye's daughters were not always perfectly paved from Odessa to Jerusalem: her motivations, strategies, and political identities were malleable, defined and redefined through the immigration process and through her interaction with the states, institutions, cities, and most of all, people she encountered. By understanding the experiences of Tevye's daughters in the Ottoman world, we can also more fully understand the volatile relationship that the Empire had with Jews who entered its domains, from Baghdad to Izmir to Jerusalem.

Immigration, Territorialism, Zionism

While the Ottoman Administration did curtail Jewish immigration to Palestine beginning in 1891, the state "had no objection to the settlement of newly arrived, industrious elements in places like Salonica and Izmir."[23] Despite the historical mythology surrounding Sultan Abdülhamid II's attitude toward Jewish immigration to Palestine--that, as the saying goes, he would have "preferred cutting off his own arm rather than hand Palestine over to the Jews"--between 1890-1914, the Ottoman Empire saw a rise in Jewish migration and in the Jewish population of Palestine, particularly.[24] While many Russian immigrants passing through the Ottoman Empire did intend to make *aliyah* and applied for Ottoman citizenship along the way, many, as I

---

22   An excellent article by Yossi Ben-Artzi, "Jewish Rural Settlement in Cyprus 1882-1935: a "Springboard" or a Destiny?" in *Jewish History*, 21.3/4 (2007): 361-383, will be discussed later in this chapter. While I agree with the author's argument, my study is different as it places settlements in Western Anatolia in conversation with Constantinople/Istanbul where the "Jewish agriculturalists" engaged with the offerings of the *métropole* rather than with Jerusalem or other cities with Zionist activities.

23   Selim Deringil, "Jewish Immigration to the Ottoman Empire at the Time of the First Zionist Congresses: A Comment," *The Last Ottoman Century and Beyond: the Jews in Turkey and the Balkans, 1808-1945*, ed. Minna Rozen (The Goldstein-Goren Diaspora Research Center: Tel Aviv University, 2002-2005).

24   Ibid, 141

will demonstrate, grew weary of farming and sometimes of Zionism or feared that the collapsing Ottoman Empire might render the value of their land useless (if their land had not already been seized by Ottoman authorities), sold what they could, and left the Empire completely for Montreal, New York, and South America. Others, like Albert Kant, sold their farms and moved to Constantinople.[25]

The founders of the Jewish Colonization Association did not identify under the official banner of Territorialism or Zionism, having predated the movements by a few years, but they did share many of the movements' ideological underpinnings. Jewish Territorialism arose in response to the British Uganda offer in 1903, and its adherents sought an alternative to a Jewish state in the biblical Land of Israel, suggesting sites in the United States and South America, its geographical boundaries determined by the Hebrew Bible. Zionism's proponents wanted to see Jews living productively and independently in the biblical land of Israel and, so, argued that post-exilic life had undermined the Jewish people in their constant encounter with anti-Semitism, especially in Europe.[26] A home for the Jews would mean a solution to the "Jewish Question," which had been occupying the minds of Jews and their European counterparts alike in the wake of the nationalist movements of the nineteenth century.

Territorialism and Zionism share aspirations for Jewish political control, for mass settlement, and for a revival of Jewish cultural and spiritual life through agricultural labor, self-reliance, and creative endeavors. Territorialists, however, believed that under no circumstances could a Jewish state arise in the Land of Israel. Recent monographs on alternative Jewish collective projects, attempt to recover microhistories that have been subverted to dominant Zionist narratives, including those by Adam Rovner (in Madagascar, Grant Island (New York), Uasin Gishu (East Africa), Benguela Plateau (Angola), Tasmania, and Suriname' as well as projects within the Soviet Union, namely Birobidzhan and Ukraine, produced by Boris Kotlerman and Jonathan Dekel-Chen, respectively. Devin E. Naar's recent book on Salonica illustrates petitions made to the World Zionist Organization in Berlin to make what

25   Kant, *Mémoires*, 114.

26   For more on the history of early Zionism, see Arthur Herzberg, *The Zionist Idea: A Historical Analysis and Reader* (New York: Doubleday, 1959) and Walter Laquer, *The History of Zionism* (London: Tauris Parke, 2003).

journalist David Florentin called the "Queen of 'Jewishness' in the Orient" into an international city (like Tangiers or Manchuria) with a Jewish administration.[27] The revival of scholarship on alternative Zionist projects is a relatively new phenomenon due in part to an academic and political emphasis on the State of Israel in post 1948.[28] As Dekel-Chen points out, during the Second World War, American Jewry "committed itself wholeheartedly to the establishment of a Jewish state in Palestine ...Consequently, non-Zionist subjects left the front page of Jewish historiography."[29]

The Jewish Colonization Association shared many goals with its younger Territorialist brothers and sisters, but it did not share in one of its most important visions: the desire for full political sovereignty. In this, it had most in common with the Soviet Union's settlements of the Crimea and Birobidzhan, funded not only by the Soviet Union but also by the Jewish Joint Distribution Committee (in the case of the Crimean settlements). Rather than the full emancipation, statehood, and sovereignty advocated by Theodor Herzl, Max Nordau, and other early Zionists, The Baron Maurice de Hirsch and the Jewish Colonization Association argued for self-sufficiency and auto emancipation within the confines of the existing empires and nation-states. This subtle yet critical distinction would lead to an important debate between the Baron de Hirsch and the Zionists and would direct the fates of Russian Jews' early years in Anatolia.

The Case for Settling Anatolia: The Baron de Hirsch, Theodor Herzl, and the Jewish Colonization Association

In 1890, approximately nine hundred Russian Jews arrived in Constantinople intending to travel further to Palestine. They were stopped by Ottoman authorities and told that they would be unable to travel further. These Russian Jews were in a bit of a bind: they had sold all of their belongings but could not travel any further, and they were wary of returning to the Russian Empire.[30] The

---

27   See Devin E. Naar, *Jewish Salonica: Between the Ottoman Empire and Modern Greece* (Palo Alto: Stanford University Press, 2016), 1-2.

28   One of the fiercest advocates is Zosa Szajkowski in his book *Mirage of American Jewish Aid in Soviet Russia, 1917-1939* (New York: Ktav Publishing House, 1977).

29   Jonathan Dekel-Chen, *Farming the Red Land: Jewish Agricultural Colonization and Local Soviet Power, 1924-1941* (New Haven: Yale University Press, 2005), 204.

30   Norman, An Outstretched Arm, 6.

Sephardic community was already overburdened with an influx of migrants in Constantinople as discussed in future chapters. The established Jewish community cabled the Baron Maurice de Hirsch.[31]

The Baron Maurice de Hirsch (1831-1896) was a wealthy Bavarian Jew who had made his first fortune in the banking industry. He had invested heavily in the railroad industry and the *chemins de fer orientaux*, a railway that connected Vienna to Constantinople and housed the Orient Express (1870-1937). During the First Balkan War (1912), the railway was limited to Eastern Thrace, but challenges to running his business informed the Baron de Hirsch's trepidation to work with Ottoman authorities on any kind of project.

The Baron de Hirsch was a deeply committed Jewish philanthropist, and devoted a considerable amount of his resources to the work of the Alliance Israélite Universelle. Encouraged by his wife, Clara, to focus his attention on the Jews of the Ottoman Empire, he believed strongly that education was a means to alleviating Jewish suffering. In 1881, he gave one million francs to the Emergency Fund to offer relief to Russian Jews fleeing pogroms, equivalent to roughly half a million American dollars today.[32] According to his contemporaries, it was a mixture of "*gewissenbisse,* of pangs of conscience, and of social ambition that made Hirsch the outstanding philanthropist of his time."[33] The Baron de Hirsch would become most well-known for his colonization projects in Argentina and Brazil, and it was the "crisis" of Russian Jewry that would be his main preoccupation. He founded the Jewish Colonization Association in 1891 and would become the primary sponsor and advocate behind Jewish settlements in Western Anatolia, the budget for which grew to approximately 180 million francs (approximately thirty-six million dollars today).[34]

Yet the Baron de Hirsch, like many of his contemporary coreligionists, never ascribed to the then-nascent Zionist movement. The Baron de Hirsch, tellingly, changed his citizenship four different times, wherever it was most pragmatic to do so, while he had homes in England, France, Moravia, and

---

31   Ibid, 7. These nine hundred Jews were shipped to the pampas of Argentina.

32   Norman, *An Outstretched Arm, 117.*

33   Kurt Grunwald, *Turkenhirsch: A Study of Baron Maurice de Hirsch Entrepreneur and Philanthropist* (Israel Program for Scientific Translation: Jerusalem, 1966) 63.

34   Ibid.

Hungary. He had a traditional religious upbringing, but was not religious as an adult. "Only on Yom Kippur did he refrain from hunting in order not to hurt the feelings of his Jewish acquaintances."[35] The Baron de Hirsch did believe in a pragmatic and strategic mode of colonization but not in Palestine. The Baron de Hirsch's politics and ideologies often overlapped with those of the Alliance: he believed in self-reliance, auto emancipation, and self-betterment, but he did not believe in the need for national statehood.[36]

In 1891, a conference was convened in Paris at the Alliance Israélite Universelle offices in response to the crisis in Russia. Members present represented most of the major Jewish aid organizations in Europe, and also indicated that the conference was an opportunity, perhaps, to provide joint funding for a Jewish Colonization Association presence in Palestine.[37] In attendance were the Grand Rabbi Zadoc Kahn (the Alsatian Chief Rabbi of France), M. Erlanger on behalf of Baron de Rothschild, Isidor Loeb on the part of Baron de Hirsch, Rabbi Mohilever (a Religious Zionist and founder of Hovevei Zion), Rabbi Dr. Azriel Hildesheimer (a Rabbi from Berlin and a founder of the Modern Orthodox Movement), S.P. Rabinowitz (a Jewish educator), Colonel Goldsmidt, and Adam Rosenberg from Hovevei Zion. The conference's goal was to raise ten thousand francs for colonies in Syria and Palestine, but, after the two barons could not agree on the colonies' location, the matter was dropped entirely.[38]

According to Baron de Hirsch, and drawing largely on reports of Jewish life relayed by Arnold White as discussed later in this chapter, the solution to Jewish suffering and anti-Semitism was auto-emancipation and mass immigration. He expressed this at the Conference and in several interviews and publications throughout the early 1890s. For example, the Baron de Hirsch held the opinion that the Jews could become productive by returning to agricultural labor. In an interview with the *Jewish Chronicle* in 1896, a few years into the colonization projects, the Baron de Hirsch remarked:

---

35   Grunwald, *Turkenhirsch*, 83

36   The Alliance's pro-Empire position would come to a head when met with an influx of Zionist Russian refugees in Constantinople, which is the subject of chapter three, "'Under One Great Fraternal Flag': Ashkenazi Jews in Constantinople."

37   Letter from Adam Rosenberg, op. cit. in Grunwald, *Turkenhirsch*, 122-123

38   Grunwald, *Turkenhirsch*, 122.

You have no conception of the good will with which they [Russian Jews] take to the soil. The predictions of our enemies that the Jews would never go back to agriculture have been falsified. The Russian Jew has grit, industry, sobriety; he is eager for work. No matter what has been at home, he takes readily to the spade... yes, they give me the greatest hope.[39]

A letter that the Baron de Hirsch had read inspired this idealization of agricultural labor. Written by Michael Heilprin (1823-1888), a Polish Hungarian Jew who had settled in the United States and argued on behalf of Russian Jewish settlements in agricultural colonies in the United States, he described the "rays of hope" emanating from Jewish agricultural projects in Oregon and North Dakota.[40] He describes the "willingness and capacity for labor of the Russian colonists," compared to the "misery of their brethren in the cities." The Russian Jews' "ability and steadiness had found their reward; a better sentiment began to prevail everywhere," and, most significantly, "a decidedly friendly and humane disposition was everywhere evinced by the non-Jewish neighbors of these victims of persecution. The hardships of their present have not ceased to be severe, but the future has ceased to appear hopeless and dark."[41] The letter deeply affected the Baron de Hirsch, and he believed that this style of agricultural settlement would not only improve the moral, social, and economic condition of the Jews but would be the antidote to what he saw as Europe's "natural" tendency toward anti-Semitism.[42] If the Jews could become productive agriculturalists within an existing government, then they would not only provide a better life than they had in the Pale of Settlement and the Jewish ghettos but also could solve the "Jewish Question."[43] To confirm these assumptions, the Baron de Hirsch did his due diligence and hired an interesting advocate, the Englishman Arnold White.

---

39   "Glimpses of Baron de Hirsch," *The Jewish Chronicle*, May 8, 1896.

40   Gustav Pollack, *Michael Heilprin and His Sons* (New York: Dodd, Mead and Company, 1912).

41   Ibid, 211.

42   Ibid.

43   There is an exhaustive literature on the history of the "Jewish Question" in Europe. For a history of anti-Semitism and the British intelligentsia, please see Sam Johnson, *Pogroms, Peasants, Jews: Britain and Eastern Europe's Jewish Question, 1867-1925* (New York: Palgrave McMillan, 2011). For an analysis of the "Jewish Question" as a broader "product of modernity," see Aamir R. Mufti, *Enlightenment in the Colony: The Jewish Question and the Crisis of Post-Colonial Culture* (Princeton: Princeton University Press, 2007). For a history of the "Jewish Question" in Germany and in German literature, Ritchie Robinson, *The "Jewish Question" in German Literature, 1749-1939: Emancipation and its Discontents* (London: Oxford University Press, 1999). For the history of the "Jewish Question" in Russia, see footnote 11.

Strange Bedfellows: The Russian Empire, Arnold White, and the Case for Agricultural Settlement

In 1916, the classic historian of Russian Jewry, Simon Dubnow, described the JCA's answer to the "Jewish Question":

> Jewish Colonization Association was to transplant 25,000 Jews to Argentina in the course of 1892 and henceforward to increase progressively the ratio of immigrants, so that in the course of twenty-five years, 3,250,000 Jews would be taken out of Russia…the brilliant perspective of a Jewish exodus cheered the hearts of the neo-Egyptian dignitaries. Their imagination caught fire. When the question came up before the Committee of Ministers, the Minister of the Navy, Chikhachev, proposed to pay the Jewish Colonization Association a bonus of a few rubles for each emigrant."[44]

Dubnow likened the exodus of Russia's Jews to the Jewish exodus from Egypt, suggesting that the JCA would be an enticing offer for the "neo-Egyptian dignitaries" of the Russian Empire. And, if successful, Russia's Jews would be free of the yoke of anti-Semitism in the Russian Empire and on the European continent.

After reading the letter written by Michael Heilprin, the Baron de Hirsch appointed a controversial figure, Arnold White (1848-1925), to travel to the Russian Empire and report back on the condition of Russian Jewry and their fitfulness to perform agricultural work. The Baron de Hirsch's goals were twofold: first, he needed to understand the Empire's Jews, to understand the population that would constitute the first colonies in Argentina. But the Baron de Hirsch was also a businessman, and he needed someone convincing to persuade the Russian authorities to allow Jews to emigrate. Who better to sell the Russians on the case for Jewish emigration to Argentina than someone who was similarly enthusiastic about Jewish emigration out of Europe completely? Arnold White was just the figure; a British nationalist and protectionist, White was a journalist and politician who made several unsuccessful runs at Parliament. From 1884 onward, heavily in debt from a failed coffee plantation in Ceylon, he became a political agitator and organized several "colonizing schemes" in South America, South Africa, Canada, and Australia.[45] In 1886, he published his first book, *The Problems of a Great City*, which describes the

---

44   Simon Dubnow, *History of the Jews in Russia and Poland, Volume 1* (Philadelphia: Jewish Publication Society of America, 1916) 415.

45   "Arnold J White," *Oxford Dictionary of National Biography* retrieved 13 February, 2015.

problems of East London according to such categories as "Unemployment," "Drink," "Emigration," and "The National Debt," a section in which he spends considerable time describing the ills that the "immigration of foreign Jews" had caused in East London.[46] After the relative success of this book, he published a series of articles that oppose unrestricted immigration (especially Eastern Europe's "destitute Jews"), and testified in front of Parliament on several occasions to support his views. He supported Britain's imperial ambitions in the colonies and was also ardently opposed to Irish home rule. He was highly worried about Germany's ambitions in England's territory and, later in his life, served on the council of the Eugenics Education Society. White was also paranoid about German unification and the ambitions of Otto Von Bismarck, and it is not unreasonable to believe that the Baron de Hirsch played on White and the Russians' mutual paranoia to his advantage.

In 1891, White traveled through the Pale of Settlement and also to St. Petersburg where he unveiled the plans to Russian dignitaries who mistook him for a member of Parliament, perhaps to his favor.[47] He also wrote letters back to the Baron de Hirsch describing the situation in Russia and the Russian Jews' "capacity" for agricultural colonization beyond Russia.[48] He had traveled from Moscow to Kiev to Odessa and visited agricultural colonies in Vilna, Ekateronislav, and Homel. "The Jews also give me the best letters of credence and everywhere I encounter the most respected Jews, and I also try to see the worst and poorest." White traveled with David Feinberg (1840-1916), or, as White recalled in his memoires, a "Russian Jewish gentleman who speaks Jargon," and who would become the president of the Jewish Colonization Association's St. Petersburg Office, an office established to aid in the affairs of would-be Russian Jewish immigrants.[49] At a certain point in their travels, Arthur White describes a situation in which Feinberg was turned away at a hotel in Kiev "because of his religion." White reports back to Hirsch:

---

46   Arnold White, *The Problems of a Great City* (London: Remington & Co. Publishers, 1886).

47   Ibid.

48   Letter from Arnold White to Baron de Hirsch, 27 June 1891. CAHJP ICA/Lon 01-2.

49   Arnold White, *The Modern Jew* (London: 1899), 52. Feinberg later familiarized himself with the Alliance Israélite Universelle and helped lobby Baron Horace Ginsburg to found several aid organizations for the Jews of Russia. See Leo Shpall, "David Feinberg's Historical Survey of the Colonization of the Russian Jews in Argentina," *Publications of the American Jewish Historical Society* 43.1 (1953): 37-69, and also Benjamin Nathans, *Beyond the Pale: The Jewish Encounter with Late Imperial Russia* (Los Angeles: University of California Press, 2002).

I do not consider that over 20% of adult men… are able to bear the physical effort of moving to a new country, under the conditions and due to physical inferiority to the Russians…Certainly, I can think of no country in Europe or the city's population that does not reach a superiority over the poor Jew in the Russian city.[50]

Informed by his observations of the social problems of East London, White reports that Jews living in Russian cities are even worse off. Despite their inherent physical inferiority to "Russians," city life has not served the Jews of Russia well. However, life in the Southern Ukrainian *oblast* of Kherson, near the Crimean peninsula, was quite different according to White:

When I compare the city with the Jewish life established by the Emperor Nicholas in the province of Kherson, the difference is astonishing. These Jews are active, although battered, tanned by the sun, they have muscles…It is an agricultural community marked by all high-class peasant characteristics. There are 30,000 of these people…they have no vices, unless early marriage, improvident and fruitful, could be regarded as vices.[51]

White is referring back to Tsar Nicholas I's April 13, 1835 edict in which he decided to create colonies of Jews in Russia. Initially, Jews had been permitted to settle relatively freely in "New Russia," the lands that Catherine the Great acquired from the Ottoman Empire (1768-1774). Prior to the edict, in 1806, Jewish families founded seven agricultural colonies in Kherson, which had several restrictions (including the inability to purchase land from a Christian village and needing to maintain a certain distance from Christian villages).[52] Many Jews headed to Odessa as well. While quantitative data varies, approximately 50-100,000 Russians made their living as agriculturalists by 1890. In these colonies, Russian Jews were given relative freedom to live and pray as they wished.[53] His description is saturated in the language of both

---

50   Letter from Arnold White to Baron de Hirsch, 27 June 1891. CAHJP ICA/Lon 01-2.

51   Ibid.

52   For more see Michael Minc, "Jewish Agricultural Settlements in Kherson up to the Bolshevik Revolution," *On the History of the Jewish Diaspora* (Tel Aviv: Tel Aviv University Press, 1990).

53   Odessa was a unique Russian city. As Patricia Herlihy remarks on her entry into the Jewish encyclopedia in Russian Jewish writers of Odessa, the city, founded in 1794, was a "frontier boomtown lacking a historical tradition. Those who sought a haven there could take with them as much (or as little) of their heritage as they wished. Whether they were Italians, Greeks, French, Russians, Poles, Ukrainians, Moldavians, or Jews who moved to the port city from abroad or from within the Russian Empire, they had the possibility to construct a fresh identity with few constraints or expectations. The young city of Odessa therefore had a cosmopolitan, diverse, fluid, and enterprising population. The historian Simon Dubnow (1860-1941), who chose to live in Odessa during his productive years and who chronicled the

colonialism and Orientalism. The emphasis on the body--the idealization of the toiling peasant--simultaneously subverts and defines the Russian Jew as the "other" who can and must remain outside of the European city. The "fruitful" Russian Jew seems naturally suited to work the Baron de Hirsch's colonies.

Indeed the contrast between the Jews in southern Russia and northern Russia is quite stark in White's descriptive reports. He depicts the Jews' resilience, strength, and ability to prosper in the Baron de Hirsch's colonies as a byproduct of the anti-Semitic conditions that they had so long endured. For example, he writes that the "nervous temperament of being a Jew" gives him or her

> An amazing ability to withstand the pressure force of existence, the uncertainty of the future, the real need tens of thousands in the present state of things...[we should] judge the character of the Jews in periods of struggle and effort as will be the case during the first years of your settlement project, as was the case in all at the beginning of world history.[54]

And that the

> The courage--the moral--courageous hope, patience, in sobriety, are worthy qualities in his worthy Jewish people. Such people, under capable guidance, are called upon to bring a good settlement plan that is well organized, whether in Argentina, in Siberia, or South Africa.

White's paternalism reifies discourses of colonialism.[55] The juxtaposition between the horrid conditions of the Jewish city and the "tanned by the sun, muscular" Jew of the Ukrainian provinces essentializes both these "types" of

---

history of Jews in Russia and Poland, called Odessa the least historical of cities, a cultural *tabula rasa.* Inhabitants could mold the city and themselves according to their own inclinations, restricted only by the prohibitions applied (rather loosely) by Russian law. Yet settlers could also bring with them their cultural, religious, and ethnic identities and form their own communities. The population of Odessa contained a mixture of both types: free uprooted spirits and community builders. As a microcosm of the population, Jews followed the same patterns. The only city within the Pale that freely admitted Jews throughout its history, Odessa attracted from the Pale of Settlement as well as from Galicia, Jews from all walks of life including intellectuals, merchants, artisans, and laborers." Patricia Herlihy, "Enzyklopädie Jüdischer Geschichte Und Kultur."*Auftrag Der Sächsischen Akademie Der Wissenschaften Zu Leipzig* (Stuttgart, Metzler) 2014. Many thanks to Professor Herlihy for providing me with the English translation as a result of an invigorating conversation about Odessa and Constantinople in the 2015-2016 Hanauer Fellowship.

54   Letter from Arnold White to Baron de Hirsch, 27 June 1891. CAHJP ICA/Lon 01-2.

55   For a critique of colonialism, see Edward Said, *Culture and Imperialism* (Vintage: New York, 1994).

Jews. White suggests a strategy for negotiating with Russian authorities and hedging the many risks of agriculture:

> The difficulties are many, and I do not think you can solve them effectively if the friendly Russian government assistance is not offered. Your first detachment must be an elite corps, as if the first kind. Nothing must be left to chance. I would advise you to choose your first detachment in agricultural colonies of Emperor Nicolas.[56]

White proposes that a central committee of emigration must be established with the "worthiest and most respected Jews in the cities" whose duties would be to select immigrants, disburse funds, control and arrange departure groups, and create a committee that worked with the government. The Baron de Hirsch followed White's recommendations and established a Central Committee, appointing David Feinberg as its Secretary in 1892. By 1894, three thousand Russian Jews had been sent to Argentina via Constantinople.[57]

White concludes his report with the following advice:

> Your project will take years to materialize, so we must look to the future. Jewish youth should be trained to handicrafts and agriculture. Nihilism comes from empty stomachs…that young people work with their hands, to prepare for their future in a colony…only then and create a new and worthy state. I cannot finish this report without mentioning the misery of children to which I was witness. I saw the famine in the Indies in 1878; I saw many evils and sorrows in different parts of the world.[58]

A committee was formed in St. Petersburg, which included Baron Ginsburg, and appointed David Feinberg (from the St. Petersburg JCA Central office) as its secretary. Back in Constantinople, *El Tiempo* was busy reporting about the Baron de Hirsch's purchasing of land in "Asia Minor." Articles stating that that the Baron De Hirsch had entered negotiations to purchase territory in Western Anatolia from the Ottoman government in order to assist Jewish immigrants "expelled from Russia" begin to appear.[59] The article details the

---

56   Letter from Arnold White to Baron de Hirsch, 27 June 1891. CAHJP ICA/Lon 01-2.

57   Norman, An Outstretched Arm, 43.

58   Letter from Arnold White to Baron de Hirsch, 27 June 1891. CAHJP ICA/Lon 01-2.

59   "El Baron de Hirsch y los Israelitas," *El Tiempo*, August 20, 1891, an issue that shared articles on the upcoming celebration of the Fourth Centennial of Spanish Expulsion. See also "El Aniversario de la Imigracion de Espanya."

size and the nature of the land, which will be "suitable for agriculture." Any emigration to Palestine is notably absent.

With this in mind, Hirsch moved to establish three separate philanthropic agencies to aid Jewish immigrants, the Jewish Colonization Association in London, the Baron de Hirsch Stiftung in Austria, and the Baron de Hirsch Fund in New York. In 1892, a committee on immigration was formed and its goals were approved:

1. To assist and promote the emigration of Jews from any part of Europe or Asia, and principally from countries in which they were being subjected to special taxes or political or other disabilities, to any other parts of the world, and to form and establish colonies in various parts of North and South America and other countries for agricultural, commercial, and other purposes;

2. To purchase in any part of the world lands that could be colonized;

3. To accept gifts for the benefit of Jewish communities or individuals;

4. To establish commercial or agricultural settlements on the lands acquired.

This fund, which still operates to this day, oversaw multiple colonies in the Russian Empire, the Soviet Union, and Latin America. But the Baron de Hirsch's most heavily publicized (and his preferred) project was a network of colonies in Argentina, Santa Fé, Entre Ríos, La Pampa, and Buenos Aires. He argued:

> The Argentine Republic is the true land of the future: there thousands of millions have hitherto been spent for railway constructions. River enlargements, harbor works; all that has been done at large cost and all this exists...Aside from the agricultural and economic status, the political social life aspect of the colonies in Argentina, I maintain, offers the Jews a point of concentration which they will hardly find elsewhere. The area of this country is nine times that of France, while its population does not reach the figure of four millions...there is room and a future for an unlimited number of Jews.[60]

---

60   Baron Maurice de Hirsch, "Memorandum on Palestinian Colonization, 1891", in Kurt Grunwald's *Turkenhirsch: A Study of Baron Maurice de Hirsch Entrepreneur and Philanthropist* (Jerusalem: Israel Program for Scientific Translation, 1966), 63.

Baron de Hirsch's vision for the salvation of Russian Jewry clashed with a nascent political ideology from Europe: the Zionism of Theodor Herzl. The Jewish Colonization Association was wary of settlement in Ottoman Palestine—both Baron de Hirsch and the Alliance, a partner of the JCA, were opposed to it, and thus the JCA took care not to contradict the pro-Empire political line of the Alliance.[61] Yet the Jewish Colonization Association also needed to appeal to potential Russian migrants (especially the Russian Societies in favor of Palestinian Colonization) who, for the most part, had hoped to settle in the Land of Israel. The Baron de Hirsch, wary from his experience building railroads in the Ottoman Empire, was, at least initially, not in favor of any settlement in Ottoman territory at all. An agreement to settle Western Anatolia would necessitate a compromise.

Hirsch and the father of modern Zionism, Theodor Herzl, clashed early on. Having heard of the creation of the Jewish Colonization Association's colonies in Argentina, Herzl requested an interview with the Baron de Hirsch in 1895 and there solicited the Baron's support. He outlined his vision for Jewish national statehood in a letter to the Baron de Hirsch, praising the national successes of German Unification and rhetorically asking him "do you know what the German Reich sprang from? From dreams, songs, fantasies, and gold-black bands worn by students. And that in a brief period of time."[62] Logistically, the Jewish "masses" would be trained through "tremendous propaganda, the popularization of the idea through newspapers, books, pamphlets, lectures, pictures, songs." He waxed, "With a flag you can lead men where you will—even into the Promised Land. Men live and die for a flag; it is indeed the only thing for which they are willing to die in mass." The Baron de Hirsch was apparently put off by the letter, refused a meeting, and refused to support Herzl (and, after his death in 1896, the Baron de Hirsch Fund again refused to finance the World Zionist Organization directly).[63] National statehood, no matter where it might be, was incompatible with the Baron de Hirsch's vision.

---

61   See Aron Rodrigue, *French Jews, Turkish Jews: The Alliance Israélite Universelle and the Politics of Jewish Schooling in Turkey, 1860-1925* (Indiana: Indiana University Press, 1990) and chapter three, "'Under One Great Fraternal Flag': Ashkenazi Jews in Constantinople."

62   Marvin Lowenthal ed., *The Diaries of Theodor Herzl* (New York: Dial Press, 1956), 37.

63   Lowenthal, *Diaries of Theodor Herzl*, 48.

Instead, Hirsch believed that colonization in Palestine was informed by "religious memories and historical traditions," and "however grand and honorable these traditions may be, they do not constitute a sufficiently solid basis wherewith to secure the immigrants in their new fatherland against new vicissitudes and new misfortunes." Hirsch was searching for a practical solution to the "Jewish Question," one that he believed would be compromised in Palestine because of its "proximity to Russia and Europe, the lack of opportunity for expansion, the climate, to which one is unaccustomed." However, what Palestine did have in its favor was "the power of legend."[64] It has been suggested that Hirsch's wariness of Palestine's proximity to Russia was based on a belief that "Palestine was destined to fall into the hands of Russia."[65] Those opposed to the colonies in the Ottoman Empire pointed to Russia as the Ottoman political nemesis and Russia's many attempts throughout ~~history to~~ have jurisdiction over holy sites in Palestine, to control Crimea as a means to access the Mediterranean and global markets. Herzl was quite disappointed in his inability to secure Hirsch's support, and later turned to Lord Nathaniel Rothschild (whose political ideals were more aligned with Herzl's) to finance the World Zionist Organization.

How did the settlement of Western Anatolia, the idea for which Hirsch was so initially skeptical, come about? The answer is both necessity and ideology: necessity because of the numbers of Russian migrants arriving in the capital, and ideology, it seems, due to its proximity to Palestine. The Baron de Hirsch warned the delegation at the Paris meeting in 1891 once more about the hazards of settling in Ottoman territory:

> I point out the danger there is in sending emigrants into Asia and Turkey. I know that land better than anybody, and better than anybody also I am in a position to judge of the misery and deceptions that await the colonists who would be sent there haphazardly.[66]

The Baron de Hirsch continued:

> From the moment that Jews emigrate, it should be done with the view, not of gaining only a few years of tranquility and respite, but with the firm purpose of securing for their posterity rest and stability in the future. Are they sure those

---

64   Grunwald, *Turkenhirsch*, 77.

65   Ibid, 79.

66   Grunwald, *Turkenhirsch*, 126.

that propose to direct the Russian emigrants towards Asiatic Turkey, that these very ones will see any useful result from their labors, and their efforts crowned with success? Are they not afraid to expose them once more to collisions, sooner or later, with their recent persecutors, the Russians? Have they considered that they thus tend to disperse the emigration movement, instead of concentrating it?

Indeed Hirsch wanted Western Anatolia to be the opposite of a *nachtasyl*, as others have suggested.[67] Literally translated as "night quarters," Hirsch's belief was that these colonies needed to be created with intentionality and longevity, something that the geopolitics of the Ottoman Empire could not promise. The colonists and the organization's administrators on the ground in Argentina and Turkey disagreed with the Baron de Hirsch in their positions on a homeland in Palestine.

Thus, the other delegates argued strongly in favor of colonization in Turkey, suggesting that it would provide much needed relief for the Russian Jews crowding Constantinople. Hirsch finally conceded that if "Russian Societies persist in their project, I am quite disposed to place at their disposal both my influence and my active co-operation with the Imperial Ottoman government."[68] The Baron de Hirsch did not stand in the way of consensus, but insisted on sufficient due diligence, and he agreed to "assist them in the negotiations to be undertaken at Constantinople…[to hire delegates to begin an] investigation of the localities more seriously to be considered for an eventual choice, as well as to obtain of the Turkish government the best possible terms."[69]

Initially, the Baron de Hirsch was able to negotiate a free lease on lands in Western Anatolia. The Ottoman administration initiated this arrangement in order to ameliorate the refugee situation in the 1890s. In 1888, the Sublime Porte had decided to

Authorize free access into Palestine to Israelites under the following conditions: their passports should expressly state that they are going to Jerusalem in the performance of a pilgrimage and not for the purpose of engaging in commerce or taking up residence there…for no more than three months.[70]

---

67   See for example Samuel J. Lee's *Moses of the New World* (New York: Thomas Yuselof, 1970).

68   Ibid.

69   Ibid, 123.

70   *Publications of the American Jewish Historical Society* 15 (Baltimore: MD, 1906) 13.

According to the historian Selim Deringil, Sultan Abdülhamid had an "obsession" with the possibility of the Jewish state in Palestine, yet purchases by settlers continued in places like Haifa by Russian settlers.[71] Immigrants, Russian Jews among them, often held Ottoman passports of dubious authenticity, but the Ottoman administration admitted by 1914 that the acquisition of land and the prevention of the "movements of people holding valid passports" were all but impossible.[72] According to a correspondence between the State Department and the American Legation to Constantinople, stories of "restrictive regulations [were] being very cruelly enforced, not only in Palestine but at the various ports around the Syrian coast."[73] Ottoman administrators in the province in Beirut wrote to the Palace and suggested that these Jewish settlers be given Ottoman citizenship and be sent to places like Benghazi. According to a memorandum from the Baron de Hirsch, two members of the Alliance, J. Navon and Michel Erlanger, after a long talk with the former, decided that "Navon believes and, it appears to me rightly so, provided Palestine be waived, the Turkish government will accept a limited number of Jewish immigrants and furnish them gratuitously, or nearly so, the necessary lands."[74] The Baron de Hirsch sent three delegates to negotiate the terms of the purchases with the Ottoman authorities.[75] It later turned out that the Jewish Colonization Association was in fact responsible for purchasing the lands, which it did sometimes in the name of a proxy or in the name of Russian immigrants themselves, but this initial concession may have encouraged the Baron de Hirsch to agree to colonies in Western Anatolia. The Baron de Hirsch would receive his colony, and the Russian immigrants would remain close to Palestine.

71 Deringil, 145.

72 Ibid, 149.

73 Publications of the American Jewish Historical Society 15 (Baltimore: MD, 1906) 14.

74 Baron Maurice de Hirsch, "Carlsbad Memorandum." Kurt Grunwald's *Turkenhirsch: A Study of Baron Maurice de Hirsch Entrepreneur and Philanthropist* (Jerusalem: Israel Program for Scientific Translation, 1966), 125.

75 Ibid, 125.

Joseph Niego, Mikveh Israel, and the Jewish Colonization Association

By the time of his death in 1896, the Baron de Hirsch had lived to see over three thousand immigrants settle in Argentina and hundreds more in Western Anatolia.[76] That same year, Herzl published *Das Judenstaadt*, and the activities of the Jewish Colonization Association in Russia and Turkey gained some ideological independence from their founder. By 1896, the Jewish Colonization Association in Russia decided that young Russians should be given an agricultural education, and a small number were sent to Mikveh Israel outside of Jaffa and Djedeida in Tunisia.[77] After his trip to Argentina in the late 1890s, describing what he thought was a near overcrowding of the colonies there, David Feinberg asked the Jewish Colonization Association to expand its activities in the Russian Empire to allow for consolidation and expansion in the Empire and in Argentina. The JCA in Russia's activities were, for the years following, focused on helping local Jewish farmers working either individually or in colonies to secure loans for the purchase of seed or breeding stock, to support a number of agricultural schools, to help with the financing and supervision of what came to be an extensive network of hundreds of loan *kassas* assistance to vocational schools for boys and girls, totaling eleven thousand pupils. Additionally, these *kassas* funded the establishment of bureaus for emigration from Russia.[78] By 1913, there were 680 *kassas* in Russia with over 450,000 members.[79]

The Russian colonies taught Russian, Hebrew, Polish, and French in their schools. They taught religion and agricultural techniques, and even exhibited their work at the International Exhibition of Horticulture in St. Petersburg in the Spring of 1913.[80] The JCA in Russia was concerned with not only existing farmers in Russia but also recruiting would-be farmers. Despite the general prohibition of owning land, some Jews were able to purchase small plots of land with the JCA's help. "Wherever there was a Jewish farm colony or farmer,

---

76   Edgardo Zablotsky, "Education in the Colonies of the Jewish Colonization Association in Argentina," *Working Paper Universidad del CEMA* (March 2016), No. 585, https://econpapers.repec.org/paper/cemdoctra/585.htm

77   This was done after the Baron de Hirsch's death as he had been vehemently opposed to sending Russian Jews to these schools without a plan for immigration.

78   Norman, *An Outstretched Arm*, 44.

79   Ibid.

80   CAHJP ICA/Lon 46-1.

whatever branch of agriculture he practiced, the tireless JCA agronomists sought him out, made him loans or arranged for the local *kassa* to do it, and gave him instruction." They did this in Minsk, in Novopoltava near Kherson, and in parts of Poland.

Isaac Férnandez (1889-1929), an Italian and Sephardic Jew from Salonica and a member of the board of the Banque de Salonique, succeeded his father as the President of the Regional Committee of the Alliance and also became head of the Constantinople JCA office. Férnandez maintained constant communication with the St. Petersburg Office and other local branches of the JCA's Information Bureaus. In 1870, an emissary of the Alliance, Charles Netter (1826-1882), founded an agricultural school on 750 acres given to the organization by the Turkish government on the outskirts of Jaffa, an important port in Palestine, and called it *Mikveh Israel*, the hope of Israel. He became its first director. Initially, the non-Zionist Alliance and Edmond de Rothschild funded the project, but it would soon take on an ideology of its own as it became a beacon for Zionism. Many immigrants of the first Aliyah passed through the halls and classrooms of Mikveh Israel, often learning agricultural skills for the first time. Netter believed that a development of agricultural techniques for the region would "enable Jews to support a modest European standard of living in Palestine."[81]

Samuel Hirsch became director of Mikveh Israel in 1879, and Joseph Niego, an Ottoman Jew born in Edirne (Adrianople), became his assistant director in 1886. Niego had studied at the Ecole Normale Israélite Orientale, a school funded by the Alliance Israélite Universelle to provide opportunities for "Oriental Jews" where he met his soon-to-be wife, Lea Mitrani, and later studied at the Montpellier and specialized in Agriculture. In 1891, Niego and Lea arrived at Mikveh Israel, pregnant with their first child. Walking through the gardens, they would have likely passed the tombstones of Samuel Hirsch's two children who died of diphtheria at Mikveh Israel.[82]

---

81   Halpern and Reinharz, *Zionism and the Creation of a New Society* (New York: Oxford University Press, 1998).

82   Amalia Levi, *Evanescent Happiness: Ottoman Jews Encounter Modernity, the Case of Lea Mitrani and Joseph Niego (1863-1923)* (Istanbul: Libra Kitap, 2015), 159.

Mikveh Israel Teachers
CAHJP ICA/Tur 369-42

Niego imported and developed an impressive faculty including experts
in zoology, veterinary medicine, horticulture, and oenology as well as
fundamentals in science, mathematics, chemistry, physics, and accounting.
He is often credited with importing eucalyptus trees from Australia in order
to dry up land and prepare it for cultivation.[83] He made it a point to have
representatives of the new Jewish settlements in Palestine attend Mikveh Israel
so that they could, in turn, return to their colonies and help disseminate the
information learned at the school. After five years of instruction at Mikveh
Israel, graduates would go on to seek employment in homes of wealthy Jews
with large properties in Alexandria or Cairo, or they would return to the
pioneering settlements such as Hovevei Tzion.[84]

---

83   Israel Ministry of Education and Culture, "Mikveh Israel," (Jerusalem, Israel: Jerusalem Post Print and
      Offset, 1970).

84   Levi, *Evanescent Happiness,* 160.

From multiple viewpoints, Mikveh Israel was a Zionist project. Many of its directors, certainly most or all of its students, were Zionists. Many of their funders, including Baron Edmond James de Rothschild, were certainly Zionist. But the Alliance maintained its anti-Zionist position. Farming was, for the Alliance, an integral part of the work of "regeneration."[85] Its mission in funding the project was to create a Jewish learning center and to "make the desert bloom." Even David Ben-Gurion, the first Prime Minister of Israel, recalled, "the State was established thanks to Mikveh Israel. If there were no Mikveh Israel, it is doubtful Israel could have been founded then. Everything started then. What we did was to complete the task politically and nationally."[86]

During his years at Mikveh Israel, Niego was careful to not cross any political lines with his employer, the Alliance. While he would later go on to become the first president of the B'nai Brith Lodge in Constantinople, a Zionist hub, he was either walking a political line with his employer or being indifferent towards Herzl's ideas. Herzl visited Mikveh Israel during his tour of Palestine in 1896 and recalls meeting Joseph Niego and Niego's anxiety at being misinterpreted as a Zionist: "I told the director of Mikveh Israel, Niego, I would introduce him to the Emperor [of Austria Hungary], should the latter recognize and speak to me. Niego begged me not to do it, as it might be regarded as a Zionist gesture and prejudice him."[87] Similarly, in a letter back to the Alliance in November of 1896, Niego recalled the visit with Herzl:

> I have the honor of reporting that Dr. Herzl and his companions...visited Mikveh Israel....and requested that I assign them places among the other colonists so that they could be present at the passage of the Emperor's procession on Friday morning....but I made a point to explain to him: "The event that we are organizing at this moment, *I told him, is to be considered under no circumstances as a Zionist event....we are organizing it in order to be appealing to the authorities of the country."*

He goes on:

> I wanted to inform you about these things because it seems to me that certain newspapers will make a lot of noise about the handshaking between the Emperor and Dr. Herzl....I saw Dr. Herzl in Jerusalem again. Because he had not found

85   Rodrigue, *French Jews, Turkish Jews,* 110.

86   Israel Ministry of Education and Culture, *Mikveh Israel* (Jerusalem, Israel: Jerusalem Post Print and Offset, 1970).

87   Marvin Lowenthal, ed. *The Diaries of Theodor Herzl* (New York: Dial Press, 1956), 280-283.

anything decent in any of the hotels…he made it clear he wanted to stay for some days in Mikveh, but in a friendly way I explained to him that I found myself in the difficult position of having to refuse him the hospitality, *because I do not want the authorities of the country to believe that Mikveh is becoming a Zionist center.*[88]

Because these sources are correspondences between Niego and the Alliance, his employer, it is difficult to say concretely whether or not these professional ideas reflected his personal political ideals. On the one hand, he had a responsibility to his employer to maintain their political line, and accommodating Herzl at Mikveh Israel might have impacted the pro-Ottoman position of the Alliance. On the other hand, if we look beyond his employment by the Alliance and the JCA, we know that Niego went on to establish the B'nai B'rith Lodge in Constantinople and became an active Zionist. In his own words in the *Bulletin de la Grande Loge de district XI*, Niego writes that he had "no political interest to support in the Orient," instead declaring "Jews independent" and responsible to work for their "own regeneration, moral and material improvement."[89] In another speech, he maintains that, while the B'nai Brith Lodge will not "take sides for Zionism but also will not condemn [it]…we will give access in our midst to the many supporters of this movement and with it their worth and respectable representatives."[90] In his lectures and talks, Niego always maintained Palestine as the focus of political and cultural regeneration for the Jewish people alongside or within the Ottoman Empire, later the Turkish state, and declared that Palestine should and is "becoming one of the best cultivated provinces of Turkey."[91] Never does he discuss independent statehood. This point is discussed further in chapters two and three.

Because of his wife's poor health, Niego needed to leave Palestine to find her appropriate medical attention. In 1904, Niego arrived in Constantinople and became the Jewish Colonization's Association's "Chief *Agronome*." With the mission of the organization less rigid after the death of the Baron de Hirsch, the Jewish Colonization Association moved to make the colonies in Western

---

88   CAHJP HM 3/338 (also in AIU Turquie LXIV E 770.3), emphasis mine in both quotes.

89   *Bulletin de la Grande Loge de district XI et de la Loge de Constantinople No 678 de B'nai B'rith* (February 1913-1921): 33

90   *Bulletin de la Grande Loge de District XI et de la Loge de Constantinople No. 678*, 1913, p. 113

91   Joseph Niego, "La Palestine," *Cinquante Années de Travail Dans les Oeuvres Juives*, 417 and 425.

Anatolia as a viable, and sometimes temporary, alternative to immigration in Palestine or in Constantinople. Russian Jews, along with Jews from the Aegean, Romania, and Galicia, began to settle in several new colonies or small agricultural settlements. The colonies of Or Yehuda, Hassan Pasha/Messilah Hadasha, Marmoura, and Salizar were funded by the Jewish farmers and the Jewish Colonization Association not only to alleviate the dire circumstances in the short term, but also, at least officially, to provide long-term homes for the Russian Jews. JCA provided support for everything from immigration (via its immigration affairs bureau) and passage to the financing of schools, land purchases, lease agreements, and agricultural equipment. Niego visited these settlements and others in Palestine and Mesopotamia, including sites near Baghdad.[92]

Or Yehuda and the Colonies of Western Anatolia

The idea for Or Yehuda, specifically, seems to have been the result of collaboration between the Alliance and the Jewish Colonization Association. In 1896, the Secretary of the Alliance in Paris, Jacques Bigart, authorized the director of the Alliance school in Izmir, Gabriel Arié, to explore the possibility of purchasing a farm nearby.[93] The following year, the Council of the Jewish Colonization Association voted to establish sixteen graduates of the Jerusalem vocational school of the Alliance Israelite in Palestine and Western Anatolia. The idea was to encourage commercial ties between the Jewish colonies and the surrounding region. In 1898, the JCA purchased 2,600 hectares on a railway line 107 kilometers from Smyrna (Izmir), the main port of Western Anatolia. Or Yehuda, the light of Judah, would become both an agricultural school and a colony.[94] Although the Alliance remained explicitly anti-Zionist and pro-Empire, a point which is central to my argument elsewhere in this monograph, the JCA found common ground with the Alliance's mission civilisatrice, its mission of regeneration through education.[95]

---

92   Joseph Niego, *Cinquante Années de Travail Dans Les Oeuvres Juives,* 20.

93   AAIU, Turquie LXXIV 29 May 1896, 23 November 1896

94   Engin Aktürk, "Osmanlı döneminde Anadolu ve Trakya topraklarında Yahudi Cemaati tarafından kurulan tarım okulları ve Akhisar or Yehuda Tarım Okulu örneğinin mimari incelemesi" (Unpublished MA Thesis: Mimar Sinan Güzel Sanatlar Üniversitesi, 2012).

95   See Aron Rodrigue, *French Jews, Turkish Jews* and chapter three.

The JCA hired an architect from Izmir, M. Magnifico, and the JCA's Central Committee of Agricultural Council in Paris approved the plan in 1900. The property included a school, preschool, cheese mill, wine cellar, dormitory, and shops for ironworking and carpentry. The property contained a vineyard of over six thousand sections where each segment was named after a prominent Jewish figure, including Montefiore (after Moses Montefiore, the British banker and philanthropist), Philippson (the Vice President of the JCA, in whose name several properties were purchased), and Netter (one of the first directors of Mikveh Israel). Budgets between the years 1903-1923 by the Jewish Colonization Association include funding for everything from the colonies in Anatolia, to a *gan,* or preschool, in the Galata neighborhood, to funding the Bank Salonique to an immigration bureau, discussed later in this chapter. As the needs and priorities of Jewish immigrants of the Ottoman Empire evolved, so did the mission of the Jewish Colonization Association.[96]

The "Light of Judah" became a microcosm of the Ottoman world. By 1900, there were ninety-four people on the domain: seventy-six of them were Jewish, and the rest were Greek. In 1919, Albert Kant visited Or Yehuda and "had the great pleasure of finding myself among this small Sephardic community. They seemed to be particularly happy as farmers, something that was very rare for Sephardic Jews in Turkey."[97] He also accounted for a number of Armenian students at the école.[98] Students at the agricultural school included four young men who had come from Mikveh Israel. Sixteen were Romanian (who had to learn French before they could study), and ten students came from the Alliance Schools and were, I assume, Sephardic. In 1910, fifteen more Russian families had landed at Or Yehuda, and by this time were relatively industrious producing grain, fruits, vegetables, tobacco, wool, olives, and grapes. The school contained approximately fifty students, and two groups of Russian immigrants were negotiating for the purchase of lands near Constantinople. A total of 450 students were trained in the school.[99] The relatively successful

---

96   CAHJP ICA/Tur 366-18.

97   Kant, *Mémoires s d'un Fermier Juif*, 122.

98   Ibid.

99   Norman, *An Outstretched Arm*, 108. Also, see CAHJP ICA/Tur 276-1.

olony relied on sharecropping and the expertise of the Palestinian Jewish students from Mikveh Israel and on Joseph Niego.[100]

The Jewish Colonization Association was optimistic after the results of Or Yehuda and another colony, Salizar, and, in 1910, formed an executive committee to expand the projects. Delegates to the committee included Mr. Guinsbourg, Dr. Victor Jacobsohn (a German Jew, member of the WZO, and head of the Anglo-Levantine Banking Company in Constantinople, which was a Zionist front), and Mr. Niego. The committee reviewed additional Russian Jews' appeals to immigrate to Anatolia.[101] At this point, the committee thought of immigration to Anatolia as "distinctly separate from the commission of immigration to Palestine."[102]

Daily life in the *école* of Or Yehuda began at seven o'clock in the morning with breakfast. Depending on the day, the students rotated between religion courses, mathematics, economics, agricultural techniques, botany, geology, veterinary medicine, winemaking, field measurement, construction, and gardening. Instruction was in French, but Hebrew and Turkish were also taught. Recreation began at five o'clock, and dinner was served at seven.[103] In 1908, several Turkish students enrolled in the school for the first time.

Around the same period of time, from 1898-1935, the JCA also became a sponsor of an existing colony in nearby British Cyprus. The idea and initial round of financing came from an organization from East London, Ahavat Zion (*Love of Zion*), which began fundraising to settle in Palestine. However, by 1896, deterred by the Ottoman ban on foreigners purchasing land and by suggestions that Jewish settlers needed "practice" in order to successfully colonize Palestine, the members of Ahavat Zion initiated a more organized and

---

100 For total agricultural exports, see "Anatolia and Istanbul, 1881-1914," Roger Owen's *The Middle East in the World Economy, 1800-1914* (Cornwall, UK: I.B. Tauris, 2002) 189-216. Reports to the Alliance and to the JCA London Office do not discuss the amount of goods sold and exported only the total operating budgets and general conditions of the farms leading me to believe that the majority of the commerce was overseen by the Russian Jews themselves (hence Kant's reluctance to leave Tikfour Tchiflik despite political uncertainly, and to hire additional workers on the farm).

101 See for example Letter from Freydman to Joseph Niego, 3 April (year unknown, but likely 1910-1912), CAHJP ICA/Lon 067-1.

102 Letter to Dr. Sonnenfeld, Director of the JCA, Paris, 6 November 1910. CAHJP ICA. Turkey Box 064, File 8.

103 Ibid.

institutionally supported effort to settle Cyprus.[104] Cyprus came under British control in 1878 at the Congress of Berlin during the conclusion of the Russo-Turkish War (1877-1878). 163 immigrants lived in the colony, sixty-three from Latakia (Syria) and one hundred from Russia.[105] By 1884, faced with tough conditions and little to no agricultural experience, these immigrants slowly filtered out to Alexandria, London, and other parts of Western Europe.[106]

Because of a myriad of factors that complicated the financing of these farms, land was often titled in the name of an Ottoman Jewish citizen. Until the 1858 Land Code, part of the Tanzimat Reforms, foreigners could not hold land in the Ottoman Empire.[107] The new code, partially devised due to foreign financing of railways in the Empire, specified that foreigners, but not foreign organizations, could hold land.[108] Furthermore, the JCA decided to purchase land under the name of specific Ottoman Jews but subtitle them to individuals likely to maintain a strategic position with contiguous plots of land.[109] Additionally, in the sources, the term "colony" is used to refer to many different kinds of agricultural projects, including small farms of just a few hectares. It seems that this was done for organizational purposes since many plots were technically "owned" by the same few names, such as Franz Philippson (b. 1851), a Belgian-Jewish banker who would become a vice

---

104 Ibid, 368. Yehoshua Eisenstadt-Barzilai, the secretary of the executive committee of Hovevei Zion in Jaffa, suggested that the "will to 'make Aliyah' must begin with the love of Zion,'…that there had been much theory, but little practice [in colonization] and this had resulted in many failures…[also] legality and proper procedures were to be scrupulously observed."

105 Yossi Ben-Artzi, "Jewish Rural Settlement in Cyprus 1882-1935: a "Springboard" or a Destiny?" *Jewish History* 21.3/4 (2007) 361-383. Relying on the historical Jewish press and some archival material from the Central Zionist Archives, Ben-Artzi gives a brief overview of Jewish settlement in Palestine and suggests that Cyprus was used as a kind of "spring board" for Zionist settlement in Palestine for a few families but that ultimately the challenges of pioneering such difficult terrain deterred many from actually moving to Palestine. See especially page 100.

106 Ibid. The JCA in Turkey received many memoranda concerning Margo Tchiflik (the Cyprus settlement) and seemed to be somewhat involved in stabilizing the colony, especially after a bad bout of malaria. It purchased additional lands, Cholmkchi and Kouklia near Margo-Tchiflik, in order to create a contiguous settlement (per the policy of the JCA) and to create an agricultural learning center in Cyprus. The JCA began to sponsor exchanges with Palestine (which was quite close) and with Mikveh Israel, recruiting its more experienced teachers. The new settlement included three families from Ahavat Zion from the first settlement but gained momentum as new refugees came from Russia and Eastern Europe.

107 See Şevket Pamuk, *The Ottoman Empire and European Capitalism, 1820-1913: Trade, Investment and Production* (Cambridge, UK: Cambridge University Press, 2010) 104-106.

108 Ibid.

109 Report from E. Krause to JCA, CAHJP ICA/Tur 237-4.

president of the Jewish Colonization Association.[110] Sometimes, properties would also be purchased in Férnandez's name or other wealthy Ottoman Jewish subjects.[111] For example, in a letter dated 11 April 1910, Férnandez, the president of the JCA Constantinople chapter, wrote to the organization in Paris that their letter to the colonies of Anatolia had been transmitted to him, the letter regarding the properties of Monsieur Taranto in whose name several properties had remained in the colony of Marmoure. Unfortunately, the Ottoman government refused to transfer the title to the settlers' names because of their foreign citizenship, and so a lien remained in Monsieur Taranto's name. A delegation from Belgium was sent to negotiate the transfer into the name of Monsieur Philippson, a future president of the JCA (1919-1929), and proof of nationality was imperative; the first document they sent in May of 1910 was "inoperable." A list of settlers, divided according to family, was produced, with the total sums loaned and the total number of securities or shares owned in the farm. Monsieur Taranto agreed to return 564,525 piasters plus interest to the Jewish Colonization Association. In Hassan Pasha (Messilah Hadasha), the property had been acquired by the name of Philippson for families coming from Novoselytsia. After three to five years, once the families were able to become Ottoman subjects and completely liquidate their affairs in Russia, the titles were transferred into their names.[112] Importantly, since Ottoman citizenship was necessary for the purchase of land in Palestine, this was an important step in the move toward owning land in the Land of Israel.

Where were these Russian Jews coming from? The records of the Jewish Colonization Association indicate immigrants traveling from Bessarabia, Kiev, Odessa, and Novoselytsia. Many of the colonists, such as the Kant family, retained their foreign (Russian) passports to move past Ottoman authorities while other colonists did apply for Ottoman citizenship. They did not seem to have problems if their final destination was not Palestine. One group in particular wanting to immigrate to Constantinople from Novoselytsia was "desperate to become Ottoman subjects," writes the delegation. [113] According

---

110 Interestingly, Franz Philippson was the son of Ludwig Philippson who founded the German paper *Allgemeine Zeitung des Judenthums.* See Ezriel Carlebach, "Allgemeine Zeitung des Judentums" *Encyclopedia Judaica* 2.1 (Detroit: Macmillan Reference USA) 670-671.

111 Letter from Niego, 5 September 1911, to Férnandez about the immigration committee. See also Rodrigue, *French Jews, Turkish Jews,* 137.

112 Letter from Niego, 5 September 1911, to Férnandez.

113 Letter from D. Yravois, Sant, CAHJP ICA/Lon 64-2. See also CAHJP ICA/Tur 369-42.

to the letters from hopeful immigrants that were preserved at the Jewish Colonization Association, these Russian Jews had at least some contact with the Information Bureaus prior to their departures and often used the Jewish Colonization Association in order to safely transport money to the next port.[114] Because of high demand, the Jewish Colonization Association argued that a separate office needed to be formed that dealt specifically with immigration. By the January 19, 1911, that office was opened and staffed by Mr. Joseph, a Russian Jew who spoke Russian, Hebrew, Yiddish, German, and French. The office was located in the Galata quarter, No. 21 Saint Pierre Han.[115] The Jewish Colonization Association helped to finance the operations of this office and, by 1912, constituted the majority of its budget.[116]

On the 5 of September, 1911, Férnandez, the President of the Committee of Immigration, sent a letter discussing the arrival of Russian Jews interested in acquiring land for agricultural settlement. Letters from Russian Jews living in Odessa, Novoselytsia, and other cities, forwarded by the St. Petersburg Jewish Colonization Association office to the Constantinople office, suggest that the Russian immigrants were willing and able to come if given the support and necessary documents.[117]

The Jewish Colonization Association's offices in St. Petersburg and in Constantinople exchanged correspondence on matters of migration. One letter, written in Yiddish, is particularly interesting because it was signed by ten Russian Jewish men, presumably on behalf of their families, working on JCA Russia projects, encouraging Ottoman and Russian Jews to join them in the colonies.[118] The September of 1913 letter, which was sent at the same time as the Botanical Exposition in St. Petersburg, describes the Kralerman Colony, which contained 40 hectares of land, as a place of "forests and lakes where fish can be caught."[119]

---

114 ICA/Turkey CAHJP ICA/Tur 237-2.

115 Letter to Monsieurs, 19 Janvier 1911, from Férnandez, CAHJP ICA/Tur 237-2.

116 CAHJP ICA/Tur 366-18.

117 CAHJP ICA/Turk 067-1. I would like to thank Elly Moseson for his help in translating these letters from Yiddish.

118 Central Archive for the History of the Jewish People, ICA/Tur 237-2.

119 Ibid.

In 1912, the Jewish Colonization Association compiled a list of Russian families either already in route to Constantinople or who were interested in acquiring land in the colonies. For the first time, the Jewish Colonization Association indicated that these families had some funds of their own (in Rubles) and designated a reference and a profession. Wary of the slow start in the colonies, the JCA needed to ensure that these families were able and trained to ensure success in Western Anatolia. A list of sixteen families, which includes fifty-five total individuals, all from Kiev, was compiled with the names, ages, current addresses, references, professions, and their "fortunes in Rubles."[120] The Friedel family, for example, intended to immigrate with eight total family members, including sons and daughters, from ages fifty-eight to five. The Friedel's family reference is an Arthur Bolomoniwitz Frankel, the proprietor of a sugar factory in Kiev. Their total assets include a building with a value of 354,000 rubles, and forty thousand rubles in cash. His profession is listed simply as an "agriculteure [sic]" or an "agriculturalist."[121] Many extended families, including the Elliokum Family, the Sohmelke, the Tchijik, the Kosorowitzky, the Kerzmann, and the Oratowsky families, are also on the list for immigration. They claimed to be agriculturalists and with anywhere between four thousand and twelve thousand rubles in cash, many of them extended family members, are also on the list for immigration. References listed include landlords, a banker, and the "*Société Alexandrowskaja des fabriques de sucre département de la fabrique de sucre de Maharinze*," suggesting that the Kosorowitzsky family had made their way to Kiev from an area near Archangelsk, in Northern Russia.[122] Another family on that list was the Kant family, from a town near the Danube River. The following year, in 1913, they would purchase plots of land on Tikfour Tchiflik.

---

120 CAHJP ICA/Tur 373- 71.

121 Ibid.

122 Ibid.

Table 1.0:
List of Russian Jewish Families Seeking to Purchase Land at Or Yehuda, CAHJP ICA/TUR 373-71

No.	List of Russian families that will acquire the property						Net worth in rubles
	Name	Age	Address	References	Profession		
1	Friedel Margulis	52	M. Pliskowo (Gov.) Kiew, Russia	Arthur Solomonowitz Frankel, owner of a sugar plant in Kiew (No. 11 Proresnaya Street)	Farmer		Furniture in Pliskow value of 3 to 4,000 rubles In cash: Forty thousand rubles (40,000)
	his wife, Chajé	43					
	his son, David	19					
	his son, Moïse	18					
	his son, Joseph	8					
	his daughter, Rachel	12					
	his daughter, Perla	10					
	his daughter, Bassie	5					
2	Elkone Margulis, son of preceding	28	M. Pliskowo (Gov.) Kiew, Russia	Smerinka (Gov. Podolsky) Russian Bank of Commerce and Industry	idem, together with his father		
	his wife, Seldé	26					
	his son, Jeschua	8					
	his daughter, Mehama	6					
3	Elliokum Margulis, son of first entry	24	M. Pliskowo (Gov.) Kiew, Russia	Land owner with Mr. Langué in Lipowitz. Village of Napodowska	idem		In cash: Four thousand rubles (4,000)
	his wife, Nehamé	23					
4	David Schmelke (son-in-law of F. Margulis)	26	M. Pliskowo (Gov.) Kiew, Russia	Wezaïmé Credit (Credit Union) in Lipowitz	Farmer with his father-in-law		In cash: 3,000 rubles (three thousand)
	his wife, Freide	24					
	his son, Abraham	4					
	his daughter, Sarah	2					

5	Wolf Tchijik	52	M. Pliskowo (Gov.) Kiew, Russia	M.B. Galpérin, sugar manufacturer in Kiev. Office in Kiev	Farmer	Furniture in Pliskow value of 3,000 rubles. In cash: 15,000 rubles. (Fifteen thousand)
	his wife, Rachel	50				
	his son, David	19				
	his son, Abraham	12				
	his son, Moïse	10				
	his son, Jonné	8				
	his son, Israel	6				
	his son, Isaac	5				
	his daughter, Rifka	20				
6	Gerz Kosorowitzky	46	Zernorutka Station (Gov.), Kiew	Alexandrowskaja company of sugar manufacturers, Department of sugar manufacuring of Maharinzé. Offices in Kiew. ———— Credit Union of Kasatine	Farmer	Furniture with a value of 3,000 rubles (three thousand) In cash: 16,000 rubles
	his wife, Malka	39				
	his son, Zundl	20				
	his son, Pinhas	12				
	his son, Kalman	7				
	his son, Herschel	6				
	his daughter, Sarah	17				
	his daughter, Deborah	14				
	his daughter, Rosa	4				
7	Baruch Kosorowitzky (son of preceding)	21	Zernorutka Station (Gov.), Kiew	idem.	Farmer, with his father	In cash: 3,000 rubles (three thousand)
	his fiancée, Manié	19				

8	Joseph Kosorowitzky	58	Zernorutka Station (Gov.), Kiew	idem.	idem.	Fortune of families number 8, 9, 10, 11, and 12 altogether is: Furniture of a value of 1,500 rubles. An oil mill of a value of 3,500 rubles. In cash: 12,000 rubles (twelve thousand)
	his wife, Sobel	56				
	his son, Israel	27				
9	Sundel Kosorowitzky (son of preceding)	36	Zernorutka Station (Gov.), Kiew	idem.	idem	
	his wife, Malka	33				
	his daughter, Sarah	8				
	his daughter, Deborah	5				
10	Pinhas Kosorowitzky (son of Joseph)	33	Zernorutka Station (Gov.), Kiew	idem.	idem.	
	his wife, Fannie	30				
	his son, Leb	4				
	his daughter, Deborah	2				
11	Abraham Kosorowitzky (son of Joseph)	31	Zernorutka Station (Gov.), Kiew	idem.	idem.	idem.
	his wife, Ethel	28				
	his son, Leb	5				
	his daughter, Bassé	3				
12	Isaac Winegrad (son-in-law of Joseph Kosorowitzky)	31	Zernorutka Station (Gov.), Kiew	idem.	idem.	idem.
	his wife, Rachel	28				
	his daughter, Tobé	3				

13	Jacob Kosorowitzky	38	Zernorutka Station (Gov.), Kiew	idem.	idem	In cash: 15,000 rubles. (fifteen thousand)
	his wife, Hanna	35				
	his daughter, Tobé	4				
	his daughter, Deborah	1				
14	Michel Kosorowitzky	42	Zernorutka Station (Gov.), Kiew	idem.	idem.	Furniture of a value of 2,000 rubles (two thousand) In cash: 4,000 rubles (four thousand)
	his wife, Miriam	38				
	his son, Haïm	13				
	his son, Schalom	10				
15	Mendel Kerzmann	37	Village of Wernirgorodok Berditschev Ouyez (Gov.) Kiew	idem.	farmer	In cash: 7,000 rubles (seven thousand)
	his wife, Sarah	35				
	his son, Jacob	12				
	his daughter, Hanna	9				
	his daughter, Bassé	7				
16	Elia Hersch Oratowsky	34	Dzunko Ouyezd in Lipowitz (Gov.) Kiew.	Credit Union in Lipowitz	farmer	In cash: 5,000 rubles (five thousand)
	his wife, Havé	32				
	his son, Idel	14				

Love, Labor, and Zionism: Albert Kant and Tikfour Tchiflik

The Kant family left their home in Kiliya in early 1913 and travelled to Odessa where they caught a steam ship heading for Constantinople. On the ship were many Jewish immigrants from their town but also from Bessarabia, Odessa, and parts of Poland. Some were en route to Palestine, others to South and North America, but all, Kant describes, were "filled with hope, with different desires and ambitions." [123]All held Russian passports.

Later that year, Zeilik Itsov Kant and his wife, Rivka, together with a few partners and with the help of the JCA, purchased two thousand hectares for 13,000 Lira (approximately 11,818 pounds sterling, or 674,000 BP in today's value) and named it Tikfour Tchiflik, five kilometers from the port city of Panderma on the Sea of Marmara.[124] Even the name Tikfour Tchiflik is symbolic. Tikfour, the French spelling of the Ottoman *tekfur,* refers to sovereign, Christian governors in Thrace and Anatolia in the early Ottoman period.[125] Tchiflik, *Çiftlik* in modern Turkish, means "the Farm." Like the name suggests, perhaps the Kants envisioned themselves as autonomous "governors" or "protectorates" of their farm under Ottoman rule.

Kant's story was common among Jewish agriculturalists in the Ottoman borderlands.[126] Despite their initial decision to join these projects because of the financial opportunity and the projects' proximities to the "historic homeland of the Jewish People in Palestine," the migrants' political and ideological affiliations turned out to be malleable once they arrived.[127] Financial constraints, familial responsibilities, and discouraging news from Palestine deterred migrants from moving on the Palestine. Kant's plans were also both inspired and complicated by falling in love with two women: Rachel

---

123 Kant, *Mémoires d'un Fermier Juif,* 29-30.

124 Kant, *Mémoires d'un Fermier Juif,* 37 and 112. Kant mentions that the seller of the property believed it to be the former land of Ali Paşa of Tepedelenli (1741-1818). For exchange rates, see Şevket Pamuk, *Osmanlı İmparatorluğu'nda Paranın Tarihi* (Istanbul: Türkiye İş Bankası Kültür Yayınları, 2017), 226.
Şevket Pamuk, *A Monetary History of the Ottoman Empire* (Cambridge: Cambridge University Press, 2000).
There is also a helpful calculator available online from the National Archives, http://bit.ly/1lpmaZK

125 Hasan Çolak, "Tekfur, fasiliyus, and kayser: Disdain, Negligence and Appropriation of Byzantine Imperial Titulature in the Ottoman World," in Marios Hadjianastasis' *Frontiers of the Ottoman Imagination* (Leiden: Brill, 2014) 5-28.

126 See Letters from Migrants to JCA, CAHJP ICA/Turk 067-1.

127 Albert Kant, *Mémoires d'un Fermier Juif,* 65

Behar, a Sephardic Jew from Panderma who later left for Palestine, as well as Masya Srebskis, a Russian migrant whom Kant seriously considered joining. These were the experiences of Kant and other Russian Jews in the Ottoman borderlands and in Constantinople that ultimately informed their decisions to remain in the Ottoman Empire.

Kant and his father spent their day monitoring and helping laborers pick and process wheat, and transporting the grain to a depot in Panderma (Bandırma).[128] In the evenings, the farmers of Tikfour Tchiflik gathered and discussed current events and issues of the farm, often breaking up into groups of men and women to socialize and discuss life in Turkey.[129] Kant and another partner on the farm, I. Goldenberg, were even kidnapped by bandits. The bandits were illiterate, and Kant wrote his own ransom notes, only asking his father to send ten thousand Russian rubles instead of ten thousand Turkish lira, worth about half.[130] Several days later, the bandits figured out the scheme and beat up Kant.[131] Goldenberg also describes another encounter with bandits: "violent blows shook the door of the house...A troop of shaggy warriors, armed to the teeth, stormed into the hall, demanding money." While his mother cried "*Aman* ['pity' in Ottoman], my father took the man who seemed to be their leader to the closet where in a box, hid the money in the household. He gave them its content."[132] He continues that the bandits left the house with Albert Kant's father, took him to the stable, took their horses, "scared him...[and] cut off half his mustache."[133] It was around this time, when life was difficult around the farm, that Kant fell in love with Rachel Behar, who later left for Palestine in 1918 with her family. Kant lamented that perhaps he should have followed her to the place that was "dear to us both,"

---

128 Kant, *Mémoires d'un Fermier Juif,* 62.

129 Kant, *Mémoires d'un Fermier Juif,* 42.

130 Kant, *Mémoires s,* 62-63. It is unclear from the source material whether there is any relation to Alfred Goldenberg.

131 Kant, *Mémoires,* 63.

132 *Les Cahiers de l'AIU,* Tuesday, 1 December 1998, 31.

133 Ibid. There is an expansive literature on bandits and vigilantes in the Ottoman provinces at the service of the Ottoman State. For the sixteenth and seventeenth centuries, see Karen Barkey, *Bandits and Bureaucrats: The Ottoman Route to State Centralization,* (Ithaca: Cornell University Press, 1994). See also Cihan Özgün, "A Town under the Shadow of Bandits in the Late Ottoman Empire: Kuşadası," *History Studies International Journal Of History* 4.4 (2012). These ideas are further elaborated in chapter four, "Memory and Memoire: Tevye's Ottoman Daughter."

but eventually, "little by little, my original kernel of Zionism went away."[134] It would not be reinvigorated until his arrival in Constantinople.

The First World War and subsequent Greek occupation (1918-1922) made life on the farm dangerous for the Kant family and their companions, and Jewish families moved between larger towns and cities as conditions worsened on the farm. The Kants continued to operate Tikfour Tchiflik by employing laborers while they sought refuge in Panderma, which Kant describes as a multi-cultural town made up of mostly Armenians, Circassians, and Greeks. Meanwhile, the Kants received word that the Ottoman authorities began to exploit the farm for newly resettled Bulgarian immigrants during the population exchanges.[135] Conditions were difficult, and an outbreak of Spanish Flu forced the Kants to move again, this time to Constantinople.[136] At the conclusion of the war, Kant and his family took an overnight ship, the *Gülcemal,* to Constantinople: "We were relatively happy to be able to go to the capital of the country that symbolized freedom and a better life to us."[137]

The period between the Balfour Declaration (1917) and the Russian Civil War (1917-1922) increased the number of Russian and Russian Jews in Constantinople. This was an exciting time for Kant, and he felt that the city became "cosmopolitan" by the presence of these Russians:

> There I could see the arrival of the first Russian émigrés who fled from the advancing victorious Bolshevik armies. All types of people were there: the rich, the poor, the lower-middle class, the aristocrats, those of the nobility and the military such as generals, officers and soldiers…In all the streets of Constantinople, you could hear Russian.[138]

He describes the "new" Constantinople, a city where "all these masses of people gave a new look to the city, half cosmopolitan, half Middle Eastern. Their dances woke up the city, which had been asleep in its orientalism."[139] Most importantly, he describes encountering the work of Theodor Herzl, "who fought for the establishment of a Jewish state in the ancient Jewish homeland,

---

134   Kant, *Mémoires,* 119.

135   Kant, *Mémoires,* 68. See chapter four, "Memory and Memoire: Tevye's Ottoman Daughter" for an analysis of Russian and Sephardic Jews' relations among various ethnic minorities, including bandits and Ottoman administrators.

136   Kant, *Mémoires,* 66-67.

137   Kant, *Mémoires,* 68.

138   Kant, *Mémoires,* 96.

139   Kant, *Mémoires,* 98.

Palestine, which seemed possible to realize after the Balfour Declaration, and it was necessary for that ideal to be ours, of all of the Jews."[140]

He began visiting bookstores in Constantinople, filling his dresser drawer in the Rubin Hotel with books and visiting with his friends, the Srouleviches, to discuss "postwar themes…communism, Bolshevism, the Russian Revolution…and the struggle for independence by a handful of Jews in Palestine which looked promising."[141] Kant met a Dr. Nemirovsky at the home of Haymovitch, who "brought a…fervent Zionism."[142] Kant writes that he

> Often went and listened with emotion to these elders talking about the role that the youth plays, particularly after the famous declaration of the British Minister Balfour. *It is necessary to go to Palestine as soon as possible in order to have our "home,"* they said. Nemirovsky's ideas and those of his friends ignited my passion, and with my whole heart I agreed with them. But the farm with all its family complications held me back. And I could not make any promises.[143]

Kant is quite obviously torn between his ideological (and perhaps, sometimes religious) longing to go to Palestine on the one hand and his commitment to the Ottoman capital and to Tikfour Tchiflik on the other. While he was happy to go to the "capital of the country that symbolized freedom and a better life," Zionism "ignited" a "passion" that he agreed with his "whole heart."[144]

Among his new Russian friends in Constantinople was a young woman named Masya Srebskis, a Russian migrant whose Zionist idealism seemed to reinforce his own. They begin to discuss Zionist ideas with friends in Turkish cafés in the city. In the "oriental environment" of the cafés, Kant and his companions spoke Russian and Yiddish:

> Late in the night, we stayed in the dining room which was well heated by the *petchka* (wall stove). Our friends told us about their lives in Russia during the First World War and the Revolution, the vicissitudes of their long journey from the Ukraine to Constantinople, which was so difficult and filled us into the current situation in Palestine where they hoped to go as soon as possible.[145]

---

140 Kant, *Mémoires*, 90.

141 Kant, *Mémoires*, 69.

142 Kant, *Mémoires*, 85.

143 Ibid.

144 Kant, *Mémoires*, 65, 68.

145 Kant, *Mémoires*, 131.

As he recalls his relationship with Srebskis, Kant begins to recount the development of his idea to move to Palestine and leads to one of two opportunities when he most seriously contemplates leaving which overlap with a love interest. Despite the fact that his feelings for Srebskis may have colored his recollections, the way that he describes Srebskis reveals his ideological motivations for moving to Palestine. Kant recalls in his memoir that she remembered a "happy and carefree" childhood in Europe, but "after the year 1917, the torments began and she barely washed ashore in Constantinople."[146] During their walks along the shores of the Bosporus, Kant describes her as having a "'Zionist' faith [that] rendered her stoic and gave her the strength to fight bravely with her younger brother to realize their plan."[147] It was in the "magnificent city" that the two would discuss Russian politics, culture, literature, "and … many new social perspectives, matters and such, which were already emerging during the formation of a new society that imposed itself in communist Russia."[148]

After expressing their love and adoration for each other, and after a brief period of separation while Kant returned to Tikfour Tchiflik to attend to business on the farm, Srebski suggested to Kant that he come with her to Palestine. Kant describes the conversation: "Masya had ruminated a lot and came up with plans so that I too could go with her to Palestine. She said she loved me very much, that we understood each other and that it was a pity for us to leave behind a happy future union."[149] Kant writes that he had agreed with Srebski but seemed to be torn mostly between his love for her and his responsibilities to his family. He recalls that

> In my heart, I agreed with what she said and proposed, but my honesty and my fidelity to my family handicapped these audacious plans…When she spoke to me with her sweet voice, and made her graceful impression, her reasoning penetrated the bottom of my heart, but when I looked at our farm and my family that lived with difficulty and in fear, I felt awful thinking about leaving them.[150]

---

146 Kant, *Mémoires*, 134.

147 Kant, *Mémoires*, 133.

148 Kant, *Mémoires*, 134.

149 Kant, *Mémoires*, 134.

150 Ibid.

Kant then shared Srebski's idea with his father and sister at the dinner table, hoping to "demonstrate to Masya the disaster that my departure to Palestine would cause," to which his father whole-heartedly agreed and his sister, Esther, immediately started to cry "when talking about the various dangers that would befall them all if I left them in this situation."[151] It is not clear from this passage what part exactly he "agreed" with, either the plans for a life together, plans for a life in Palestine specifically, or a mix of the two. Despite the impossibility of Kant following Srebskis to Palestine, the Kant family nonetheless affirmed the importance of her plan, and their full support of it. When they ask her about her future life in Palestine and her plans there, she replied: "that she was going there as a pioneer and that she would do everything necessary to help strengthen the position of the Jews in their former homeland."[152] In his recollections, Kant supported this vision of Zionism, representative of the more ideologically motivated of the Second Aliyah (1904-1914). He interjects his opinion regarding her decision to leave for Palestine and reveals his support of the Zionist pioneers:

> Her ideals were well anchored in her heart. It was absolutely necessary to overcome the difficulties and pave the way for millions of suffering Jews who were experiencing a degrading life in the majority of countries in Europe, the Americas and elsewhere. My father watched this frail and young person, and shaking his head he told her with little conviction: "My child, I wish that God comes to your aid." To which Masya answered immediately: "You have all been waiting for 2000 years for God to help you and bring you out of the miserable situation in which you are trapped. This continual waiting on prayers has given nothing. We must act with other ideals and we will succeed because we believe otherwise.[153]

Kant certainly paints Srebskis as an idealist, as almost an early Manya Shochat kind of figure who believed in a self-help vision of Jewish settlement in Palestine.[154] Kant and his father agree with her sentiments, which they express as offering prayers of support, but, as Srebskis interjected, faith alone would not help her accomplish her goals in Palestine.

---

151 Kant, *Mémoires*, 165-166.

152 Kant, *Mémoires*, 165-166.

153 Kant, *Mémoires*, 169.

154 Raḥel Yanait Ben-Zvi, *Before Golda, Manya Shochat: A Biography* (New York: Biblio Press, 1989).

After Srebskis departed for Palestine, Kant's own ideas surrounding Zionism and immigration to Palestine began to develop. He remained in touch with the Srebskis and other families who moved to Palestine and read about the goings on in the various foreign presses available in Constantinople.

Indeed, it seemed that Kant's Zionism was ignited more so in Constantinople than it was in the realities of agricultural life in Tikfour Tchiflik; in fact, his experiences there, if anything, kept him away from Palestine. For example, Kant describes a Russian "back to the land" Zionist named Falic who came to work on a farm nearby:

> He was a good man, tall and strong. With help from his sons, he began plowing in some Bessarabian clothes, plowing his fields, surrounded by our Muslim farmers who were continually surprised by his gestures. Without resources or opportunities, the children in this colony, a girl of 9 and two boys of 10 and 12, did not study apart from their prayers that their father, who was very pious and very devout, taught them. Although the new arrivals pleased us with their presence, I personally had no interesting contact with them. This Falic wanted to impose the Zionist system of "back to earth" here at the farm, but among a population who had other ideals ... it all meant very little.[155]

Unfortunately Kant does not say much about this Bessarabian family working on Tikfour Tchiflik, but the "back to earth" Zionism clearly does not resonate with Kant or the "population with other ideals," and this theme resounds throughout the memoir. From this passage and others, it seems like Tikfour Tchiflik was more of an economic opportunity that relied on hiring labor rather than a proto-nationalist project. For Kant, despite his desire to move to Palestine, his ideals seem to be more impressed upon him during his time in Constantinople.

It was something in the nexus between family commitments and the news that increased Jewish immigration had caused friction between Jews and Arabs in Palestine that prevented him from going:

> All my explanations, maps and promises that they would come and join me one day did not squash their justified opposition. Sure, I could have gone without their consent, but we were bound together by exceptional familial links *that did not allow me to do what I should have done.* My struggle with my family and other issues continued for some held off on my plan to go to Palestine.[156]

---

155 Kant, *Mémoires*, 109-110.

156 Kant, *Mémoires*, 100, my emphasis.

Thus, the reasons for not moving to Palestine were often practical rather than ideological. Many Jewish farmers such as Kant chose not to go to Palestine, deterred by yet another international move, "complete insecurity," and the fact that the majority of their wealth was tied up in their land, which, in some cases, came into government possession.[157] Despite his feelings that moving to Palestine was what he "should have done," the practical outweighed his initial ideological goals. Kant remained in the Ottoman Empire (and after 1923, the Turkish Republic) for these reasons, but he still proselytized the Zionist cause to his Russian friends, who,

> Although they listened to me sympathetically...[they were not] enthusiastic about the idea of going to Palestine, which for them was distant and unknown. They were generally religious practitioners, but their civic duty was hardly developed, and so I had to awaken in them other considerations and feelings as permanent as the founders had hoped.[158]

Kant's invocation of "civic" duty as something that is developed, rather than inevitable with religious affiliation, suggests that Kant's politics and identity are linked to secular ideas of nationalism and statehood, consistent with the ideas of many early Zionists. It is also a fascinating reversal of the claims we see Sephardic Jews and the Alliance Israélite Universelle making throughout this period: that Zionism is a dangerous byproduct of overly religious, backward, Russian Jews, unlike the modern, patriotic "Ottoman" (Sephardic) Jews.[159]

Despite his Zionist sympathies and affiliations, Kant nonetheless interacted with and engaged in Ottoman life and culture. He describes his father eventually shaving off his own beard, a physical symbol of religious observance, and begins to learn Ottoman from the Hodjas, a neighboring Turkish family.[160] He also expresses particularly nationalist sentiments surrounding his description of the Greco-Turkish War (1919-1922):

---

157 Kant, *Mémoires*, 85, 92.

158 Kant, *Mémoires*, 90.

159 See for example, *El Tiempo* 26 December 1910; *El Tiempo* 6 January 1911; *El Tiempo* 1 June 1911; *El Tiempo* 5 June 1911; and *El Tiempo* 9 August 1911. See also the letter from Bigart to Nahum, Esther Benbassa, *A Sephardic Chief Rabbi in Politics, 1892–1923*, trans. Miriam Kochan (Tuscaloosa: University of Alabama Press, 1995).

160 Kant, *Mémoires*, 69, 88.

They thought this invasion would be easy and quick after the defeat of the Turkish armies at the end of the World War in 1918 and the occupation of Constantinople and other Turkish territories by the Allies with the help of the English supplies and money. If they had known then the types of defeats they would so enthusiastically encounter, they would not have so easily and cheerfully left their country. Their plan of easy conquest was perhaps normal when looking at the political horizon of a feeble Turkey. Who could have imagined that a Turkish general, a pawn of a definitively defeated army, would arrive with a broken army to hunt all the invaders of the Turkish national territory, in particular the Greeks, in such an energetic manner and almost throw them into the sea.[161]

By the time of Turkish Statehood and the "reforms" of Atatürk, the Kants' farm was employing Circassians and Muslim laborers, and the Kants moved back to Constantinople.

Interestingly, Kant seems to maintain a cultural orientation toward Russia. He describes the period when he arrived in Constantinople from Bandırma "thirsty to talk with the young people from Russia who were generally cultivated and intellectual, and I took great pleasure talking to these young men and women."[162] Although Bandırma had some Jewish families, including Sephardic families, Kant preferred to discuss Russian high culture and literature with others well versed in those topics. At multiple points of his memoir, Albert Kant invokes his Russophile taste in literature and in culture. He "admired Tolstoy" and recalls sitting by the stove and discussing the ideas of "Turgenev, Zola, and Hugo,"[163] and central to his relationship with Masya Srebskis was her understanding of these authors and their conversations about them.[164]

Benjamin Sperer (1921-2021), the grandson of Russian migrants who arrived in Galata decades prior, recounts a much different orientation. Sperer's father, Samuel "Shmulik" Sperer, worked for an Austrian company, and was raised speaking German and Yiddish rather than Russian.[165] While Sperer was too young to recount the Russian Civil War, Kant describes the Russian migrants and migrants who arrived in Constantinople at the Hotel Gendelman,

---

161 Kant, *Mémoires*, 69, 88.

162 Kant, *Mémoires*, 128

163 Kant, *Mémoires*, 11. While these are not all Russian authors, Russian high literary culture regarded French literature and culture in the highest esteem.

164 Ibid.

165 Benjamin Sperer, *Under Turkish Skies* (Istanbul: Libra Kitap, 2017), 17

The Jewish youth of Russia was much more distraught spiritually after the debacle of the Russian monarchy. Many young people had great hope of a better life through the socialism of Kerensky, and then Lenin, and everyone especially hoped that the new government would be a regime of liberty and equality, which could finally be enjoyed by the millions of beings belonging to the Jewish minority.[166]

It is clear to see that Kant is quite sympathetic with the idealism of these "Russian youth," and he understands that there still exists a possibility of returning to Russia. While these descriptions happen well into Kant's memoir, they reflect the overall nostalgic tone of his memoir. His descriptions of Kiliya, his affinity for Russian high culture, and of course later, his politics—contrast starkly with the realism of Sperer's descriptions. On the very first page of his memoir, Sperer describes his family as part of the Russian Jews who arrived in Constantinople "fleeing the long knives of marauding Cossacks who frequently galloped through Jewish villages, the vodka bottle in one hand and their sharp sabers in the other, killing and raping whoever crossed their paths."[167]

The End of the Jewish Colonization Association in Western Anatolia and "Enchanting Constantinople"

Tikfour Tchiflik was seized and disposed of by the Turkish government at the end of the First World War. The Jewish Colonization Association decided to stop investing any money into Tikfour Tchiflik, and Kant spent more and more time on the farm to try to make it profitable. By 1919, they were able to repurchase the farm by sowing wheat, barley, oats, and flax.[168] Later, they added livestock to the production of the farm, and as Kant describes, it was through "much effort, attention, patience and above all perseverance."[169] By February of 1919, additional lands were still being purchased under Franz Philippson's name. Férnandez updated the Jewish Colonization Association office in London; it was difficult to buy and sell parcels as the military government made claims on large pieces of land.[170] Russian subjects slowly left for Palestine during the First World War and immediately after, during the

---

166 Kant, *Mémoires d'un Fermier Juif en Turquie,* 128-29

167 Sperer, *Under Turkish Skies,* 13.

168 Kant, *Mémoires,* 117.

169 Kant, *Mémoires,* 117.

170 CAHJP ICA/Tur 11-40.

British Mandate period. Smaller numbers of Russian Jews tried their fortunes in other Turkish cities, like Izmir and Istanbul, and some even made it to North America (to cities like Montreal and New York) and made claims to lands left behind in the colonies.[171]

Colonists experienced firsthand the imminent collapse of the First World. In a letter to the Commanding General of the British Army, the Jewish Colonization Association wrote to beg for protection for the Mesila Hadasha colony just outside of Istanbul, eighteen kilometers from the Üsküdar district of today's Istanbul. The British army had been camping nearby, and the Jewish Colonization Association offered the army accommodations in exchange for some protections. The "neighboring Turks" had taken "advantage of the foreign states of the colony" and had occupied these lands.[172] The colony had been "consistently ruined by a band of Kemalists and had suffered from forest fires," likely because these same "Kemalists" had been uprooting trees in forests near the colony for their use. In Panderma (Bandırma) and the surrounding farms, there was no foreign military, but Kant recalls British officers coming out to the farm to hunt, and navy officers coming ashore to shop, stroll, and visit the train station.[173] In fact, because the title of Tikfour Tchiflik was technically in the name of a British member of the Jewish Colonization Association, the Kants put up British flags to protect themselves from the Greeks (who were allied with the British).[174] While the Turkish authorities in Panderma depended on sultan Mehmet VI (1861-1926), the final sultan of the Ottoman Empire, and were responsible for order and security there, a feeling of general insecurity pervaded the colonies, and, because of this, families like Kant did not return until the conclusion of World War I.[175]

The Treaty of Lausanne (1923) forbade foreigners from purchasing lands in the Turkish Republic, and the JCA decided to suspend all of its operations in Western Anatolia. By this time, many of the immigrants had left either for the Turkish capital of Istanbul, for Palestine, or for other places in the

---

171   CAHJP İCA/Tur 366-16.

172   CAHJP ICA/Tur 368-34.

173   Kant, *Mémoires*, 91.

174   Kant, *Mémoires*, 202-203.

175   Ibid.

United States and Western Europe. The letters encouraged Ottoman Jews to join them on their Jewish agricultural project—not in Palestine—but rather in Russia. Kant describes Russians and Russian Jews seeking temporary refuge in Constantinople after the Bolshevik Revolution and the Russian Civil War.[176] But their stay was temporary. Many intended to move on to Haifa, the northern port in Palestine, and await their visas in Constantinople.[177] He writes that the Russian Jews "had confidence in the English Minister Balfour's Declaration who benevolently proclaimed the creation of an independent Home in Palestine for the millions of Jews scattered around the world. The lives of Jews were very difficult and all wanted to go to their ancient homeland."[178] Yet many could not go because of "their precarious situation" and they waited in Galata until they were able to leave.

The colony, in the words of Joseph Niego, had "little success," at least in how the story ended.[179] Many of the funds were then transferred into the *Caisse de Petits Prêts,* or small loans fund, and Niego became director of the program. The small loans fund acted similarly to the JCA's credit funds in Russia, Poland, and Romania.[180] In 1925, the JCA sold the farm to a Turkish farmer named Ahmet Kayalı who later donated the complex to the Turkish government in 1944. From 1944-1997, the colony served as a Turkish primary school.

Goldenberg went on to study at the Alliance school in Paris and later served as a teacher in Djedida, Tunisia, and in Marrakesh, Morocco:

> Or Yehuda had enchanted my childhood. Today, it is a simple small Turkish village called Tchiflik Oured. Our agricultural school is the village school, the administration building is the seat of the town hall, the first floor of the house we lived in was burned and Turkish peasants have divided the old domain. When many years later, my daughter Lucette and her husband made the pilgrimage there during the summer of 1970, our old living room was filled with melons and now a police post is found in the main square, once bustling with activity.[181]

---

176 Kant, *Mémoires d'un Fermier Juif en Turquie,* 96.

177 Kant, *Mémoires d'un Fermier Juif en Turquie,* 128.

178 Kant, *Mémoires d'un Fermier Juif en Turquie,* 128.

179 Niego, *Cinquante Années de Travail Dans les Oeuvres Juives,* 21.

180 Ibid.

181 *Les Cahiers de l'AIU,* Tuesday, 1 December 1998, 34.

Neither Kant nor Goldenberg ever made it to Palestine. Goldenberg became a teacher for the Alliance, and Kant hired help on Tikfour Tchiflik and moved to Constantinople. "Disoriented after so many years in the Anatolian countryside," Kant describes rushing "through all the streets, shops and other places to discover new things and a different life."[182]

---

182 Kant, *Mémoires*, 68.

Epilogue

Reorienting Jewish Geographies

Lazar Weinstein was a religious man. He left Kishinev, then a part of Bessarabia, in 1880 with his mother and siblings for Constantinople, because he thought it could be a safe haven for his family until they had saved enough money and received the necessary paperwork to secure passage to the United States. He had heard that the conditions were relatively favorable for Jews in the Ottoman Empire, and, along with other Russian Jewish migrants, the Weinsteins settled in the Galata quarter near the Schneider Tempel.[1] The proximity to the synagogue allowed Lazar Weinstein to pray and study in the synagogue's *beit midrash*, or house of study, while his mother worked as a seamstress to support their family. Although the family was poor, Weinstein became invigorated by religious life in the city that served as a kind of *entrepôt* for Jews of various backgrounds as well as other religious minority groups. Sephardi, Ashkenazi, German, and Russian Jews and other Ottoman and foreign subjects made their home in the neighborhood just steps away from the port. According to family legend transmitted two generations to Leah Weinstein Yahya, whom I interviewed in Istanbul in 2015, by the time the requisite immigration papers arrived a few years later, Lazar dramatically tore up the visa and announced that the family would remain in Constantinople. He married Rosalie Friedman and had two children, Frieda and Leah, both of whom resided in Istanbul.

The Weinsteins were one of many Russian Jewish migrant families that chose an alternate route of exit from the Russian Empire—yet their paths were not canonized in Jewish historiography and historical memory like the

---

1   Sarah Zaides, Interview with Leah Weinstein Yahya, May 2015

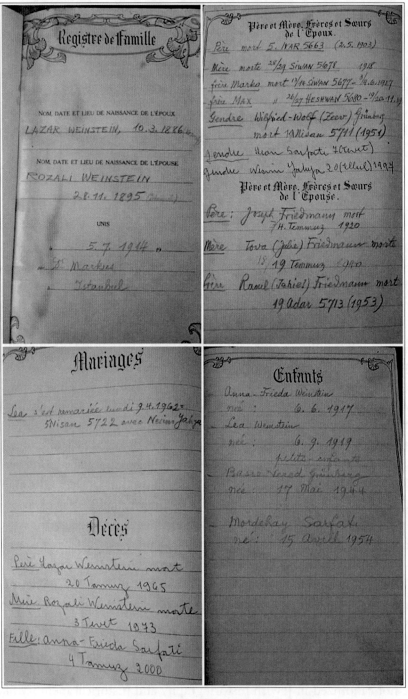

Weinstein Family Registry-
Rozali and Lazar were married by Rabbi David Markus in 1914.
C/O Leah Weinstein Yahya

paths of Tevye's daughters Tsatyl, Beilke, and Hodl. Perhaps if all the Russian migrants' stories had similar codas to the Weinstein's story, they may have been transmitted by way of Jewish or Ottoman history, historiography, and memory. Yet following the trajectories of Tevye's daughters in the Ottoman Empire has demonstrated that the routes of exit from the Russian Empire were neither clearly defined nor clearly oriented—indeed, Russian migrants had many choices to make once they arrived in the Ottoman Empire. Perhaps they struggled, as Albert Kant and his family did, with their decision to leave their home country and purchase a farm in Western Anatolia—only then to consider, and then reconsider, moving to Palestine. Perhaps they were inspired by secular Jewish nationalism, just as Masya Srebskis found her inspiration, who then joined her young friend Albert on Tikfour Tchiflik until she decided to continue on to participate in the Second Aliyah in Palestine. Or, perhaps they would join the revolutionary Soviet project after all, as Albert Kant's friends staying at the Hotel Gendelman had.[2]

Migration is not unidirectional, yet it is often told as such. Arrows directing the paths of exit did not exclusively point west; in fact, they often pointed in many directions.[3] Kant's acquaintance Duniya and her family, for example, returned to Odessa after the Russian Civil War.[4] The point is, there were many paths available for Russian Jews on the eve of the Bolshevik Revolution—and indeed, there were many paths still available *after* the Bolshevik Revolution.

The story of Tevye's Ottoman Daughter is not only about historical recovery and helping to understand the motivations and ideologies of a subaltern migrant group: it allows us an important opportunity to reconsider our understandings of Jewish geography. The "centers" of Jewish thought in the modern period have long been understood as the major cities of Europe, Paris, Berlin, Vienna, as well as revolutionary hotbeds in the Russian Empire. Yet the experiences of Russian Jews like Kant and Goldenberg and others demonstrate the importance and indeed the uniqueness of the Ottoman Empire to the development of Jewish political and communal identities.

---

2   Kant, *Mémoires d'un Fermier Juif en Turquie*, 128-29

3   For an excellent study of how migration back and forth between Lebanon and North America helped shape the Lebanese middle class at the turn of the century, please see Akram Fouad Khater *Inventing Home: Emigration, Gender, and the Middle Class in Lebanon, 1870-1920* (Oakland: University of California Press, 2001).

4   Kant, *Mémoires d'un Fermier Juif en Turquie*, 196

Through the lens of the experience of Russian Jews, we can see the ways in which political ideologies, especially Jewish nationalist ideologies (including political Zionism), were made and unmade, and how Ottoman as well as Eastern and Western European Jews attempted to define the contours of terms like "Ashkenazi" and "Sephardi." Indeed, claims to identities like Ashkenazi and Sephardi were directly informed by these political ideologies, highly contingent upon the political and historical climate in the late Ottoman milieu. Importantly, these identities and definitions did not evolve solely in the Ottoman capital, but had important ties to the social and economic experiments of Jewish collective farming in the shatterzones of empire and political currents taking shape in Europe. Thus, Tevye's Ottoman Daughter has also elaborated the importance of the movement of people, but also of ideas.

Ultimately, Tevye's Ottoman Daughter urges us to reconsider what geographical "hubs" as well as "spokes" existed in the *fin-de-siècle* and how relationships existed between more than one hub, and often, existed among many hubs and spokes. In other words, Jews in Constantinople were in communication with not only Jews in Jerusalem, Paris, or Berlin, but also, with Jews in Cyprus and in Western Anatolia. Thus, in order to understand the developments of political ideologies, we cannot only look to the "shatterzones of empire," to places like the Ottoman borderlands, as scholars have suggested, but to the *relationship* between the borderlands and the city.[5] Identities for Jews like Albert Kant were not impressed upon in a singular place, but rather, in the movement and intersections of different places, empires, and ideas. Several cities competed with those in Ottoman or Mandate Palestine for significance in the political and ideological lives of Jews in the twilight years of the Ottoman and the Russian Empires.[6] Yet, as this book has demonstrated, they were looking not just to Constantinople, to Salonica, or to Jerusalem (in the Ottoman Empire) or Paris or Berlin (in Western Europe) or New York (in the New World) for their routes of exit – be it ideological or physical—but also to small agricultural towns like Tikfour Tchiflik or Or Yehuda. Thus, to help them understand their own identities and place within the Ottoman milieu, they not only looked to traditional harbingers of Western European mores of

---

5   Bartov and Weitz, *Shatterzone of Empires*, 2. See also Reynolds, *Shattering Empires*.

6   Devin Naar has pointed out that Jewish leaders proposed Salonica as a kind of autonomous Jewish city-state to the World Zionist Organization. See Naar, *Jewish Salonica*, 1.

identity, but also to Russia and Russian Jews, who effectively transformed the political and social fabric of the Ottoman Empire's Jewish community.

One of the dimensions through which the Ottoman Empire and Russian Empire exercised imperial power was through the administrative organization of confessions.[7] However, just as scholars have cautioned that the confessional element of rule did not eliminate conflict or produce consensus in the Russian case, so, too, should we be wary of exaggerating harmony and minimizing tensions in the Ottoman case.[8] Indeed, the communal tensions that arose in response to the arrival of Russian Jewish migrants in the Ottoman Empire demonstrate that this system of governance was more complex and the Jewish case in Constantinople helps us to illuminate the diversity-and indeed the tensions and conflict- that existed within a particular religious millet. The 1890 Agreement, published by the office of the Chief Rabbi, the growth of Ashkenazi organizations under the leadership of Rabbi David Markus, and the establishment of the *meclis-i-cismani*, challenge our understanding of Ottoman governance as simply between the Sephardic Chief Rabbi and the Sublime Porte.[9] Rather, the Jewish millet had to negotiate among its own membership as it interacted with the Ottoman Empire, and the challenges with the *Haham Başı* were not purely politically motivated, as scholars have suggested.[10]

In addition to broadening our understanding of how the Ottoman Empire governed, *Tevye's Ottoman Daughter* also allows us also to broaden our understanding of how Jewish subjects of the Ottoman Empire understood themselves vis-à-vie other Jews. While some scholars have suggested that, similar to the Russian Empire, Ottoman Jews understood themselves as imperial subjects, they also understood themselves in relation to other members of their millet.[11] In other words, the critical links in their identities were not just the Ottoman state, but more importantly, were other Jews living in the Ottoman Empire and in Western Europe. Horizontal, as well as vertical

---

7   See Crews, *For Prophet and Tsar.*

8   Michael Khodarkovsky, "Robert D. Crews. For Prophet and Tsar: Islam and Empire in Russia and Central Asia," *The American Historical Review,* Volume 112.5.1941

9   *El Tiempo,* 30 June 1890

10 See Esther Benbassa, Zionism and the Politics of Coalitions in the Ottoman Jewish Communities in the Early Twentieth Century," Retrieved Online 8/17/2017, http://bit.ly/2uUyIzy

11 See Julia Phillips Cohen, *Becoming Ottomans* and Robert Crews, *For Prophet and Tsar.*

relationships constituted the development of the identities of the Jews of the Ottoman Empires.

In fields of critical theory and in American Studies, scholars have made considerable strides to interrogate the socially constructed nature of race and of ethnicity. The field of Jewish Studies has also been influenced by this scholarship and while it has implicitly understood that terms like "Sephardi" and "Ashkenazi" are themselves social constructs, has yet to really interrogate these terms or to engage them in a comparative and categorical analysis and consider them in the highly political contexts in which they are used. Rather, more attention has been paid to interrogating the socially constructed nature of Jewish identity and community in the diaspora and in Israel, and in particular, to its political expressions and manifestations, but what the Ottoman context makes explicitly clear is that terms like Ashkenazi and Sephardi have themselves been assumed static and left unproblematized.[12] If we can break down Jewish communities and understand how claims to these identities were made, more complete and nuanced understanding of the formation of Jewish political ideas and ideologies could also be achieved.

Instead, scholars of Ottoman History and the early Mandate Period have also focused on *inter*ommununal politics and tensions among Jews, Muslims, and Christians, in an attempt to identify, as one recent documentary put it, the "seeds of conflict" in the Arab/Israeli Conflict.[13] Other scholars have also looked at moments of intercommunal cooperation and political organization, working against the historical teleology of Israeli statehood in 1948 to demonstrate the importance of non-statist opportunities after the Young Turk Revolution. As Michelle U. Campos argues, "by tracing how Muslims, Christians, and Jews became imperial citizens together," historians can learn how the "Ottoman nation" became a "shared field of social and political contestation."[14] However, what this monograph has demonstrated is that attention should also be paid to the *intra*communal relationships among various kinds of Jews in the fin-de-siècle. Jews did not constitute a monolithic millet in the Ottoman Empire. Examining the discursive natures of Jewish

---

12   For example, see David Biale, *Power and Powerlessness in Jewish History* (New York: Schocken Books, 1984).

13   Ben Loeterman PBS Documentary *1913: Seeds of Conflict,* Retrieved online in May 18, 2017, http://www.pbs.org/program/1913-seeds-conflict/

14   Michelle U. Campos, *Ottoman Brothers,* 17.

identities, and especially, how they played out in relation to political and historical contexts, can give us insight into the diversity of political and social choices and opportunities that Jews had at the end of empire.

Tevye's Ottoman Daughter allows us to reconsider many of our modalities of analysis of Jewish history. By studying Russian Jewish migrants in the Ottoman Empire, we are able to not only interrogate traditional routes of migration, but also categories of people in their Ottoman imperial contexts. As the political and social context of the late Ottoman Empire became more precarious in the wake of nationalist separatists movements in the Balkans, and demonstrating allegiance to the sultan or to the Second Constitutional Period became increasingly politically important, Sephardi and Ashkenazi Jews alike began to depict Russian Jews as morally, socially, and politically subversive.

Indeed, the tendency to place blame on migrants, especially in times of economic and political instability, is not a phenomenon unique to the Ottoman Empire. For many Americans in the 1890s, new immigrants from Southern and Eastern Europe personified the economic and social problems of the decade. As Irving Howe pointed out, "new immigrants" became "the symptom and the cause of a spreading social malaise."[15] "German Jews" similarly depicted their Russian and Sephardic coreligionists as a kind of "double other" the United States.[16] It is fascinating that these very same migrants that were so politically subversive were also the catalyst for many important political questions, including those of nationalism, Ottomanism, and the future of Jewish communities in the Ottoman Empire. As I have demonstrated, the discourses surrounding Russian Jews refracted various groups' anxieties as well as political priorities and aspirations, which of course, shifted and evolved with their historical contexts.

In chapter one I suggest that "every *other* has their *other*." This study is unique because it examines the ways in which Sephardic Jews imagined and represented their other, who also happened to be their self-proclaimed "coreligionists" and brothers. They used Russian Jewish migrants as a counterpoint to assist in their identification with enlightened, emancipated German Jewry. They also

15   Irving Howe, *World of Our Fathers: The Journey of East European Jews to America and the Life They Found and Made* (New York: Harcourt, 1976), 51-61.

16   See Devin Naar, "Fashioning the "Mother of Israel": The Ottoman Jewish Historical Narrative and the Image of Jewish Salonica." *Jewish History* 28, no. 3 (2014): 337-72.

did this in order to assist in demonstrating their "civic Ottomanism" and European status. Yet Russian Jews inevitably had their own vantage point from which they understood both themselves, and their coreligionists in the Ottoman Empire. Kant, for example, describes coming from Panderma to Constantinople "thirsty to talk with the young people from Russia who were generally cultivated and intellectual, and I took great pleasure talking to these young men and women."[17] Although Panderma had some Jewish families, including Sephardic families, Kant preferred to discuss Russian high culture and literature with others well versed in those topics. At multiple points of his memoir, Albert Kant invokes his Russophile taste in literature and in culture, positioning himself as a Russian Jew, distinguishing himself from other Jews, including Sephardim, in Western Anatolia. Coincidentally, after the Bolshevik Revolution and his time in Constantinople, he seems to have lost touch with Kiliya and considers himself affected by the "dazzle" of the city and perhaps, even, influenced by his decision to remain in Turkey.[18] When he returns to his hometown to Kiliya to meet his old friend, he describes her as completely changed; "There was no trace of the beautiful, radiant girl with us in Turkey" and "she had become a real Russian peasant, heavy with age and above all from the tough living conditions that she endured."[19]

Recovering this history has been especially difficult, as sources discussing these historical actors --migrants, women, and minorities – are especially rare. And indeed there is more work to be done, and more archives to be visited. What were the relationships—personal, intellectual, and political—between the Russian Jews of Constantinople and the Ottoman Borderlands, and the Jews of Russia? And how did these exchanges change, if at all, across two major historical ruptures—the formation of the Soviet Union and the Turkish Republic?[20] Indeed, the "end" of these two empires, and the beginnings of other governments of other kinds, allowed for the materialization of Israeli Statehood in 1948 in the wake of genocide committed against the Jews of Europe during the Second World War. Remembering that nearly half a century before, Ashkenazi and Sephardi

---

17   Kant, *Mémoires*, 128

18   Kant, *Mémoires*, 128

19   Kant, *Mémoires*, 196

20   James Meyer, *Turks Across Empires: Marketing Russian Identity in the Russian and Ottoman Borderlands, 1856-1914* (London: Oxford University Press, 2014).

Jewish communities did live under the same proverbial roof and contested many issues that would resonate with contemporary communities – t about the fates, paths, and routes of exit, available to Jewish people around the world.

BIBLIOGRAPHY

Archives

Alliance Israélite Universelle, Paris, France (AIU)

Central Archives for the History of the Jewish People, Jerusalem, Israel (CAHJP)

Central Zionist Archives, Jerusalem, Israel (CZA)

Joint Distribution Committee Archive, New York City, United States (JDC)

Library of Congress, Washington, DC, United States

Periodicals

Allgemeine Zeitung des Judentums (Leipzig and Berlin)

La America (New York City)

La Boz de Türkiye (Istanbul)

El Amaneser (Istanbul)

L'Aurore (Istanbul)

La Jeune Turquie (Paris)

The Jewish Chronicle (London)

New York Sun (New York City)

New York Tageblatt (New York City)

El Tiempo (Istanbul)

La Vara (New York City)

Alpersohn, Mordechai. *Dreissig Jahren in Argentina*, vol. 1. Berlin, 1923.

American Jewish Historical Society. *Publications of the American Jewish Historical Society* 15 (1906): 13-14.

Ben-Gurion, David. *Zichronot*. Tel Aviv: Am Oved, 1971.

Cohen, Lucy. *Lady de Rothschild and her Daughters 1821-1931*. London: John Murray Publishers, 1935

Cohen, Samuel. "Report of an Inquiry Made in Constantinople on Behalf of the Jewish Association for the Protection of Girls and Women." In *The Jews and Prostitution in Constantinople 1854–1922*, by Rıfat N. Bali, Istanbul: Isis, 2008.

Congressional Record (Senate). 52nd Congress, 1st session, February 15, 1892, vol. 33, pt. 2, 1132 (speech of Senator W.E. Chandler).

Hirsch, Baron Maurice de. "Carlsbad Memorandum." *Turkenhirsch: A Study of Baron Maurice de Hirsch Entrepreneur and Philanthropist*, by Kurt Grunwald, 125. Jerusalem: Israel Program for Scientific Translation, 1966.

———. "Memorandum on Palestinian Colonization, 1891." In *Turkenhirsch: A Study of Baron Maurice de Hirsch Entrepreneur and Philanthropist*, by Kurt Grunwald, 63. Jerusalem: Israel Program for Scientific Translation, 1966.

———. "My Views on Philanthropy," (1891). *North American Review* 153, no. 416. The Nineteenth Century in Print: The Making of America in Books and Periodicals. Cornell University Library and the Library of Congress, http://memory.loc.gov/ammem/ndlpcoop/moahtml/snchome.html.

Kant, Albert. *Mémoires d'un Fermier Juif en Turquie*. Edited by Rıfat N Bali. Istanbul: Libra Kitapçılık, 2013.

Levy, Avigdor. "The Appointment of a Chief Rabbi in 1835." *The Jews of the Ottoman Empire*, edited by Avigdor Levy, 425-439. Princeton: Darwin Press, 1994.

League of Nations. *Report of the Special Body of Experts on the Extent of the International White Slave Traffic, Part 2 (1927)*.

Lowenthal, Marvin, ed. *The Diaries of Theodor Herzl*. New York: Dial Press, 1956.

Niego, Joseph. *Cinquante Années de Travail dans les Oeuvres Juives: Allocutions et Conférences. Bulletin publié à l'occasion du soixante-dixième anniversaire du Frère Grand Président J. Niégo, sous les auspices du District XI de la Béné-Bérith, avec une préface de J. Shaki*. Istanbul: Babok & Fils, 1933.

———. "La Palestine." *Cinquante Années de Travail Dans les Oeuvres Juives*, no. 417 and 425.

Norman, Theodor. *An Outstretched Arm: A History of the Jewish Colonization Association*. New York: Routledge, 1985

Pappenheim, Bertha. *Sisyphus-Arbeit: Reisebriefe aus den Jahren 1911 und 1912*. Leipzig: Paul E. Linder, 1924.

———. "The Burning Shame of a Terrible Scandal: Jewish Conference in London on the White Slave Traffic." *The Jewish Chronicle*, April 23, 1910.

White, Arnold. *The Modern Jew*. London: Frederick A. Stokes Company, 1899.

———. *The Problems of a Great City*. London: Remington & Co. Publishers, 1886.

Secondary Sources

Aktürk, Engin. *Osmanlı Döneminde Anadolu ve Trakya Topraklarında Yahudi Cemaati Tarafından Kurulan Tarım Okulları ve Akhisar Or Yehuda Tarım Okulu Örneğinin Mimari İncelemesi*. unpublished MA Thesis, Istanbul: Mimar Sinan Güzel Sanatlar Üniversitesi, Aralık 2012.

Alroey, Gur. *Bread to Eat and Clothes to Wear: Letters from Jewish Migrants in the Early Twentieth Century*. Detroit: Wayne State University Press, 2011.

———. *An Unpromising Land: Jewish Migration to Palestine in the Early Twentieth Century.* Stanford: Stanford University Press, 2014.

American Jewish Historical Society. *Publications of the American Jewish Historical Society* 15 (1906): 13-14.

Anderson, Benedict. *Imagined Communities: Reflections on the Origin and the Spread of Nationalism.* New York: Verso, 2006.

Anderson, Bernhard W., Bruce M. Metzger, and Roland E. Murphy. *The New Oxford Annotated Bible with the Apocryphal/Deuterocanonical Books.* New York: Oxford University Press, 1991.

Arbeit Zeitung, New York, February 12, 1892. Op. cit. in *Quarantine! East European Jewish Migration and the New York City Epidemics of 1892,* by Howard Markel. Baltimore: John Hopkins University Press, 1997.

Aschheim, Steven E. *Brothers and Strangers: The East European Jew in German and German Jewish Consciousness, 1800–1923.* Madison: University of Wisconsin Press, 1982.

Bakić-Hayden, Milica. "Nesting Orientalisms: The Case of Former Yugoslavia." *Slavic Review* 54, no. 4 (1995): 917–31.

Bali, Rıfat N. *The Jews and Prostitution in Constantinople 1854–1922.* Istanbul: Isis, 2008.

Barkey, Karen. *Bandits and Bureaucrats: The Ottoman Route to State Centralization.* Ithaca: Cornell University Press, 1994.

Bartov, Omer and Eric D. Weitz. *Shatterzone of Empires: Coexistence and Violence in the German, Habsburg, Russian, and Ottoman Borderlands.* Bloomington: Indiana University Press, 2013.

Ben-Artzi, Yossi. "Jewish Rural Settlement in Cyprus 1882-1935: a 'Springboard' or a Destiny?" *Jewish History* 21, no. 3/4 (2007): 361-383.

Benbassa, Esther. *A Sephardic Chief Rabbi in Politics, 1892–1923,* translated by Miriam Kochan. Tuscaloosa: University of Alabama Press, 1995.

———. "Associational Strategies in Ottoman Jewish Society in the Nineteenth and Twentieth Centuries." In *The Jews of the Ottoman Empire,* edited by Avigdor Levy. Princeton: Darwin Press, 1994.

———. *Ha-Yahadut ha-'Othmanit beyn Hitma'arevut le-Ṣiyyonut, 1908–1920,* translated by Me'ir Yisra'el. Jerusalem: Merkaz Zalman Shazar, 1996.

———. "Zionism and the Politics of Coalitions in the Ottoman Jewish Communities in the Early Twentieth Century." *Ottoman and Turkish Jewry: Community and Leadership,* edited by Aron Rodrigue, 225-251. Bloomington: Indiana University Press, 1992.

Ben-Gurion, David. *Zichronot.* Tel Aviv: Am Oved, 1971.

Benor, Sarah B. "Lexical Othering in Judezmo: How Ottoman Sephardim Refer to Non-Jews." In *Languages and Literatures of Sephardic and Oriental Jews: proceeding of the sixth International Congress for Research on the Sephardi and Oriental Jewish Heritage,* edited by David M. Bunis, 65-85. The Bialik Institute Misgav Yerushalayim, Jerusalem, 2009.

Ben-Zvi, Rahel Y. *Before Golda, Manya Shochat: A Biography.* New York: Biblio Press, 1989.

Bernstein, Deborah. "Gender, Nationalism and Colonial Policy: Prostitution in the Jewish Settlement of Mandate Palestine, 1918–1948." *Women's History Review* 21, no. 1 (2012): 81–100.

Bernstein, Laurie. *Sonia's Daughters: Prostitutes and Their Regulation in Imperial Russia.* Berkeley: University of California Press, 1995.

Birnbaum, Pierre and Ira Katznelson. *Paths of Emancipation: Jews, States, and Citizenship.* Princeton, NJ: Princeton Legacy Library, 1995.

Bornes-Varol, Marie-Christine. "The Balat Quarter and its Image: A Study of a Jewish Neighborhood in Istanbul." Translated by Eric Fassin and Avigdor Levy. *The Jews of the Ottoman Empire*, edited by Avigdor Levy, 633-646. Princeton: Darwin Press, 1994.

Bristow, Edward. *Prostitution and Prejudice: The Jewish Fight against White Slavery 1870–1939.* Clarendon: Oxford University Press, 1982.

Brubaker, Rogers. *Nationalism Reframed: Nationhood and the National Question in the New Europe.* Cambridge: Cambridge University Press, 1996.

Bulletin de la Grande Loge de District XI et de la Loge de Constantinople. No. 678, *Février 1911-Février 1913*, "Rapport de la Commission de secours aux éprouvés israélites de la guerre balkanique lu dans la séance extraordinaire du 30 Janvier 1913," (1913).

———. "Rapport de Israel Auerbach: Délégué de la Grande Loge No. XI aux lieux du désastre cause pour tremblement de terre du 9 Août 1912," (1913).

Bunis, David M. *Voices from Jewish Salonika.* Jerusalem, 1999.

Campos, Michelle U. *Ottoman Brothers: Muslims, Christians, and Jews in Early Twentieth-Century Palestine.* Stanford: Stanford University Press, 2011.

Cohen, Julia Phillips. *Becoming Ottomans: Sephardi Jews and Imperial Citizenship in the Modern Era.* Oxford: Oxford University Press, 2014.

Cohen, Lucy. *Lady de Rothschild and her Daughters 1821-1931.* London: John Murray Publishers, 1935

Cohen, Naomi W. *Encounter with Emancipation: The German Jews in the United States, 1830–1914.* Philadelphia: Jewish Publication Society, 1984.

Colak, Hasan. "Tekfur, Fasiliyus, and Kayser: Disdain, Negligence and Appropriation of Byzantine Imperial Titulature in the Ottoman World." In *Marios Hadjianastasis' Frontiers of the Ottoman Imagination*, 5-28. Leiden: Brill, 2014.

Cooper, Frederic. *Citizenship between Empire and Nation: Remaking France and French Africa, 1945–1960.* Princeton: Princeton University Press, 2014.

Dekel-Chen, Jonathan. *Farming the Red Land: Jewish Agricultural Colonization and Local Soviet Power, 1924–1941.* New Haven: Yale University Press, 2005.

Deringil, Selim. "Jewish Immigration to the Ottoman Empire at the Time of the First Zionist Congresses: A Comment." In *The Last Ottoman Century and Beyond: the Jews in Turkey and the Balkans, 1808-1945*, edited by Minna Rozen, Tel Aviv: Tel Aviv University, 2002-2005.

Der Matossian, Bedross. *Shattered Dreams of Revolution: From Liberty to Violence in the Late Ottoman Empire*. Stanford: Stanford University Press, 2014.

Diner, Hasia R. *A Time for Gathering: The Second Migration, 1820-1880*. Baltimore: The John Hopkins University Press, 1995.

Dreyfus, Jim. "The Economic Aryanization of Brothels: An Illumination of Some Jewish Prostitution and Procurement in Occupied France, 1940-1944." *Revue des Etudes Juives* 162, no. 1-2 (2003): 219–46.

Dubnow, Simon. *History of the Jews in Russia and Poland*, vol. 1. Philadelphia: Jewish Publication Society of America, 1916.

Encyclopedia Judaica, 13ᵗʰ ed., *s.v.* "Population." Jerusalem: Keter, 1972.

Encyclopedia Judaica, 2ⁿᵈ ed., *s.v.* "Allgemeine Zeitung des Judentums," by Ezriel Carlebach. Detroit: Macmillan Reference USA, 670-671.

Encyclopedia of Jews in the Islamic World, s.v. Brill, edited by Norman A. Stillman. "David Feivel Markus," by Aksel Erbahar.

———. "Fresco, David," by Julia Phillips Cohen. Accessed May 3, 2017.

———. "L'Aurore (Istanbul)," by D. Gershon Lewental.

———. "Levi (Ha-Levi), Moshe," by D. Gershon Lewental. Accessed September 21, 2016.

———. "Sciuto, Lucien," by D. Gershon Lewental.

First International Congress for the Suppression of the White Slave Traffic. London, 1899.

Fitzgibbon, Edward M. *Alexander I and the Near East: The Ottoman Empire in Russia's Foreign Relations, 1801–1807*. Columbus: Ohio State University Press, 1974.

Foucault, Michel. *Power/Knowledge: Selected Interviews and Other Writings 1972-1977*. New York: Pantheon, 1980.

Frankel, Jonathan. "Assimilation and the Jews in Nineteenth-Century Europe: Towards a New Historiography?" In *Assimilation and Community: The Jews in Nineteenth Century Europe*, edited by Jonathan Frankel and Steven Zipperstein. Cambridge: Cambridge University Press, 1992.

Frary, Lucien J., and Mara Kozelsky. *Russian-Ottoman Borderlands: The Eastern Question Reconsidered*. Madison: University of Wisconsin Press, 2014.

Fuhrmann, Malte. "Down and Out on the Quays of İzmir: 'European' Musicians, Innkeepers, and Prostitutes in the Ottoman Port-Cities." *Mediterranean Historical Review* 24 (2009): 169–85.

Gartner, Lloyd P. "Anglo-Jewry and the Jewish International Traffic in Prostitution, 1885-1914." *Association for Jewish Studies Review* 7 (1982): 129–78.

Grunwald, Kurt. *Turkenhirsch: A Study of Baron Maurice de Hirsch Entrepreneur and Philanthropist*. Israel Program for Scientific Translation: Jerusalem, 1966.

Gurock, Jeffrey S. *When Harlem Was Jewish, 1870–1930*. New York: Columbia University Press, 1979.

Halévy, Aron. "Les Israélites Polonais De Constantinople Leur établissement à Constantinople–leurs mœurs," March 16, 1890. AIU/Tur 1C17.

Handlin, Oscar. *A Continuing Task; the American Jewish Joint Distribution Committee, 1914-1964*. New York: Random House, 1964

Halpern, Ben and Jehuda Reinharz. *Zionism and the Creation of a New Society*. New York: Oxford University Press, 1998.

Herlihy, Patricia. "Enzyklopädie Jüdischer Geschichte Und Kultur."*Auftrag Der Sächsischen Akademie Der Wissenschaften Zu Leipzig*. Stuttgart: Metzler, 2014.

Herzberg, Arthur. *The Zionist Idea: A Historical Analysis and Reader*. New York: Doubleday, 1959.

Heschel, Susannah and Umar Ryad, eds. *The Muslim Reception of European Orientalism: Reversing the Gaze*. New York: Routledge, 2020.

Hirsch, Francine. *Empire of Nations: Ethnographic Knowledge and the Making of the Soviet Union*. Ithaca: Cornell University Press, 2014.

Galante, Avram. *Histoire des Juifs de Turquie* 2. Istanbul: İsis, 1985.

Howe, Irving. *World of Our Fathers*. Harcourt: New York, 1976.

Hyman, Paula. *Gender and Assimilation in Modern Jewish History: The Roles and Representation of Women*. Seattle: University of Washington Press, 1995.

International Bureau for the Suppression of Traffic in Women and Children. *Traffic in Women and Children: Past Achievements, Present Tasks*. London, 1949.

Israel Ministry of Education and Culture. *Mivekh Israel*. Jerusalem, Israel: Jerusalem Post Print and Offset, 1970.

Johnson, Abigail. *From Empire to Empire: Between Ottoman and British Rule*. Syracuse: Syracuse University Press, 2011.

Johnson, Clarence R. *Constantinople to-Day; Or, The Pathfinder Survey of Constantinople; A Study in Oriental Social Life*. New York: Macmillan, 1922.

Johnson, Sam. *Pogroms, Peasants, Jews: Britain and Eastern Europe's Jewish Question, 1867-1925*. New York: Palgrave McMillan, 2011.

Kappeler, Andreas. *The Russian Empire: A Multiethnic History*. Essex: Pearson Education, 2001.

Karpat, Kemal H. *Ottoman Population, 1830-1914: Demographic and Social Characteristics*. Madison: University of Wisconsin Press, 1985.

Kasaba, Reşat. *A Moveable Empire: Ottoman Nomads, Migrants, and Refugees*. Seattle: University of Washington Press, 2009.

Kauffman, Reginald Wright. *House of Bondage*. Mofat: New York, 1911.

Kayali, Hasan. "Elections and the Electoral Process in the Ottoman Empire, 1876–1919." *International Journal of Middle East Studies* 27, no. 3 (1995): 265–86.

Kazhan, Alexander, ed. *Oxford Dictionary of Byzantium*. New York: Oxford University Press, 1991.

Khalid, Adeep. *The Politics of Muslim Cultural Reform: Jadidism in Central Asia*. Berkeley: University of California Press, 1999.

Kleeman, Faye Y. *Gender, Ethnicity, and the Spectacles of the Empire*. Honolulu: University of Hawaii Press, 2014.

Klier, John. *Russia Gathers Her Jews: the Origins of the "Jewish Question" in Russia, 1772-1825*. DeKalb: Northern Illinois University Press, 1986.

Kochan, Lionel. *The Jews in Soviet Russia since 1917*. London: Oxford University Press, 1972.

Köse, Yavuz. "Vertical Bazaars of Modernity: Western Department Stores and their Staff in Istanbul, 1889–1921." *International Review of Social History* S17, no 45. (2009): 91-114.

Laqueur, Walter. *The History of Zionism*. London: Tauris Parke, 2003.

Lee, Samuel J. *Moses of the New World*. New York: Thomas Yuselof, 1970.

Levi, Amalia. *Evanescent Happiness: Ottoman Jews Encounter Modernity, the Case of Lea Mitrani and Joseph Niego (1863-1923)*. Istanbul: Libra Kitapçılık Ve Yayıncılık, 2015.

Lowenstein, Steven M. *Frankfurt on the Hudson: The German Jewish Community of Washington Heights, 1933–1983, Its Structure and Culture*. Detroit: Wayne State University Press, 1989.

Makdisi, Usamma. "Ottoman Orientalism." *The American Historical Review* 107, no. 3 (2002): 768-796.

Maksudyan, Nazan. "'This Time Women As Well Got Involved In Politics!' Nineteenth Century Ottoman Women's Organizations and Political Agency." In *Women and the City, Women in the City: a Gendered Perspective on Ottoman Urban History*, edited by Nazan Maksudyan. New York: Berghahn, 2014.

Marks, Lara. "Jewish Women and Jewish Prostitution in the East End of London." *Jewish Quarterly* 34, no. 2 (1987): 6-10.

Mays, Devi. *Forging Ties, Forging Passports: Migration and the Modern Sephardi Diaspora*. Stanford: Stanford University Press, 2020.

Martin, Terry D. *The Affirmative Action Empire: Nations and Nationalism in the Soviet Union, 1923–1939*. Ithaca: Cornell University Press, 2001.

McCarthy, Justin. "Jewish Population in the Late Ottoman Period." In *The Jews of the Ottoman Empire*, edited by Avigdor Levy, 377-378. Princeton: Darwin Press, 1994.

Minc, Michael. "Jewish Agricultural Settlements in Kherson up to the Bolshevik Revolution." *On the History of the Jewish Diaspora*. Tel Aviv: Tel Aviv University Press, 1990.

Morris, Benny. *The Birth of the Palestinian Refugee Problem 1947–1949*. Cambridge: Cambridge University Press, 1989.

Mufti, Aamir R. *Enlightenment in the Colony: The Jewish Question and the Crisis of Post-Colonial Culture*. Princeton: Princeton University Press, 2007.

Naar, Devin E. "Fashioning the 'Mother of Israel': The Ottoman Jewish Historical Narrative and the Image of Jewish Salonica." *Jewish History* 28, no. 3 (2014): 337–72.

———. *Jewish Salonica: Between the Ottoman Empire and Modern Greece*. Stanford: Stanford University Press, 2016.

———. "'The Mother of Israel' or 'Sephardi Metropolis': Sephardim, Ashkenazim, and Romaniotes in Salonica?" *Jewish Social Studies* 22, no. 1 (2016): 81-129.

Nabokov, Vladimir. *Speak, Memory: An Autobiography Revisited.* New York: Knopf, 1999

Nahum, Haim. Letter to Monsieur le Président, 27 April, 1919. Op. cit. *A Sephardic Chief Rabbi in Politics, 1892–1923*, by Esther Benbassa, trans. Miriam Kochan. Tuscaloosa: University of Alabama Press, 1995.

Nathans, Benjamin. *Beyond the Pale: the Jewish Encounter in Late Imperial Russia.* Los Angeles: University of California Press, 2002.

O'Farrel, Claire. *Michel Foucault.* London: Sage, 2005.

Owen, Roger. *The Middle East in the World Economy, 1800-1914*, 189-216. Cornwall, UK: I.B. Tauris, 2002.

Oxford Dictionary of National Biography, n.v. "Arnold J White." Accessed February 13, 2015.

Özgün, Cihan. "A Town under the Shadow of Bandits in the Late Ottoman Empire: Kuşadası." *History Studies International Journal of History* 4, no. 4 (2012).

Pamuk, Sevket. *The Ottoman Empire and European Capitalism, 1820-1913: Trade, Investment and Production.* Cambridge, UK: Cambridge University Press, 2010.

Pappé, Ilan. *A History of Modern Palestine: One Land Two Peoples.* Cambridge: Cambridge University Press, 2006.

Perez, Emma. "Queering the Borderlands: The Challenges of Excavating the Invisible and Unheard." *Frontiers: A Journal of Women Studies* 24 (2003): 122–31.

Pollack, Gustav. *Michael Heilprin and His Sons.* New York: Dodd, Mead and Company, 1912.

Reynolds, Michael A. *Shattering Empires: The Clash and Collapse of the Ottoman and Russian Empires 1908–1918.* Cambridge: Cambridge University Press, 2011.

Robinson, Ritchie. *The "Jewish Question" in German Literature, 1749-1939: Emancipation and its Discontents.* London: Oxford University Press, 1999.

Rodrigue, Aron. *French Jews, Turkish Jews: The Alliance Israélite Universelle and the Politics of Jewish Schooling in Turkey, 1860-1925.* Indiana: Indiana University Press, 1990.

Romano, Juda. "Lucien Sciuto Murio." *La Boz de Türkiye*, March 1, 1947, 199.

Rovner, Adam. *In the Shadow of Zion: Promised Lands Before Israel.* New York: New York University Press, 2014.

Said, Edward. *Culture and Imperialism.* Vintage Books: New York, 1994.

———. "New History, Old Ideas." *Al-Ahram*, May 27, 1998.

———. *Orientalism.* New York: Vintage Books, 1979.

Schechtman, Joseph. *The Life and Times of Vladimir Jabotinsky.* Silver Spring: Eshel Books, 1986.

Schild, Robert, Erdal Frayman, and Moşe Grosman. *A Hundred Year Old Synagogue.* Translated by Erdoğan Ağca. Istanbul: Galata Ashkenazi Cultural Association, 2000.

Shaw, Stanford J. *History of the Ottoman Empire and Modern Turkey.* Cambridge: Cambridge University Press, 1976.

Shmuelevitz, Aryeh. "Zionism, Jews and Muslims in the Ottoman Empire as Reflected in the Weekly Hamevasser." In *Jews, Muslims and Mass Media: Mediating the "Other,"* edited by Tudor Parfitt and Yulia Egorova, New York: Routledge, 2004.

Shpall, Leo. "David Feinberg's Historical Survey of the Colonization of the Russian Jews in Argentina." *Publications of the American Jewish Historical Society* 43, no. 1 (1953): 37-69.

Slezkine, Yuri. *The Jewish Century.* Princeton, NJ: Princeton University Press, 1984.

Soyer, Daniel. *Jewish Immigrant Associations and American Identity in New York, 1880–1939.* Detroit: Wayne State University Press, 2001.

Srebrnik, Henry F. *Jerusalem on the Amur: Birobidzhan and the Canadian Jewish Communist Movement, 1924–1951.* Montreal: McGill-Queen's University Press, 2008.

Stein, Sarah A. *Making Jews Modern: The Yiddish and Ladino Press in the Russian and Ottoman Empires.* Bloomington: Indiana University Press, 2004.

Suny, Ronald. *The Revenge of the Past: Nationalism, Revolution, and the Collapse of the Soviet Union.* Stanford: Stanford University Press, 1993.

Szajkowski, Zosa. *Mirage of American Jewish Aid in Soviet Russia, 1917-1939.* New York: Ktav Publishing House, 1977.

Taki, Victor. "Limits of Protection: Russia and the Orthodox Coreligionists in the Ottoman Empire." *Carl Beck Papers in Russian and East European Studies,* no. 2401. (2015) https://doi.org/10.5195/cbp.2015.201

"Turkish Press and Zionism, Then." *Ha-Herut,* January 21, 1910. Op cit. *Ottoman Brothers: Muslims, Christians, and Jews in Early Twentieth-Century Palestine,* by Michelle Campos. Stanford: Stanford University Press, 2011.

Van Den Boogert, Maurtis H. *The Capitulations and the Ottoman Legal System: Qadis, Consuls and Beratlis in the 18th Century.* Leiden: Brill, 2005.

Wolfe, Rachel S. "From Protestant Missionaries to Jewish Educators: Children's Textbooks in Judeo Spanish." *Neue Romania* 40 (2011): 135–51.

Wyers, Mark. D. *Wicked Istanbul: The Regulation of Prostitution in the Early Turkish Republic.* Istanbul: Libra Kitapçılık, 2013.

Yahni, Aslan, ed. *90 Yıl Kuruluşundan Bugüne İhtiyarlara Yardım Derneği.* Istanbul: İhtiyarlara Yardım Derneği, 2006.

Yerushalmi, Yosef H. "Exile and Expulsion in Jewish History." *Crisis and Creativity in the Sephardic World, 1391-1648,* edited by B. Gampbel. New York: Columbia University Press, 1997.

———. *Zakhor: Jewish History and Jewish Memory.* Seattle: University of Washington Press, 1982.

———. "Servants of the Kings and Not Servants of Servants: Some Aspects of the Political History of the Jews." In *The Faith of Fallen Jews: Yosef Hayim Yerushalmi and the Writing of Jewish History,* edited by D. Myers and A. Kaye, 245-76. Waltham: Brandeis University Press, 2013.

Yıldız, Hülya "Limits of the Imaginable in the Early Turkish Novel: Non-Muslim Prostitutes and Their Ottoman Muslim Clients." *Texas Studies in Literature and Language* 54, no. 4 (2012), 533–34.

Zablotsky, Edgardo. "Education in the Colonies of the Jewish Colonization Association in Argentina." *Universidad del CEMA Working Papers Series* (March 2016), No. 585, https://econpapers.repec.org/paper/cemdoctra/585.htm

INDEX